RICHARD WINNINGTON

Film criticism and caricatures
1943–53

Richard Winnington, 1952

Previous page: Winnington at the *News Chronicle,* 1948

RICHARD WINNINGTON

film
criticism and caricatures
1943–53

SELECTED WITH AN INTRODUCTION BY

PAUL ROTHA

BOOKS
10 East 53d St. New York 10022
(a division of Harper & Row Publishers, Inc.)

To
the Memory of
RICHARD WINNINGTON
who saw it all through
and saw through it all
but still loved what
was left of the real
CINEMA

Rotha on the Film, 1958

Published in the U.S.A. 1976 by
HARPER & ROW PUBLISHERS, INC.,
BARNES & NOBLE IMPORT DIVISION

First published 1975 by Elek Books Ltd., London

This edition and Introduction copyright © 1975 by Paul Rotha

ISBN 0–06–497766–8

Printed in Great Britain

Contents

Preface

When Richard Winnington made a selection of his criticisms and caricatures from his column over five-and-a-half years in the old *News Chronicle* to form the volume *Drawn and Quartered*, published in late 1948, I assume, obviously, that he chose those which he thought the most expressive. In this new selection I have included a substantial number of the criticisms and caricatures in *Drawn and Quartered*, together with further material dating from the last five years of Winnington's life. For the latter I have gone back over the *News Chronicle* files at the British Museum Newspaper Library, whose services were most helpful. From April 1943, until September 1953, only a few days before he died, I have made this new selection, so far as written criticism is concerned, mainly, but not wholly, on the grounds of the importance of the films themselves. As for the caricatures, these have been chosen for their satirical brilliance, not necessarily for the quality of the films depicted.

Unfortunately, many of the caricatures in the newspaper files were too small and too grey to allow new reproductions to be made. Even more unfortunate is the fact that when the *News Chronicle* was merged with the *Daily Mail*, a very large number of Winnington's drawings were destroyed. However, with the help of Mr Keith Mackenzie, himself a distinguished caricaturist, a number of originals have been located, some in Winnington's ex-wife, Pearl Falconer's, possession (now in the Victoria and Albert Museum and the British Museum Print Room), some with his brother, Geoffrey Winnington, some carefully kept by his colleague, Stanley Baron, who also treasures two sketchbooks kept when they made their journeys together, described later, and some in my own keeping. Ronald Ingles, who designed the format for *Drawn and Quartered*, also came up with a few. Another useful source was a symposium of film criticism, *Shots in the Dark*, published by Allan Wingate in 1951, which included some of Winnington's work that had already been used in the *News Chronicle*. All these people are hereby thanked. Several of his friends made tape-recordings of their memories of Winnington; his two brothers, Geoffrey and Alan, were especially helpful in this respect. Partly as a result of a letter in the *New Statesman* (1 September 1972) asking for reminiscences, as well as from personal contact, many people wrote to me of their memories. They included Bernard King, Stanley and Betty Baron (Elizabeth Frank), Ralph McCarthy, Patrick Brangwyn, Jack Davies (who kindly allowed me to use the drawing that Winnington made on the fly-leaf of his book given to the young John Howard Davies for his role in *Oliver Twist*), S. John Peskett, Gwen Holmes, Constance Keel, Jympson Harman, Gladys Boyd, Stephen Watts, Matthew Norgate and Ronald Ingles.

Alistair Cooke is thanked for permitting me to quote from his Preface in a new edition of *Garbo and The Nightwatchmen*. I am obliged to Mrs Peggy Tyler for loaning me her copy of *MacDonald Medley* (1947) and Messrs Collins for the use of *Convoy* magazine (1945). The Associated Newspaper Group is also to be thanked for permission to use so liberally material from the now defunct *News Chronicle*; also *Sight and Sound*, Penguin Books, *New Theatre* and *Harper's Bazaar*.

My especial gratitude is due in two quarters. First, to the Granada Group and for Denis Forman's personal aid in obtaining a subsidy from them to help the publishers publish at all; second, to the British Film Institute for defraying some of the expenses during my period of research and then making me a grant to enable my work on the book to be completed. Without these two aids, this new edition and preservation of Richard Winnington's work would not have been possible.

Further gratitude is expressed to those who have shown their appreciation of Winnington in pieces which follow my Introduction: Nicolas Bentley, who has amended his piece which he contributed to *Drawn and Quartered*; and Mr Keith MacKenzie, now in charge of the cartoon department at Associated Newspapers. Mr Mackenzie's very generous help in collecting the drawings for this book and discussing the selection of what should be used needs my warmest thanks. I should also like to thank Mr Tom Baistow, a good friend and colleague of Winnington's, who is now Deputy Editor of the *New Statesman*, for giving me his extensive reminiscences.

To end, my gratitude to Pearl Falconer, herself such a good artist, for memories of when she and Dick were together. And I do not forget the close collaboration given by Mr Antony Wood of my publishers in preparing the book as it now appears.

P.R. April 1975

Introduction

Criticism in the cinema during the eighty odd years of the medium's history has not been overall of a quality and perception comparable to that found in literature or music or theatre or other arts. I am here referring to film critics writing for newspapers and journals, not to authors of books about the cinema. This has not always been the fault of the critics. Films are a universal popular entertainment first, and a form of art second. As a result editors and proprietors of newspapers and magazines have mostly required their film writers to be not critics but descriptive journalists and gossip collectors. It was not until the mid-twenties and the thirties that a few journalists — like Iris Barry, Caroline Lejeune and Robert Herring in England, Eric Knight and Meyer Levin in America — fought for space in the journals for which they wrote to print informed criticism and achieved the status of film critics.

Today, bookstores abound in books about the cinema in all its intriguing aspects, some of which come my way by courtesy of their authors or publishers, and I find many of them unreadable because of their obscurity. Their writers are prone to hide their meanings in intricate sentences about some poor, simple little film which, if at all, deserved a few astringent words. Purposes are found in films which their makers never intended. Alistair Cooke, himself once a very good film critic before he became concerned with wider issues, put this very well in the Preface to the new (1971) edition of his anthology of film criticism, *Garbo and The Nightwatchmen*, first published in 1937. He writes:

'What I admired, and admire, most in a critic is a personal point of view and the ability to express it crisply, or passionately, or drolly, or entertainingly, but above all intelligibly. I could name half a dozen eminent contemporary critics who would never have been invited into the company of these Nightwatchmen because in various wordy ways they illustrate the grinding solemnity which Otis Ferguson so richly parodied in his piece here on *Three Songs of Lenin.*'

Ephemeral indeed is the work of most film critics and not many have dared to make an anthology of their work — Agee, Lejeune, Graham Greene, and Grierson come to mind. Seldom does a critic, as Cooke requires, establish a viewpoint, an attitude to the art and entertainment he criticises; rarer still to maintain and to develop that attitude to a medium which by its very nature is ever in a state of change over the years. Richard Winnington splendidly achieved this. An unwavering thread of continuity runs through all his criticism whether in words or drawings, an attitude reached only after years of close observation and knowledge of the medium he loved so much. He wrote as he drew, with discipline and care for words and line.

He belonged in the company of James Agee, Eric Knight, Otis Ferguson, André Bazin and Louis Delluc — all no longer here, and it would be distasteful for me as a member of the Critics' Circle to name any contemporary critics — he was one of the great critics in cinema history. His economy of style, apart from his brilliant satirical caricatures, is something to be emulated. Someone once said of him, 'He wrote and drew like an angel, but with a devil's pen.'

Winnington grew up with the cinema with a passionate devotion and brought an adult eye to its works from whatever country they came. He knew its origins and roots and growing pains. He knew the struggles of its genuine exponents. He never wrote about a film from the past (as I've known some critics do) unless he had seen and judged it for himself. He saw each new film and he saw every film he could see, as an honest theatre critic or an honest literary critic sees a new play or reads a new book — in perspective with the growth of the art form in question. But his criticism, while being deadly true, was never destructive. If you did not resent criticism of your work, there was much you could learn from a Winnington review — if you chose.

Tom Baistow, Winnington's friend and colleague on the old *News Chronicle*, has written: 'To understand Winnington's importance as a film critic, it is vital to know that, first and foremost, he was a critic of society: the quintessential English radical — a true non-conformist, enemy of all Establishments, Left, Right or Centre, scourge of all phoneys, hater of cant and compromise: above all, a lover of the truth — when, however rarely, it could be found. It was this tireless pursuit of the truth — although he would have slapped the phrase down as "sentimental liberal crap" — that gave Winnington his unique authority in a branch of journalism that has been noted more for wordsmiths and freeloaders than believers in the cinema as an aesthetic expression of the eternal verities.'

He was quick to detect the pompous, the precious, the smug and the sham — all the pseudo-intellectualism that grows up around the arts, the cinema especially. He exposed the cult of the rarified few: the snobbery of the clique. All this because he knew that the cinema was the art of the people and he asked that it should be used to bring out the best in people, not the worst. No wonder, then, that so many of the cinema's promoters and money-men failed to grasp or even understand what Winnington wrote; they just feared him. To them he was someone odd indeed, a man who loved with a deep sincerity a medium to which he devoted much of his life for reasons other than personal gain.

If only a few of the promoters, financiers, producers, executives and their inevitable entourage of accountants had had over the past thirty years a tenth of the knowledge and devotion to the film medium and its audiences that Winnington had, the British film industry might not be once again in the perilous position that it is today, television notwithstanding.

My first meeting with Winnington was, inevitably, in a pub. At that time I had a small flat in Cliffords Inn, just up Fetter Lane from Fleet Street.* It was near to the

* The first reference to Winnington in my diary of that time is 1 July 1943. It must have been some time before that we first met.

throb of the machine-rooms, to the skills of the print-men and in contact with those who opinionated and criticised and reported on the world about us morning by morning, night by night, week after week. Newsprint was short in supply then and newspapers scarce in pages.

One of my locals was the Clachan in Mitre Court, between the Post Office and El Vino's wine bar, that antheap of lawyers and newspapermen and gossip-mongerers. The pub was managed by the indomitable, ample-girthed and genial Mrs Rothwell, who was once, it was said, a prison wardress. It could well be. She was tough, she had to be, but warm if she liked you. She liked Dick Winnington.

This particular evening I was with Herbert Jones, a publisher and a lover of good typography and hence a friend. Winnington came into the pub with the bravado that I was to know so well. Herbert introduced us. 'If you wrote the bloody *Film Till Now*,' said Winnington, 'I'll buy you a drink. It is my Bible.' 'If you're the bloody film critic of the *News Chronicle*,' I replied, 'I'll have one because I admire your film column, but not now, I'm late for a meeting.' 'Then bugger off', said Dick, and I did.

The next morning, crossing the street from Fetter Lane into Fleet Street, I caught sight of Winnington lighting his pipe outside the then *Manchester Guardian* office. I said to him, 'Mr Winnington, I did not intend to be rude to you in the Clachan last night, but I was very late . . .' 'Forget it, Cock,' he said airily. 'Let's go and have a beer.' We did and for the next ten years were the closest of friends. Not only did we agree about films, our main love in life, but also, we found, on most other matters, political and anywise, even including women. He lived nearby in Temple Chambers close to the *News Chronicle* office at the bottom of Bouverie Street where he worked. When I was not otherwise busy, we went to film Press shows together and we often shared breakfast at a café in Fleet Street. He would also spend an occasional week-end at my cottage in Buckinghamshire.

Richard Winnington was born in Edmonton, North London, on 10 September 1905. He was the eldest of a family of seven. His father was an accountant for the Essex Insurance Committee. Later, the family moved to a typical middle-class house in Queen's Road, Buckhurst Hill, Essex. Richard went to a minor public school called Bancroft's. He had no kind of formal art training but he drew, his two brothers, Geoffrey and Alan, recall, continuously from an early age. He was thus wholly self-taught. From the outset, his aim was caricature.

He left school during the great Depression. Neither he nor Alan, his younger brother, could find work. Their father would give them ten shillings a week each for beer and tobacco money. They would go into pubs and Dick would draw carica-tures for a shilling apiece, or a pint of beer. 'I remember him sitting up in that attic at Queen's Road,' recalls Geoffrey. 'He used to send me out to buy an ounce of St Bruno Flake tobacco and he'd give me a penny for getting it. He would stay up there all day and just draw and draw and then throw them away. He used to say, "I have to develop my own line." He was not influenced by any other caricaturist but had a great admiration for Gillray and Hogarth. He did not try to find any commercial outlet for his work. He just drew and drew and discarded. Unhappily none of those early drawings has survived. Most of them were of film people — stars and all that. From his earliest years, I remember that Dick was passionately keen on the cinema.'

Then somehow, it is not known how, Winnington found work in areas far from where his real talent lay. He sold Tungsten Tipped Steel in Cardiff for Hall and Pickles Ltd. He was not a successful salesman. Someone who knew him well at that time (Mr S. John Peskett) remembers: 'He hated and despised whatever work he was supposed to be doing. For a while he served behind the counter in Thomas Cook's, the Continental travel agents. He would talk with good humour about the acquaintanceships he made across the counter with lady travellers to whose hotel rooms he would sometimes contrive to deliver their tickets in person. This may have been one of his many fantasies but he was assuredly a good-looking, tall and very entertaining young man. When he was once again out of work, I was looking after export trade for the Heinz canned food people at Harlesden in West London and I contrived to get him an interview for a job as a salesman. With his rather diffident manner, he did not make a good impression. He had a wry sense of humour which did not go down well with the executive he saw. But he was tall, had personality and that was what Heinz wanted.

'Of course, it was a disaster. Dick had to pay calls on grocers and to hold sampling and tasting sessions in their shops for potential lady customers. He had to offer them cups of soup and plates of baked beans. Reports of his activities began to filter back to London; they were not exactly encouraging. From the Midlands, where his territory lay, it was said that he would approach the prettiest young housewives with a cup of soup, at the same time declaiming from *Alice in Wonderland*, "Soup of the evening, my dear! Beautiful, beautiful soup!" Most grocers thought he was mad. The climax came over window-dressing. To sell tins of soup, grocers knew that their shop-windows had to be filled with tins, row upon row, tier upon tier. Winnington cleared the window, bought some black velvet and draped the window with it. In the centre he then placed a single tin of baked beans. That abruptly ended his career as a grocery salesman.'

How Winnington came to break into the newspaper world is obscure. According to his brother Geoffrey, he got a freelance job around 1936 with the *Daily Express*. He did a strip on the features page about two pigeons called Bib and Bob for £2 a drawing, but Alan, his other brother, says it was more like ten shillings a time. He was not happy but it was work, it was Fleet Street, however menial, and it was using his real talent for drawing. Sometime in 1936 Ralph McCarthy, then Deputy Features Editor on the *News Chronicle*, spotted his work and offered him a full-time staff job to do any drawings, except for fashions and maps, that the paper needed. Later, he was asked to do drawings to illustrate the five-day story serials which were a feature of the paper in those pre-war days. Among others, he did illustrations for Richard Hughes' *A High Wind in Jamaica* and Hemingway's *To Have and Have Not*. Actually, his wife, Pearl, would sometimes do these for him when he was too hard pressed with other work, but the paper never knew this.

Winnington married Pearl Falconer in 1938. She was an artist of very considerable merit. (Many of us now who admired her drawings regret that she has done little in recent years; one day her work will be regarded in high esteem.) 'I don't know how or when he met her,' says Geoffrey, 'he just walked into the house in Queen's Road one day with Pearl, whom none of us had ever seen, and said, "Mother, I got married yesterday. Meet my wife!" '

Some admirers of both Pearl Falconer and Richard Winnington's work say that he was influenced by her. Perhaps it would be more true to say that they influenced each other. A comparison of their story illustrations makes it hard sometimes to determine who had done which. Their divorce in 1947 was a great sadness to both of them. It had been, and this is important, a working as well as a living relationship.

At the time Winnington joined the *News Chronicle*, its film criticism, if such it could be called, was being written by an amiable but elderly gentleman called A. T. Borthwick, who was both unwell and unknowledgeable about the cinema. On occasions — and there were many — when Mr Borthwick was unable to attend Press shows, Winnington would stand in for him. This was his first written and printed film criticism. It was unsigned. When Mr Borthwick retired through ill health, Winnington, at his own suggestion, was offered the column in spring 1943. Gerald Barry, the Editor, liked the idea, especially when Dick suggested that if space allowed he would also contribute a satirical caricature. Thus the Winnington film column, which was to become so influential and widely read, was born.

The *News Chronicle* under Gerald Barry's editorship from 1936 to 1947 was a mildly liberal journal with a national readership of some one and a half million, owned by members of the Cadbury family. In 1930 the old *Daily News* had merged with the *Daily Chronicle* to become the *News Chronicle*. Sir Walter Layton was Chairman of the latter company. Its general outlook was unmistakably liberal. It was anti-Franco during the Spanish Civil War and fiercely anti-appeasement at the time of the infamous Munich Agreement between Hitler and Chamberlain. Over these years it had a loyal staff of very talented, professional newspapermen, proud of their paper. Among them, in no special order of merit, are now remembered: A. J. Cummings (political commentator), Vernon Bartlett (diplomatic correspondent), Robert Lynd (on books), L. F. Easterbrook (on agriculture), Ritchie Calder (on science), Robert Waithman (American correspondent), Alan Dent (on theatre), Philip Jordan (a foreign correspondent), Ian McKay (gossip columnist), Vernon Brown (air correspondent), Stanley Baron (travel and countryside correspondent), Frederick Laws (the arts in general), Elizabeth Frank (also the arts but especially ballet), Stephen Potter (on books) and, of course, the brilliant political cartoonist Vicky, who was so sadly to commit suicide in 1966. Behind this sparkling team there were many skilled members of the editorial staff like Ralph McCarthy and Tom Baistow.

It was one of the major tragedies of Fleet Street when its owners decided to sell the *News Chronicle* to the Associated Newspaper Group and the paper was absorbed into the *Daily Mail* in 1960. Britain lost a fine and outspoken newspaper. One of the saddest casualties of that absorption was that a very large number of original drawings by both Winnington and Vicky was destroyed. So were also the file copies of the newspaper; the only record today is that at the British Museum Newspaper Library.

Among the many reminiscences I have received from those who worked alongside Winnington in that building at the bottom end of Bouverie Street, off Fleet Street, the following give, I hope, a good idea of the man, the critic, caricaturist and highly professional journalist, and the conditions and atmosphere in which he worked.*

'Dick Winnington would glower and rage and thump and chew viciously on the stem of his cold pipe. Suddenly he would chuckle gleefully and laugh aloud,' writes Bernard King, at that time Features Art Editor. 'He sat in the top right-hand corner of the big Features Room on the third floor. Vicky had his drawing-desk to the right of him but on the other side of the room. My large lay-out table was in close proximity to Dick, almost shielding him from the others in the big room. Not that he was aware of his surroundings. Passionately absorbed, he was wholly unaware of the noise and confusion of the big room. To a Features Art Editor, Winnington was a joy and a gift. Where he learned the newspaper craft I do not know, but his knowledge of type faces and sizes and illustration reproduction was profound. He was a complete professional. Given an inch of space on a page, he would fill it exactly even allowing for the 30 pt. lower case head × 3, open brevier merging into s/c minion. He never, repeat never, overwrote as do so many journalists.

'Of course he could be exasperating and unreasonable. He would never deviate from the perfection of his column — cutting, revising and rewriting up to the last minute. Watching him at work, I was immune from the urging and cursing telephone calls from the Head Printer down below. "Where the hell is Winnington's piece? He's holding up the stone." Eventually Winnington's galley proof arrived and a relieved Head Printer called to say that the piece dropped in perfectly to the space which was waiting for it, as I knew it would.

'At his drawing-board Winnington was wonderful to watch. This was a time when my ulcer was soothed in sympathy with his mood, his gleeful and mischievous chuckling as his acid pen unerringly demolished the stars and their films each week. I never detected the slightest resort to imitation or to well-established tricks favoured by so many caricaturists. In my many years in the newspaper world I have worked closely with dozens of well-known artists, some with impressive art training. Not one, and I write this with conviction, approached the insight, the exposure, and the humour, above all, as did Dick Winnington. A finer, kinder, generous and more dedicated man it would be hard to find. His dedication was so utter that I risk adding the following scene:

'The Features Room in the *News Chronicle* was packed with an unusually early morning crowd, shouting and waving morning papers. In Banner Headlines 150 Tempo Extra bold caps they had the heading — ALLIES LAND ON FRENCH COAST! Everything in all papers had been cleared or cut for the story for which the world had been waiting. Into this tumult strode Dick, pipe in mouth as always,

---

* Some of these came to me by personal contact and tape-recordings, and others as a result of my letter in the *New Statesman* (1 September 1972) asking for reminiscences. The letters have been telescoped.

pushing his way through to his desk. I went across to him and shouted, "Hi! Great news, Dick!" "Oh, yes," he says, "But they cut eight inches from my piece and why in hell did you let them drop my drawing?" Hard-boiled operator that I am, I always felt humbled by his genius.'

Tom Baistow on the editorial side worked closely with Winnington and has this to say of his working methods and his influence on Vicky, and especially of the difficulties in the years after Gerald Barry resigned as Editor. He writes:

'Winnington's dual brilliance as critic and caricaturist was a weekly feat that looked deceptively easy as seen on the printed page. But those taut, perceptive and witty reviews and savage likenesses in line — each in itself a critique — were the distillation of long hours of painstaking chopping and changing in a search for the *mot juste* or the right vapid pout on a silly starlet's ripe mouth. I have seen him draw five heads of Joan Crawford before deciding to have another go the next day. However demanding his current girlfriend, she had to play second to the final page proof of his column on Friday nights. His film column was his first — maybe his only — love. To such a perfectionist any interference with his final version was the sadistic sport of unfeeling philistines. To ask him for a ten-line cut in his proof for reasons of space and watch him agonise over the self-inflicted wound was a chastening experience, even for a hardened sub-editor as I was. Yet we admired rather than resented such egotism for art's sake. For we all on the *News Chronicle* knew that Dick Winnington really cared — not merely about his own standards but about everyone else's.

'In that long glass-walled room on the third floor, Winnington exerted a seminal influence that touched us all. The Features Department in the immediate post-war days was an exciting place under Ralph McCarthy. He had the priceless gift of getting better out of people than they believed they could deliver. The result was an ideal ambience for creative journalism. Vicky's genius, translated by Hitler into an alien culture, was still not fully blown.* But if Gerald Barry as Editor gave this little refugee from Nazi Germany his unrivalled command of British idiosyncrasy by making him familiarise himself with every source from Shakespeare to Max Miller, it was Winnington who bullied him into a much more mature draughtsmanship and taught him nuances of caricature that were to help make him the foremost political cartoonist of the post-war years. Dick's coaching of Vicky was not always of the gentlest — "You clever bloody foreigners always get it wrong about the English — Ernie Bevin should be batting at wickets *chalked on a wall* and not on the bloody playing fields of Eton." But Vicky knew that Dick had to do his kindnesses the hard way, an idealist protected by his cynicism, and in later years Vicky generously acknowledged his great debt to Winnington.

'Sadly, that era of the easy-going and hard creative approach was doomed to be short-lived. Its decline undoubtedly shortened Winnington's own life. In 1947 Gerald Barry relinquished his editorship of the paper to plan for the Festival of Britain to be held in 1951, and Robin Cruikshank, a talented writer but hopelessly weak and pussyfooting as an editor, took over. Irritated by Ralph McCarthy's

* Vicky's first cartoons in England were commissioned by *World Film News*, in 1936 (Vol. I, No. I), before he joined the *News Chronicle*.

vigorous professionalism and his attempts to instil some decisiveness into the editorial leadership, Cruikshank exiled McCarthy to Manchester as Northern Editor in 1949. It was then that the rot really set in, the moral and professional decay that was to bring the paper down, and Nemesis moved in on both Winnington and Vicky. McCarthy's successor as Features Editor was Robert Reid, a plain Yorkshire practitioner of the hard-news school with a deep suspicion of all that was "arty-crafty" — anything more *avant-garde* than the Huddersfield *Messiah*. The reshuffle made life doubly difficult for both Vicky and Winnington. Not only was Reid not on their wavelength but the new Editor was implacably pro-American — he had been the paper's American correspondent and he had an American wife — and reacted hysterically to any questioning of U.S. policies or the American way of life. With the outbreak of the Korean war and the rearmament of Germany, Cruikshank's hyper-sensitivity became almost pathological. Vicky and Winnington, fierce critics of America's strong-arm methods abroad and her rat-race culture at home, found themselves in ever more frequent conflict with the paper's new and ultimately disastrous attitudes.

'The strain of working in such an unsympathetic atmosphere began to tell on both men. In an attempt to come to terms with the Editor's dislike of his ruthlessly honest evaluation of Hollywood's plastic ethos and synthetic values, as well as Reid's taste for the emollient and banal, Winnington compromised for the first and only time — he experimented with a comic-strip technique which relegated his previous written words to caption form. It only appeared once. It was a predictable failure. Although he got his column back, Dick never really recovered his confidence or zest. A year later he was dead.'

Among Winnington's fellow critics, several have vivid reminiscences. The late G. Allen Hutt, who, as well as being on the *Daily Worker*, wrote about films under the name of 'George Pitman' for the now defunct Sunday *Reynold's News*, remembers: 'At some gathering or other, Dick was put out by an offensive member of the company. Turning to him and taking the pipe out of his mouth, he said in his icily calm voice, "Let's face it . . . you're a shit!" Richard had a disconcertingly quiet, even sardonic, way of lobbing blockbusters at people of whom he disapproved.'

Stephen Watts, for twenty years writing about films for the Sunday edition of the *New York Times*, also has memories: 'I must tell you of one thing about Winnington that I shall never forget. We were both waiting for an elevator in one of those Wardour Street offices to see a Press show when Dick suddenly put an arm round my shoulder and said, "You're all right. You've never sold out." I was taken completely by surprise but you will recall that Dick was very severe with a certain kind of film critic who in his view had "sold out", either by writing to please his proprietor or editor, or his friends in the film business.'

Matthew Norgate, who for many years contributed film criticism to B.B.C. Radio, writes: '"This is a nice sugary, family musical (for there are songs, how there are songs!) to which you can safely bring the kiddies. Never mind if the kiddies are sick." Pure Winnington, you will say? But you won't find it anywhere in his writings because he didn't write it. I did, in 1946, when Dick was at the peak of his brilliance. In those days I, and I think most other critics, found it difficult not to try and write in his style. If one wasn't careful, even one's views came under his influence. Partly because his were usually such sensible views, partly because he was one of the few film critics who had no compunction about discussing a film with his colleagues, or airing his views if there was no one worth discussing them with after a Press show.'

I do not myself wholly agree that Winnington would freely discuss films with his fellow critics. Some of them doubtless admired his acerbic style and respected his knowledge of the cinema. Others were certainly envious of his reputation. At the usual Press show drink session (to which I sometimes went with him), given by the film's producers or distributors, some critics could be seen hovering around hoping to hear what he thought about the film we had just seen. On more than one occasion I remember him analysing a film with me in a corner and, sensing a snooper trying to overhear our words, Dick saying loudly, 'Shit, let's get out of here and go to a decent pub away from the creeps.' Frankly, I do not think that Winnington had a high opinion of his fellow critics with one or two exceptions, of whom Dilys Powell was one. A question often heard was, 'What will Winnington say about it?' There was one critic in particular whose column appeared before Dick's who was a frequent eavesdropper, usually in El Vino's, and thus Winnington's views would appear elsewhere before his own column came out.

Late at night in my flat, every now and again, Winnington would read over to me what he had written about a picture before delivering his copy the next morning for typing. We would rarely disagree about a film's qualities. Never would I try and change his opinion. That would have been insulting and useless anyway. One of the very few films upon which we did not, at first, agree was Jean Renoir's *The River*, made in India in 1951. We saw it together at the Press show. He enthused about it; I had reservations. We then agreed each to see it again but separately. When we next met, he had modified his first enthusiasms while I had found qualities that had first escaped me. We thus came to a happy compromise.

Many times I have been asked what were Winnington's political views. In addition to his weekly column for the *News Chronicle*, he also wrote film criticism for the then *Daily Worker* under the pseudonym of 'John Ross', from early 1943 until November 1948. If these reviews do not appear in this book, it is because they were for the most part a repeat of his *News Chronicle* pieces. He did no drawings for the *Worker*, presumably because his unique style would have been recognised by the *News Chronicle* executives. I do not think, but do not know, if he was ever a member of the Communist Party, and I care less. He once told Stanley Baron (a colleague on the paper) that he had been a member for a very short time but was expelled because he preferred the company he found in the local pub to that of the Party's cell meetings. That to me sounds characteristic of Dick Winnington. My notion is that during the ten years that I knew him so well, he asked too much and cared too deeply for the freedom of the individual to make his or her choice in life to submit to any kind of political discipline no matter how much he may have believed in its ideology.

It has sometimes been said that had opportunity arisen, Winnington would have turned his double skill from the cinema to the world of politics. This I find hard to believe and think that the notion arose from a brilliant drawing he made of the interior of the House of Commons in session in 1945. It was made as a result of dashes between the *News Chronicle* office and the House; actual drawing, like photography, being not allowed in the House. He was far too cynical and disillusioned about politicians and their hypocrisy to have found their world his. I can imagine his language in the Parliamentary lobby.

He used no hammer but a stiletto with the initials R.W. clearly marked on the handle. He would prefer, God bless him, to drink in the old Clachan (now, alas, tarted up) off Fleet Street than in the smart Screenwriters Club (now defunct). I remember that when in 1951 I had, as Chairman of the British Film Academy, to present Max Ophüls with his award for *La Ronde*, I had to wear an old dinner-jacket. Dick refused to come. 'D'you think I'd be seen drinking with you afterwards looking like that!'

I have been asked if Winnington had any influence on his fellow critics. I do not think very much. His attitude towards the cinema was certainly admired and respected. His opinions were sought, but so many critics were not free to write all they may have wished. His admiration for Helen Fletcher, film critic of the *Daily Graphic*, was unbounded as the dedication of *Drawn and Quartered* showed, and her death was a grievous blow to him. Of her he wrote, 'She so specially made films live in print.' He liked and perhaps influenced slightly the work of Siriol Hugh-Jones in *Vogue*. The young writers of *Sequence*, Lindsay Anderson and Gavin Lambert, to my knowledge admired his work; to them he was the only film critic of whom they wholly approved.

Gwen Holmes, who worked on the *News Chronicle* in the Features Department, remembers: 'Soon after becoming film critic, Dick put his foot down about the Christmas gifts lavished by Wardour Street and told the publicity men that he wanted none of it. It was a unique attitude for a film critic and was not liked in some quarters of the film trade. It was a kind of approach to the cinema that was foreign to them.'

In connection with the possible corruption of film critics by the film business, Winnington's own evidence before the Royal Commission on the Press (10 June 1948) is worth quoting. In his written memorandum, he said: 'I happen to consider that to accept work of any sort from a film company is incompatible with the highest pursuit of film criticism, but I acknowledge that each person has his own code of ethics. Colleagues whose integrity cannot be doubted have to my knowledge contributed rough script treatments to film companies for which they were paid, although their work was subsequently shelved.' In his oral evidence, he said: 'The critic should be a contact between the cinema and the public. I think that he must find himself in opposition to the commercial side of the cinema. I find myself disapproving of, and opposing, Wardour Street so constantly that to accept any money from them would be invidious in the extreme, but, there again, I have my own standards and other people have theirs.'

It has been said of Richard Winnington that he was intolerant. He was — intolerant of exploitation, of phoneyness, of unprofessionalism. His high regard was for the basic understanding of human qualities, especially of dignity and integrity.

That is why the flesh-peddlers of Wardour Street, Pinewood and Elstree could not understand him.

More than once he was asked to make a film himself. However, he wisely refused on the grounds that he had not the technical expertise demanded by the film medium and was too old to learn. He agreed to try his hand at writing a script but no one took up the offer. Once when I pressed him to say what subject he would choose, he said maybe the Cleft-Chin Murder as the Press labelled it at the time. But the risk of libel would have made it too difficult. He had an amateur's interest in criminology. One of his favourite books was William Bolitho's *Murder for Profit*. He was a devotee of Hammett, Chandler and Simenon, none of whom he thought had been done well in the cinema except perhaps for *The Maltese Falcon* and *Double Indemnity*. He agreed with me that the only possible Philip Marlowe was Bogart, and the only really acceptable Maigret was Gabin.

His only great love — apart from human relationships — was the cinema and what it could interpret about life — and that cannot be said too often. He hated, and it really hurt him, as it does me, to see this wonderful medium for which he cared so deeply debased, prostituted and exploited in the aim of naked commercial greed. He fully recognised the medium's economic dependence on being an industry but could not, and would not, see why this should not be decently and efficiently equated with its being a great art — the art of our time — an interpreter of life and of human endeavour. From time to time he saw this fulfilled in films from Europe like *Casque d'Or* or *Les Jeux Interdits* or *Bicycle Thieves*, and even sometimes from America like *Sunset Boulevard* or *Double Indemnity* or *They Live by Night* — but why not, he asked, from England? He was quick to praise the realism and artistry of Lean's *Brief Encounter*, Reed's *Odd Man Out* and *The Third Man*, and Hamer's *Kind Hearts and Coronets* but he despised such *kitsch*, or crap as he called it, as the Box films and most of Rank's pollution at the time.

Winnington always took pleasure in writing the headlines to his reviews, which were often brilliantly witty: 'The Grapes of Rotha', 'The Belles of St Mary's', 'A Slight Case of Orson'. The descriptive captions that accompany many of the caricatures reproduced in this book are his own.

Although the publicity men in Wardour Street, especially those working for British companies, feared Winnington for his unbuyability, there were one or two employed by American distributors in London who respected his outlook and his influence. Sometimes a Hollywood B picture would arrive about which its makers were already cool and it would be quietly unleashed into suburban cinemas without even the occasion of a Press show. Ernie Player at Warner Brothers and David Jones at R.K.O. (that was), I remember, would espy such films and show them privately to Winnington. On more than one occasion he liked them very much and got the Film Section of the Critics' Circle to ask for a Press show, and he himself would give the film a long and usually favourable review which had significant bearing on its subsequent bookings and certainly led to a West End showing. Two such films were Nicholas Ray's *They Live by Night* (1948) and *The Window* (1948) by Ted Tetzlaff. As a direct result of Winnington's column, both films had a successful showing, which would not have been the case without his backing. Another film he supported was John Huston's *Red Badge of Courage* (1953). Its producers, M.G.M., already embarrassed by a film they neither liked nor understood, did not intend to screen it to the London critics, but at Winnington's instigation a Press screening was made and the film then played at M.G.M.'s Ritz Cinema, Leicester Square. In this way, Winnington fought the battle for good pictures which might otherwise have been crucified by the soulless machinery of the distribution side of the film industry. I do not know if these three films made a profit for their producers — the first two were low budget productions — but I cannot believe that they made a loss. If they did, it was due to faulty distribution methods and not to the films. Distributors, as Robert Flaherty once proved with *Moana*, are notoriously bad at promotion. They know only how to sell sex and violence, which anyway sell themselves.

In the summer of 1953 Winnington was gravely ill. Elizabeth Frank more and more took over his column. He had told me from time to time that he was being given injections by a doctor in Harley Street, but he was shy of saying more. In 1950 he had spent some five weeks in the Forest Hill Hospital in Buckhurst Hill, who cared for him well. When I went to see him, all he wanted were books and tobacco. We talked, I remember well, about the wonderful cinematic qualities of Simenon and he was very angry when I told him that my offer to direct *The Man Who Watched the Trains Go By* had been rejected by its producer, Raymond Stross. In the summer of 1953, a short time before he died, he refused a reservation for a hospital bed because it would have meant him missing the Press show of *Shane*, a film to which he much looked forward. We saw it together. He did his review, which is included here, but it was the last one that he to write.

A few days later I called in at the Clachan to find him. He was not there. Mrs Rothwell leaned across the counter and said in a low voice, 'Dick was in earlier. He looked dreadfully ill. He's gone to his room. I wish you'd go and see him.' This put me in a predicament. Although I knew exactly where Dick lived in Temple Chambers, he had made me swear never to go and see him there. I decided to break my promise.

The room was high up in the building and approached by winding passages. A knock on his door brought no reply. It was unlocked, so I went in. The light was on. Dick was lying on a divan or bed. In a low voice, he said he was all right. I suggested that I call a doctor. He said, No, he was just tired. I knew that his stubbornness would not let him see a doctor if I called one. He did not speak more. The room was barely furnished; a big table littered with papers and books, and a curtained-off wardrobe. Books were everywhere. So was dust. Presently I left. He was asleep, I think.

Back in my flat I sat and thought about the room in which Dick isolated himself. He was not at that time in any need of money. He made his mother a small allowance but had no other commitments. Why, then, did he choose to live in such shabby and uncomfortable surroundings? There was no need for it. True, the room was near to the *News Chronicle*, but why this uncared-for state? It was a kind of mortification. Perhaps that was why he did not want me to see it.

A few days later Dick's mother called me to say that he had been admitted to the German hospital in South-East London. I visited him; he had a room to himself but for once was not smoking his pipe. On 16 September, I was alone in my flat. The rain was falling heavily. Mrs Winnington called to say that she was at the hospital. Would I come at once? I caught a taxi in Fleet Street. It must have been about 10 p.m. when I got there. His mother, Pearl Falconer (who had been there all day), and Joan, his sister, were in his room. I looked for a few moments at a face I knew so well, but, as always at such moments of death, I did not now recognise. He would not last out the night. 'Goodbye, Cock,' I said as I had done so often, and took the waiting taxi back to Cliffords Inn.

First I had a big drink. Then around midnight I walked down Fleet Street to the *News Chronicle* building. The rain, I remember, had stopped. The night doorman knew me and asked after Dick. He let me go up to the Features Room, now empty. On Winnington's desk were a number of his drawings. I took all of them and a dog-eared copy of the first edition of my book, *The Film Till Now*. When I got back to the flat, I wrote the obituary notice which appeared in the last edition of the *News Chronicle* that morning. It was one of the most painful things I have ever done.

Winnington was buried in St John's Cemetery, Buckhurst Hill. The death certificate, dated 17 September 1953, gave several causes for his death, the most serious of which was anyloid of the kidneys. I do not rightly recall who was at the funeral ceremony except for his family, but Jympson Harman, for many years film critic of the *Evening News*, which had the biggest circulation of London's evening papers — Winnington had a warm and rather unexpected relationship with him — remembers that he just 'resisted dropping a copy of that morning's Press show synopsis on to the coffin. It seemed to me then, and it still does, that, extravagant as the act might have been, it would have been a fitting tribute of my respect and admiration for a great lover of the cinema.'

A Memorial Service was held in St Dunstan-in-the-West, Fleet Street, on Friday 23 October. I was honoured to be asked to give the Address. It was attended by some members of his family, many people from the newspaper world, a few film critics, some friends and a vague sprinkling of film trade persons who no doubt brought bottles of gin. After the tension of the service, a few of us who had known Dick well went across the road to El Vino's. 'This is the only part of the ceremony to which Dick would have subscribed,' someone said. I think it was Stephen Watts. Whoever it was, I thanked them deeply for such a fine comment.

It was not only his friends and colleagues who paid tribute to him, but many among the printing staff of the paper for which he worked but whose names do not get in the paper. Men with whom Dick would always have a beer. They later printed for free distribution a copy of my Memorial Address which I falteringly gave, and which the *Guardian* liked so much, and many people wrote to ask for copies. There were many obituary letters in the *News Chronicle* for several days. Perhaps Augustus John's telegram sums them all up. 'ALL HERE DEEPLY REGRET LOSS OF BRILLIANT DRAUGHTSMAN AND TRUE CRITIC RICHARD WINNINGTON' — Fordingbridge, Hants.

About Winnington's criticism and drawings I shall write little here because I think they speak too strongly for themselves. Only a few points need to be made. It is well known that during the war and in the immediate post-war years, newsprint shortage forced journalists to curtail their copy. But this did not dictate Winnington's astringent, terse style. He always wrote with an economy of words. He wrote short, sharp sentences with a blasting effect. If he had been given more space in his weekly column, I doubt if he would have used it. His pen scorched the slick glamour off many painted faces. The gormless publicists of Wardour Street cringed beneath such astringent flail. It was a kind of criticism that could not be muted by a free bottle of gin. To expose and make mock of the sordid publicity that was erected around the cinema, to deflate its shady promoters, this was one of Winnington's main ambitions, in addition to his aim to reveal all that was creatively good and worthwhile. He hated, above all, the accountant mind that came to dominate the British film, a kind of mind that had no understanding whatsoever of the artistic integrity necessary for the making of significant films. Here many names of the guilty could be given, but why give them the pleasure of such publicity? They will rot in obscurity while the name of Winnington and others will live on.

Here is an example of what he wrote about a really bad film: *Possessed* (1947). 'You have what the Trade lovingly calls Drama wherein the camera painfully follows every flick of Joan Crawford's eyelashes through 108 minutes and scarcely anything else. As she is a schizophrenic with persecution and homicidal mania, a paranoic and addicted to coma, trauma and hallucinations, it is acting with bells on. The film contains flashbacks, pyschiatrists, dream sequences, Raymond Massey and Van Heflin. After she has killed the latter and wronged the former and everybody else within reach, the jolly psychiatrist locates the golden heart that guarantees her a fair trial and a happy laughing future. What utter crap!'

His caricatures, we may note, were made *after* he had written his criticism. Is it not a high tribute that today they are as alive, vital and barbed as when they were made? It will be noted that Winnington seldom made a caricature of a film which he particularly liked. No drawing went with his review of *Bicycle Thieves*, *Open City* or *Paisa*. Bogart, Bette Davis, Cagney, Lorre, Gabin, Lauren Bacall, Granger, Crosby and all the others live more in his drawings than all their glossy studio photographs. His skill lay not just in his devastating caricatures of the main players in a film but in an exposure of their roles. He could sum up the whole *sense* of a film in a single drawing without text. The scenic background to his characters was often as important as they were. Many of his drawings were the whole film, not just its exponents. See, for example, those of *Brief Encounter*, *Love Eternal* and *King of Siam*. But my own favourite is of *Blanche Fury* in which the house is all. The text is blistering and one wonders that the makers of the film could ever have had the audacity to make another picture.

When he very occasionally interviewed film people, Winnington was as probing as a court prosecutor played by Spencer Tracy. I was present at some of these meetings (indeed I sometimes set them up). Two were with such disparate characters as Max Ophüls and Roberto Rossellini. With the first there was utter affinity, a wholly sympathetic contact between the two men. They understood and respected each other. With Rossellini, however, there was an air of suspicion. Winnington greatly admired *Open City* and *Paisa* (did not we all?) but sensed that others than Rossellini had contributed to the high qualities of those films which the director was shy to admit. (Only after the interview, which took place in my flat, did I tell Winnington of the part played by Sergei Amadei in the making of these films.) With a third director, the late Vittorio de Sica, he was wholly *simpatico*. There was instant harmony between the man who had made *Bicycle Thieves* and *Umberto D* and the sensitive, human, film critic. I can remember that when we were secretly shown the latter film, of which Korda owned the British rights but would not let the film be shown because he feared poverty, we were both unashamedly in tears. Winnington was not perhaps at his best as an interviewer, but in a book review, included here, of Grierson's collection of essays and criticisms, *Grierson on Documentary*, he wrote with a burning sincerity. So far as I know, the two men never met. Winnington had an instant ability to detect and then expose the spurious and the dishonest, discern the genuine from the fake. He could smell out like a Labrador the second-rate whether in a person or a film. And he did not hesitate to say so.

Away from the world of the cinema, Winnington's straight drawings were as brilliant as his caricatures. In the summer of 1946, the Editor of the *News Chronicle* asked Stanley Baron (travel and countryside correspondent) and Winnington to contribute a series of feature pieces to the paper to be called 'August Days and Nights'. The idea was that they should 'discover the post-war resorts of Britain'. Southend was the first and then they went to Brixham, Scarborough, the Norfolk Broads and a Butlin's holiday camp at Clacton, on the East Coast. They did not always go together; usually Baron went first and wrote his piece and Winnington, having read it, followed later to make notes in his sketchbook which would form the basis for his final drawings.

'On the Broads,' recalls Stanley Baron, 'we did go together. I seemed to meet many of my friends but Dick was busy proving to everybody that they were having a miserable time. He concentrated on the wives, who were, of course, having a wretched holiday as their husbands spent all the time fishing and boating. When Dick had finished with the wives, they were all convinced that they were having a miserable time.'

About this time, too, at Elizabeth Frank's suggestion, Winnington dropped into a ballet rehearsal room and made one of his best drawings which unhappily the paper did not use, but it is reproduced in the present volume. In addition to these satirical drawings, he also made many serious drawings, mostly of architectural subjects. His sketchbooks are filled with the most sensitive observations. There are many revealing pub interiors with their frequenters. They show a mastery of line.

The year after Winnington's death I was searching for some way by which his wide reputation both as a critic and a caricaturist could be kept alive. *Drawn and Quartered* was already out of print. I wanted a permanent tribute to his unique talents and the quality of his integrity. Some kind of annual award to a film and its maker seemed appropriate. In France there were the Louis Delluc and Jean Vigo awards, much sought after by French film-makers. They did not give some *kitsch* statuette but a simple verbal presentation. They were not surrounded by the kind of vulgar spectacle that is associated with Hollywood Oscars. So I contacted about fifty persons who had known Winnington as a friend and colleague and informed them of the project. Would they care to make a small donation towards the cost of having a diploma designed and printed, and towards notepaper and postal charges? It would also enable twelve copies of *Drawn and Quartered* to be bought, all the publisher could find. At first I had in mind that the Award might be linked with the Critics' Circle, of which Winnington had been an active member, especially at the time of M.G.M.'s libel case against Arnot Robertson. The Hon. General Secretary, however, Matthew Norgate, replied that 'while we are wholly in sympathy with your scheme, we feel that we cannot depart from the Circle's policy as to annual awards in the Circle's name'. I had previously approached the Council of the then British Film Academy (of which I was a Fellow) to see if the annual award could be given at the Academy's ceremony each year, but the idea was met with 'only a moderate interest' according to its Director, Roger Manvell. I then decided to go ahead and form a small committee representative of all the arts, which would meet once a year to select the film publicly shown in the United Kingdom during the previous year which best reflected Winnington's ideals of artistic and social integrity. The Winnington Award itself was to be a diploma signed by the members of the committee and a copy of his book, also signed by the members. Each year the winner would be invited to attend the ceremony. The following were asked to be members: Michael Ayrton, Nicolas Bentley, Paul Dehn (who had succeeded to Winnington's column), Graham Greene, Alan Rawsthorne, Michael Redgrave, Rex Warner, Norman Wilson (Chairman of the Edinburgh Film Festival) and Basil Wright. Only Graham Greene declined on the grounds that he was too closely involved in film production, indicating that one of his films might be eligible for an award. Basil Wright and I ran the same risk.

In 1955, the first award was given to the Soviet director, Mark Donskoi, for his trilogy *The Childhood of Maxim Gorki* (1938), *My Apprenticeship* (1939) and *My Universities* (1940). We knew that Winnington had a particular respect for these films but they had only been presented as a complete trilogy that year in England at the Everyman Cinema. Next year the Award went to the Sanders brothers in California for their brilliant, short, anti-war film, *Time Out of War*. In 1957, it was given to Robert Bresson for the outstanding *Un Condamné à Mort S'est Echappé*. Following that, it was awarded to Henri George-Cluzot for his magnificent *Mystery of Picasso*, and the last year to Jack Clayton for *Room at the Top*. During these years the Award presentation was moved from Edinburgh to the London Film Festival because of the impracticability of members attending the Edinburgh event. Norman Wilson withdrew from the Committee, his place being taken by Miss Dilys Powell. In 1960 and '61, my work took me to Germany from where it was impossible to organise the Committee's meetings. Alas, the Award was allowed to lapse on the grounds that some members found themselves unable to see the short selection of films each year.

I feel, finally, that this Introduction would not be complete without some words of appreciation of Winnington's graphic genius by two caricaturists who greatly admired his work. Nicolas Bentley needs no introduction. Keith Mackenzie, a skilled cartoonist himself, who did drawings for the *News Chronicle* after Winnington's death from 1955, is now in charge of the Cartoon Department at Associated Newspapers.

Paul Rotha, April 1975

NICOLAS BENTLEY:

Richard Winnington's knowledge of art may have been less profound than that of Ruskin or Pater, but his powers of observation and the accuracy of his criticism within his own sphere were no less acute than theirs. Yet to start with he had no thought of becoming an artist, nor, I believe, a critic. The selling of travel tickets and steel had not left him much time to learn or practise drawing. Both these occupations helped, however, in his development as an artist, and particularly as a caricaturist. They sharpened his wit and his judgment of character; and they put a still keener edge on his appetite for significant details.

With his passion for the cinema and true flair for humorous illustration, matured and disciplined by his apprenticeship in Press illustration, this critic-cum-caricaturist was an office made as clearly for him as by him. For many years readers of the paper for which he drew delighted in his weekly drawings. No other artist of his *genre* could bite out the character of his victims with a more shrewd or more economical wit. In spite of his sometimes extravagant distortion, Winnington's likenesses were too near the truth to be unkind. It is only when distortion is practised for its own sake, or for the artist's, that it becomes truly malicious, that it ceases to be valid comment and degenerates into abuse.

As a rule it is possible to trace in an artist's work the sources from which his inspiration and his style derive. With Winnington, however, this isn't easy; no doubt because he himself was more aware of general than specific influences in his work. Nevertheless, there was one artist to whom he recognised a half-conscious debt. In the insubstantial oddities of Edward Lear one can see cousins, not far removed, of some of those curious beings who have their unnatural habitats in the world of commercial cinema. Many of Lear's characters have that same air of wide-eyed, witless gaiety (or wide-eyed, witless tragedy) that one sees so often on the screen; that same determined glare and glitter in the eye that bespeak a mind utterly devoid of resolution; that same melting simplicity, molten in the flames of hard experience.

The mock heroics of a Stewart Granger, the celluloid sufferings of a Lana Turner, aren't difficult to caricature. But it wasn't enough, as Winnington knew, to catch a likeness. The setting for suffering or for mock-heroics, whether it was a Georgian manor house or a bar parlour or the Arizona desert, were used by him to point the mood — and sometimes the moral — of the scenes he drew.

25

Not only all things that catch the eye, but all those that catch the imagination, are the business of the caricaturist. And no one knew his business better than Richard Winnington.

January 1975

KEITH MACKENZIE:

A trained caricaturist has a mind which works like a camera. It retains an image which, with subtle distortion, emerges via the hand and the pen as a drawing crystallizing the essence of its subject. Many 'pure' caricaturists of whom the greatest is perhaps Max Beerbohm, worked wholly from memory. It would be hard to think of Max working from a sitting model or from a series of photographs.

Richard Winnington was a 'natural' caricaturist. He was, as we know, self-taught. He and his colleague, Vicky, influenced each other as a comparison of their drawings will show. Caricature being a specialist art, it was unusual to find two such expert exponents working not just under the same roof but side by side in the same room. They would argue not about their relevant styles but over the finer points of their political viewpoints.

Films that left him lost for words that were legally safe Winnington criticised in drawings, something no other critic could do. It left defenceless those whom he satirised. He developed his own individual style based on a fine, slightly 'Baroque' line, strengthened by a bold use of Indian ink applied with a fully-charged brush. His linework was wholly unlike the thick brush-drawn work of David Low, the brilliant cartoonist whose work enlivened the *Evening Standard,* the *Daily Herald,* the *Manchester Guardian* and at times *Picture Post* and the *New Statesman.* As anyone who has ever tried to draw caricatures will agree, the line between capturing a true likeness and just failing is a very fine one. Winnington developed his own method of coping with this hazard which was also used by Vicky. Having drawn his figures, their background scene and action, he would redraw any head which was not in his view wholly satisfactory. The new head would then be pasted on to the appropriate figure. He might do this several times until happy. Most of his film drawings were done on flimsy layout paper which makes them hard to preserve. They are not particularly good-looking as originals, being pasted together with Cow Gum and corrected with process white, but as in the case of all newspaper work, the finished product was the printed drawing made from a line-block on to the newsprint.

The difficulty of making drawings from memory after seeing a film and at the same time studying it critically for a written review may be imagined. It is of value to read now what Winnington himself wrote about this. Let him have the final word.

'The true caricaturist, the satirist, is a lover of his fellow-men and women. He is also, like the practised lover, a privileged person: he rarely gives offence in spite of the outrageous liberties he takes. Breughel, Rowlandson, Hogarth, Cruikshank, they had all the malice in the world and all the love.

'I have not all the love in the world for film stars — if for the cinema — but I try to give them the benefit of looking at them as human beings in the drawings which sometimes attend my film notes. Mostly these poor-rich are not allowed to look or sound human. When they do, usually at the beginning of their careers, the critics tend to acclaim them wildly. Then the processes of Hollywood get to work to make them unrecognisable outside the husky voice, the hair-do, tricks that imprison them in celluloid, never to break into life.

'For some years now I have been drawing for newspapers. If I have seemed to specialise in caricaturing film stars, it is perhaps because the latent instinct of a film critic was stirring within me. Things could and still can be said in a drawing, critical things, that put in any other form might bring in the threat of libel.

'A mixed attitude of love for the cinema and dislike of the way it's being used commercially leads me to protest in drawings against the universal tendency to glamorize the film stars. Never does the camera lie so unbearably or so elegantly as in its output about films and film stars, which makes the caricaturist a useful commentator.

'The opportunities of studying your models are prolific; a constant stream of profiles, angles and studied glamorizing of every little bit of personal trick, make the job of drawing your film stars far harsher than making a two-minute sketch of, say, your Features Editor, or favourite pub companion. As these stars flash by on the screen you can pick on the whole impression and try to photograph it on the mind while following the story and assessing the film. Those beautiful, shiny stills sent out by the studios are of little help. Even in the case of rugged character actors, the polishing and refining obscure the view.

'The only way of making a caricature is from the inward exposure of the eye and mind. Else it is a mere exaggeration distorting physical peculiarities, or representational romantic likeness. The comment that bites home is between the two and cannot be defined. I am not claiming that my caricatures possess this rare element. But when I try to depict film stars or politicians or, more easily, the ordinary man or woman, that is my line of approach.'*

January 1975

On pages 28–31: drawings by Winnington on general subjects

---

* *Convoy*, a wartime magazine published by Collins, London 1945.

Ernie Quick, landlord of Shurton Inn (pencil)

'August Days and Nights' 1: Lovelies Competition, Butlin's, 1946

Vera Volkova's Dance Rehearsal Studio, St Martin's Lane,
London (unpublished). 'It's good — it's sweaty!'

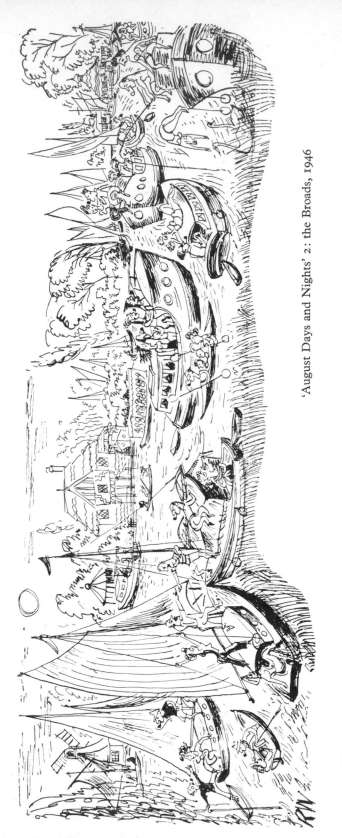

'August Days and Nights' 2 : the Broads, 1946

Below:

The Labour Government, 1945. On the front bench are Attlee, Dalton, Bevin, Morrison, Cripps, Ellen Wilkinson, Bevan, Dr Edith Summerskill. On the Opposition front bench are Churchill, Eden and others.

To conform with Parliamentary rules forbidding photographs or sketches when the House is sitting, Winnington first drew the interior after the House had risen, then while Hugh Dalton, Chancellor of the Exchequer, was speaking, memorised the positions of the figures. He completed the sketch in the *News Chronicle* office in time for the same night's editions

Winnington at the Czechoslovak Film Festival, New Gallery
Kinema, London, May 1947

Criticism and Caricatures
1943–53

Dream Indian — Ginger Rogers and Cornel Wilde in *It Had To be You*

Previous page: Panache — James Cagney in *Johnny Vagabond*

34

Custom seems to demand that the author of a collection of previously published articles conceals his eager welcome of easy money (the jam on the bread and butter) by some sort of coy disclaimer. I have always possessed so avid an appetite for collected criticism of films as they come week by week to the critic that I could not, in sincerity, apologise for adding to their slender stock. Such reviews, written fresh from the film previews, have a mood and flavour of times and occasions not to be caught in weightier and more deliberate assessments. Moreover (and invaluably for the addict) they preserve from oblivion the contemporaneous lunacy of the out and out bad film.

R.W. 1948

NOTE

The date at the head of each piece is that of the film's showing in Britain and not necessarily that of its actual production.

P.R.

BALTIC DEPUTY: *Directed by* JOSEF HEIFITS *and* ALEXANDER ZARKHI:
18 April 1943

The thing about a film like this, which in acting, dialogue, story, treatment and photography, is even more adult, is the effect of exhilaration it leaves on you afterwards. I do not see how it could have been better handled.

The story itself has the sharp drama of truth and it is obvious that everybody participating believed in it utterly.

Professor Palezhayev was the only scientist to welcome the 1917 revolution. He was also the greatest Russian physicist, honoured by European universities, worshipped by his colleagues and students — until he supported the Bolsheviks. He supported them because he saw that the emancipation of the workers and of science were interdependent. He was spurned by his fellow scientists, but adored by the revolutionaries; he became the Deputy of the Baltic sailors to the Petrograd Soviet.

N. K. Cherkassov, whose acting is sheer perfection, gives a portrait you won't forget of a great and good man. The power, integrity and simplicity of a man of genius are in every gesture he makes and every word he utters.

There are four or five other principal characters. Each one is a full and rounded portrait drawn with sympathy and stark economy. The dialogue throughout is impregnated with wit and intelligence. Very wisely, it has not been dubbed, but is done by means of sub-titles. Seeing this film was a great experience which I shall repeat with enthusiasm.

35

WORLD OF PLENTY (M.O.I. Documentary): *Directed by* PAUL ROTHA: *31 May 1943*

Its subject, Food, is dramatically handled by the use of some beautiful film sequences from all over the world, graphs and a commentary by experts, including Lord Horder, Sir John Orr and Dr Wellington Koo, etc. It makes an impassioned plea for a 'world strategy of food', for giving to every inhabitant of the world all that he needs of food from a world of plenty.

The production by Paul Rotha is brilliant. It is good that the M.O.I. should set their seal to this not unreasonable demand, but there is one word that persists — how ?

NEW EARTH: *Directed by* JORIS IVENS: *18 September 1943*

I have just seen a film which brilliantly reinforces one's belief in the art of the cinema. It is a documentary made about eight years ago in Holland, and it tells the story of the building of the great dam across the neck of the Zuyder Zee with the consequent reclamation of vast tracts of land from the sea.

The director, Joris Ivens, has recently added to it, in America, a superb musical score by Hanns Eisler and an English commentary. The result is a mature, vital and beautifully composed work which is right in line with the great documentaries *Turksib, Drifters* and *The River*, and which in sheer dramatic power excels all but the very best fiction films.

Here the perfect weaving of sound, movement and texture into the story — and it is a great story — creates an effect, through mind and heart, that no other medium could so quickly or so generally achieve — a belief in man and in the universal purpose of man. It is democracy in celluloid.

It is to be hoped that nothing will prevent this film from being widely released as soon as possible.

FIRST COMES COURAGE: *Directed by* DOROTHY ARZNER: *16 October 1943*

When we see a beautiful woman being shunned by her fellow-townsmen in Norway we know that she is the leader of the underground. We know that because we are film-goers and we are familiar with that look of acute self-sacrifice and abnegation accompanying the exquisitely designed clothes and perfect make-up and because she is Merle Oberon. The Nazis don't know it.

Along comes Herr Commandant, Major Dichter. He knows it least of all because he loves her. She is stringing him along. With artless little tricks that wouldn't deceive a two-year-old child she extracts information from him and relays it to England.

But, poor saps though the Nazis are, they begin to smell a rat. So out from England comes parachuted Capt. Brian Aherne. And here a surprise is packed for us. These two have met before. They used to go ski-ing together. They are lovers.

But she must marry the German to quieten suspicion. There is a slap-up Nazi wedding. Before the worst can happen the Commandos arrive. Laconic British greetings. 'Hello, old chap, how are you?' The German is shot. All set, you think, for England, Home and Beauty. You're wrong. Miss Oberon is a push-over for punishment.

She must go back to her one-woman underground movement, and with such excruciating fortitude that it almost seems the gallant captain gets the notion that life with her would be a serious business. Do we detect a slight air of relief as he goes back without her to the happy hazards of Commando life?

DIVIDE AND CONQUER: *Produced by* FRANK CAPRA: *27 November 1943*

This magnificent documentary, one of seven films made by the U.S. Office of War Information for American consumption, is the second to be seen in this country. Frank Capra ransacked the film libraries of Britain and America, the latter being well stocked with German newsreels up to Pearl Harbor.

German photographers were in the thick of the fighting from the beginning, so most of the material is from their cameras. The irony is that their pictures should

Anti-Fascism and water —
Betty Davis and Paul Lukas
in *Watch on the Rhine*

play such an important part in what will be the historic document of the rise and fall of the Wehrmacht.

In 50 minutes a complete picture is built up of the German Blitzkrieg, from the invasion of Norway to Dunkirk.

The editing seems to me to be near perfection. The whole scene is laid bare — the vile savagery, the vicious logic of Nazi strategy and the anguish of its victims.

A lucid composition of sound and movement, pointed here and there with the face of a blinded man, a bereft woman, a wounded child which becomes the concentrated image of humanity on the rack. This film is harrowing, it is unforgettable.

The general principle is to preserve anonymity of the men concerned in the making. It is known that Lt.-Col. Frank Capra made this film as he did *The Battle of Britain.*

This is a strange development from the maker of whimsicalities like *It Happened One Night,* and pseudo-serious sociological comedies like *Mr Deeds Goes to Town* and *You Can't Take It With You.*

They all had the same brilliant, brittle touch and were all colossal successes. They made him something like £80,000 a year.

Capra is 48, short and dark. He went steerage with his family to America from Italy in 1903; began by selling newspapers and singing in cafés while educating himself. His film career was started by writing gags for Mack Sennett. During the last war he served as a lieutenant of artillery.

Lt.-Col. Anatole Litvak, director of *Mayerling* and *This Above All,* is known also to be associated in the making of this series. Another is Capt. Anthony Veiller. The entire group is composed of directors, actors, producers, cameramen from Hollywood.

I gather it is intended to show only three of these films in this country. It is difficult to understand why.

The official reason given for withholding them from the British public is that they are too remote in time, but the U.S. War Department thinks it is good for American troops.

One thing is certain — the public after seeing *Divide and Conquer* will want to see the whole series, all of which carry the same high quality and integrity.

THE CHILDHOOD OF MAXIM GORKY: *Directed by* MARK DONSKOI: *4 December 1943*

Like *Baltic Deputy,* this is for grown-up minds. It is episodic and sprawling, the photography is by no means good — quite inferior to the polished camera work of the average Hollywood product — but it touches the mind and heart as no film within years has done.

A small boy, endowed with the wide sympathetic observation of the creative artist, watches the unfolding drama of life in a community where people 'are strangers in their own land'.

'Those were the days of living,' he exclaims and where but in Russia under Tsarism could people, kept relentlessly on the poverty line, exhibit such violent extremes of strength and weakness? It is a rich panorama lit by humour, accompanied by the slow sad music of the Volga.

These people live, everyone of them; they illuminate our own childhood memories and we know that it is all true. Here the high tensility of courage withstands the stupid meanness, the stupid slyness, the chicanery and greed. Every one of young Gorky's family lives precariously, their warm generous impulses distorted by the dominating and fantastically difficult task of getting enough bread to eat.

The boy, played by Alyosha Lyarksy, is quiet and sympathetic, mutely observing, always resisting. He must get to know everything. He must fight back. The outstanding player in a cast exhibiting all the highest qualities of Soviet acting is the grandfather of M. G. Troyanovsky. This is inspired — a taut, beautiful performance.

You will find the slowness unimportant (even those seemingly endless vistas of river and field have their relevance), for the content of the picture is more tremendously packed than anything in celluloid I remember. *The Childhood of Maxim Gorky* is not only the truest interpretation of a book by movie (it can almost be said to transcend the original), but is one of the three greatest films ever made.

MY UNIVERSITIES: *Directed by* MARK DONSKOI: *22 April 1944*

It is with wonder and gratitude that I turn to a film which does not debase mankind's varied agonies into box-office fairy tales. This revival of the third of the Gorky trilogy (the middle section has never reached this country) has none of the facile technique which can put over the cloudy dreams of intimidated writers and artists.

The Russian tempo in movies is slow to the Western eye and ear. (The film has been cut to an hour and forty minutes and shows distinct traces of the surgery) but nothing can disguise the integrity of Donskoi's interpretation of the truth as Maxim Gorky saw it 'the truth that is above compassion'.

This account of Gorky's young manhood in Kazan is packed with the horror, the poetry, the weakness and the courage of men. N. Valbert in the central part of Gorky exemplifies the care taken by Soviet directors of historical films in the matter of physical resemblance to the original and suggests, as few actors could, the imprisoned mind of the as yet inarticulate writer.

Lemoyonov the baker, always in his nightdress, lovingly addressing his pigs as 'my dark little hermits', while brutally and sadistically ill-using his employees, is, by S. Kapukov, brought to glowing life — the richly deep Russian life-stream which Gorky apostrophises and faces with the clear eyes of a man and conscious artist — as the film ends.

THE SONG OF RUSSIA: *Directed by* GREGORY RATOFF: *4 April 1944*

Film studios have evolved a new tongue — the broken accent deriving from no known language to be used by foreigners on all occasions. Useful because the slightly comic air thus given them emphasises the superior qualities of the laconic, quizzical, resourceful Westerner.

In this acutely self-conscious tribute with music from M.G.M. to Russia the thing is taken to the pitch of having an actor made up like Stalin reciting the 'Scorched Earth' speech with comic accenting. Only world-famous conductor Robert Taylor and his manager Robert Benchley, on a musical tour of Russia just before the invasion, talk straight American — now this is the wrong way round, surely these two should have the accent as they are all of them talking the same tongue — Russian? However, with the exception of Susan Peters, who slips badly at times, the entire cast keep it up with energy and industry.

Although the music of Tchaikovsky flows in and out of every sequence, none of it is ever completed, and while our ears are tantalised by brief excerpts of the 'Pathétique' Symphony superbly conducted by Albert Coates, we get an eyeful of Robert Taylor looking desperately stern and sawing the air with a baton.

Music brings together the venerated conductor and the beautiful young pianist, though they never discuss it. Nobody in all the coterie of Soviet musical experts ever discusses it. For them the endless, empty litany of screen courtship under the lambent Russian moon with some village junketings thrown in. This fiesta is a little Broadway musical in itself.

And the message? That the Russians are brave, simple, musical, lovable and above all quaint. And how is it conveyed? By the return of the two lovers to the West, with the urgent approval of the Soviet Union, so that they can go around playing the Tchaikovsky Piano Concerto. Simple.

Sisters under the skin — Lucille Ball (Du Barry) and Barbara Stanwyck (Gypsy Rose Lee)

THE FORGOTTEN VILLAGE: *Directed by* HERBERT KLINE: *13 May 1944*

John Steinbeck, it is said, wrote the story and script of this film as a spiritual relaxation from Hollywood. With directors Herbert Kline and Alexander Hackensmid, photographer Agustin Delgado and their crew, he went to a primitive Mexican village. Here they lived, talked, listened, and then created.

Their actors were the villagers. Says Steinbeck, 'Most of them had never seen a movie, but they understood our story well: it is part of their lives.'

One family is brought close to us, and the human constants of joy and sorrow, birth and death, play upon and illumine each member. We know them well.Typhus threatens the children's lives and the village is torn with the clash between medicine and magic. The young son of the family leads the revolt against the primitive, is driven out by his fellows, but even as he travels to the city is conscious of victory.

It is difficult to avoid extravagance in praising a film that from beginning to end is full of a deep and brooding beauty. There is scarcely one momentary framed design of light and shadow, of sculptured Indian faces, of the stilled chiaroscuro of the Mexican countryside that is not wholly satisfying. A subdued and perfectly cut-in commentary, spoken by Burgess Meredith, tells the story. The music of Hanns Eisler is what film music seldom is — a reflection of the mood, shape and meaning of the film itself. It lasts for one hour.

NIGHT SONG: *Directed by* JOHN CROMWELL: *1944*

A microcosm of the star system can be observed in the case of Dana Andrews, who managed to exist as a very satisfying actor in some of the best films of our times until stardom hit him.

The directors and writers of these films have either toed the line or fallen into disgrace. Dana Andrews, a handsome star with a good voice, has acquired heart-throb status and is apparently ready for anything.

To occupy, for instance, the sticky end of a typical Joan Crawford triangle, or to put contact lenses over his eyes and fit his fingers in the right places on a piano as a blind musician in *Night Song*. See what can be done to a sensitive and efficient screen actor:

Forced by his blindness (caused by an accident) to play in the small San Francisco night club orchestra of his friend Hoagy Carmichael he stares into space and intermittently flings out curses and resentment. As with all screen composers he is stuck half-way through a piano concerto and simply won't finish it out of grouch, although he will keep tinkling at it in between numbers.

He is ripe to be discovered, saved from himself, cured of his blindness and led to a triumphant rehabilitation at the Carnegie Hall by Merle Oberon, a sad, discontented millionairess with a yen for Art and High Thought.

She has a tougher proposition than with Chopin (who only coughed and got political), but she wins through by masquerading as a poor blind girl begging piano lessons and, after a lot of tantrums and loose talk about music, breaking him down into finishing that concerto.

What is simpler than that it should win the 5,000 dollar prize cunningly instituted by her rich self so that he could afford the operation to cure his sight; that he should become infatuated with wealthy Miss Oberon and forget poor blind Miss Oberon until the surging notes of his concerto (played in full by Artur Rubinstein and the New York Philharmonic) send him back to his true love (Miss Oberon having arranged the switch by taking a fast aeroplane to San Francisco)?

Merle Oberon, acting as a girl acting blind and as two ends of a triangle, is distinguishable from George Oberon Sand by the absence of a top-hat and indistinguishable from Merle Oberon in any other film. Dana Andrews gets by with contact lenses, rudeness and much spinal manipulation at the piano.

The concerto, in the screen tradition of one movement, sounds like background music that has strayed frontwards.

DOUBLE INDEMNITY: *Directed by* BILLY WILDER: *16 September 1944*

This is the sort of film making which revives a critic from the depressive effects of bright epics about the big soul of America or the suffering soul of Europe and gives him a new lease of faith. Why? Because Billy Wilder, director and part writer, is, from beginning to end, the complete master of his story, tells it with consummate economy and packs it with visual subtlety.

It is a sordid triangular murder story from the pen of James M. Cain, melodramatic, lusty, and well knit. The crime, an ingenious one with only a few improbabilities, is seen from the inside through the mind of Fred MacMurray, insurance salesman, lured by Barbara Stanwyck into killing her husband for the twin rewards of love and the insurance money.

The terrific tension as the fates close in on them is heightened by the casual seeming detail with which Billy Wilder stresses character and underlines terror and by the perfect logical employment of the flash-back. The idiom is harsh and salty, the deliberately vulgar atmosphere primed with the sultry, cruel, passion of shoddy, selfish, violent characters. There is a minimum of cliché.

Barbara Stanwyck plays the seductress with lascivious power. Fred MacMurray is better cast, as an insurance salesman, then ever before in his career and Edward G. Robinson by this one taut performance as a claims investigator and the instrument of Nemesis atones for a succession of dreary and unsubstantial parts.

WESTERN APPROACHES: *Directed by* PAT JACKSON *for the Crown Film Unit: 9 December 1944*

There has never been a film so surrounded by modesty and self-effacement as this magnificent British story of the Atlantic convoys. When by the merest chance I discovered its existence last May and wrote about it in the *News Chronicle*, mine was the first news of it to appear, although the film was then complete.

For a whole year we have known we are going to see that epic production *Caesar and Cleopatra* some time in 1945; *Wilson* and *Till You Went Away* already loom large in our lives. How can they — how could any film — live up to these premature

Barbara Stanwyck in *Double
Indemnity*

ecstasies? But if advance publicity has its drawbacks, so too has the complete absence of it. For citizens like me can get comfort from the thought that such films as *Western Approaches* lie ahead.

The film is devoid of heroics although it is impregnated with heroism. The wrecked crew in the lifeboat who try to warn their rescuers of the lurking U-boat and the captain of the *Leander* who suddenly decides to alter his course to pick up the lifeboat are men playing the parts they normally live and they give us the common currency of bravery as no screen actors could. They are seamen, and their selflessness in danger is automatic and unstated.

I have seen this film three times and its quality becomes more marked with each viewing. It is perhaps the feel of the sea itself evoked at moments with an exquisite blend of colour, sound and shape — the flapping of a sail, the cry of a bird, the clanking of chains, the elusive changing face of the Atlantic. In this delicate use of sound, embracing at times the best Technicolor effects of the sea ever photographed, lies perhaps the film's great freshness.

Refreshing, too, are those ordinary British voices whose accents sound without false emphasis and a story that, although fictionally conceived, mirrors a thousand untold tales of the Western Approaches during the most vicious sea war the world has ever known. And that story has shape and drama and austerity.

You will not find here the suave technique of the commercial product; you may think it in some ways an untidy sort of picture; but you will have been as near to the Atlantic as the imagination of a first-class director and the camera can get you. And the life of a merchant sailor is not noted for tidiness.

SUNDAY DINNER FOR A SOLDIER: *Directed by* LLOYD BACON: *20 January 1945*

This is a quiet film about a poor, ramshackle American family living in a ramshackle houseboat in Florida. The family consists of an improvident grandfather and his four grandchildren. They are Charles Winninger, Anne Baxter, Connie Marshall, Bobby Driscoll and Billy Cummings, and they are all drawn with a warmth of honest sentiment that is irresistible.

The whole tension of the film hangs on whether (a) the family can afford to invite an unknown soldier to Sunday dinner, and (b) if, when they have scraped together the food, he is going to turn up anyway. And the audience is made to share every small frustration and sudden hope and little sadness until the last breathless minute of waiting for the guest to arrive.

The film could have so easily been but never is, mawkish. It is good because it captures and convinces you from the beginning, because the camera is never stinted and gives you vistas of sand and palm and delta, follows convincingly the movement and play and fears of children, and because imagination reinforces its honesty.

One scene will go for ever into my private gallery; wherein Anne Baxter pours all the longings of youth into a dance with an imaginary partner in the ruined ballroom of a de-luxe coastal hotel that was half built and forgotten. That dance in the moonlight with no accompaniment beyond a hummed tune from Miss Baxter is the purest screen poetry. *Sunday Dinner for a Soldier*, simple, true and tender is the best propaganda America has put out in the current year. It got no advance boosting, one week at the Tivoli and poor distribution.

TO HAVE AND HAVE NOT: *Directed by* HOWARD HAWKS: *16 June 1945*

I remember thinking when I read and illustrated it as a serial in the *News Chronicle* that Ernest Hemingway's book *To Have and Have Not* would film. It still would.

The book is simple Blood and Thunder with a splash of Sex, given by Hemingway's abbreviated prose the necessary speed and tenseness.

Warner Bros. have taken it in hand, invoked the distinguished pen of William Faulkner for screen adaptation and, by advance publicity, made us sick with longing to set eyes on Lauren Bacall — the 'sizzling, slinky, husky, sultry' newcomer to the Warner firmament.

To Have and Have Not is remarkable at least for the ingenuity and industry by which the original story and the individualities of Faulkner and Hemingway have been rendered down into Hollywood basic.

This indeed is just another of these Resistance films from which it is about time we were liberated. Here we are in Martinique in 1940 in a murky, multi-accented and joylessly phoney world. Of all such pictures *Casablanca*, though no less false, alone has any buoyancy or self belief.

Among simple-minded Resisters and Keystone Vichyites, Humphrey Bogart and Lauren Bacall, bored, disillusioned, cynical, find love and in an inert way some faint stirring of anti-Fascist sentiment. This does them much credit for it is a long way to Pearl Harbour. Children of pulp thrillers and Hemingway, they clip their phrases, throw away their lines and strive for the immobility of Yogis.

Miss Bacall is an extract of several stars — Dietrich, Bankhead, Harlow, Lake and Garbo. She is much more handsome than Humphrey Bogart but not nearly as talented. I have to confess that in spite of the 'down under look' to which she attributes her success as a 'wolverine' I was pretty generally dampened down by the whole outfit.

LERMONTOV: *Directed by* ALBERT GENDELSTEIN: *23 June 1945*

This week I have seen a film which left me with a tingle of exhilaration that is the periodic reward and revivifier of the film addict. But only those who are in London can, if they are so disposed, confirm or dismiss my claim that *Lermontov* is a distinguished movie. For to book this film for the provinces would not fit in with the plans of any of the distributing groups; it might make less money than a Hollywood musical; it might only just pay its way.

Lermontov has avoidable disadvantages. It has been mauled in the cutting and badly copied. Yet these flaws become unimportant as the rarer magic of the screen begins to possess you. Russian film makers have a perfect and individual gift for evoking the flavour of their own history.

And here, despite the tinge of propaganda, despite the toning up of Lermontov's character, is the authentic Russia of Gogol, Pushkin, Lermontov; an era of duels and Byronic raptures, suicides and passion, with the decadent glitter of the Tsarist Court in the background. It was the age of the romantic revolt against oppression by poets, writers and musicians, and the film has rightly been given a romantic flourish.

There are sequences which rank high as cinema, which I shall see again and perhaps again for the sheer visual pleasure they afford. And there is the music which Prokofiev wrote for the film with an exquisite feel for the subject and the age. The slow tempo, quickened here and there by a ballroom scene, a duel or a carouse, does not drag; it is necessary to the nostalgia of the film and stimulates its mood.

Mikhail Lermontov was a great Russian poet who in 1841 died at 26 in the last of the several duels he fought. He has been well served by this film which should endear the man and perhaps his poetry to many persons who had previously gone in comparative ignorance of either.

45

Russia with barely 500 years of historic tradition has paid a dozen such tributes to her past. Britain, packed with the material for a thousand historical films, can boast only of the tepid charms of *Tudor Rose* and the successfully vulgar, jingoistic and inaccurate *Henry VIII*. What about John Wilkes, Byron, Shelley, Chatterton and all the rest whose lives are, if anything, over-rich in colour, in courage, in genius, and, even for Hollywood, sex-appeal.

THE SOUTHERNER: *Directed by* JEAN RENOIR: *1 September 1945* (*See also page 169*)

I cannot imagine anybody failing to be spellbound by this first successful essay at Franco-American screen collaboration. The result of Loew's production and Jean Renoir's direction is an evocation of America's deep South, unusually pointed by Gallic emphasis.

Superficially it is the old saga of one man in a two-handed fight against nature and poverty, sustained only by a deep love for his few acres of earth. Illness, through malnutrition, strikes his child. Storm and flood wreck his cotton crop and drive him almost to the wild surrender of despair. Yes, you say, we have had it. But this film, revealing itself as something true and fresh from its opening shot, shows that we haven't.

For here is something of the lyricism that as well as its deep compassion, fastens *La Grande Illusion* for ever in our minds. And here too is shape in the seasonal flow of image, in the symbolism of flood and drought, for water is the dominant; water prayed for and water cursed.

The rhythm is sure; against hot, rich dusty landscapes the characters solidify: the young farmer (Zachary Scott), his wife (Betty Field), the grandmother (Beulah Bondi), the two children, the faithful friend, the morose, embittered neighbour (J. Carrol Naish), the casual trollop of the bar.

There is no Spiritual-singing chorus, but an apt accompaniment composed by Werner Janssen; there is in a story thick with opportunities scarcely one of even the more honourable clichés. The grief of a mother over her sick child, the helplessness of the husband to comfort her (watch the sensitive acting of Zachary Scott and Betty Field), a fight in a saloon, a fight in the farmyard — these and other sequences have a suggestiveness both intelligent and tender, a sophistication behind the simplicity.

I cannot let pass this short review of a fine and beautifully acted film without referring to superb playing of the grandmother by Beulah Bondi. It merits at least a couple of dozen Oscars at current rates.

LOVE STORY: *Directed by* LESLIE ARLISS: *7 October 1944*

This is the story of three brave, suffering, genteel hearts. And how tender and self-abnegating is this triangular love bond between a beautiful girl pianist with only six months to live, a handsome airman, who is gradually going blind but conceals it all under a gay and irritating stream of banter, and his girlfriend from schooldays, who knows his secret and loves him hopelessly. These parts are played by Margaret Lockwood, Stewart Granger and Patricia Roc.

In psychology and dialogue this is straight out of *Mabel's Weekly* extended to admit sundry comical turns from the lower orders and a piano rhapsody which was born on the lovers' first meeting as they were poised in a Kodak composition on the Cornish headlands. Need I say that this piece of music is given *in toto* at the end, played by Harriet Cohen and the British National Orchestra, while Miss Lockwood dreamily fits her fingers into the right places. It has the cries of seagulls, the surge of the waves and is a blood or rather bloodless relation of the Warsaw Concerto.

Tom Walls with a music-hall Yorkshire accent, acting as a pawky old Cupid, brings the only breath of life, if you like that sort of life, into the scene. Apart from all this the film, which embarrassed me, will do well, but I do hate to think of the

French casualty — Jean Gabin in *The Imposter*

Love at Milford Junction — Trevor Howard and Celia Johnson in *Brief Encounter*

appalling caricature of British bus conductresses, a race I respect and admire, going in front of American audiences.

BRIEF ENCOUNTER: *Directed by* DAVID LEAN: *24 November 1945*

Four people remarked separately to me after its preview that *Brief Encounter* was more like a French film, finding about the highest praise they could for it. What they meant is that the film among other things, is emotionally grown-up. But let us be hopeful and say that it is more like a British film.

Love in the suburbs is an endlessly and treacherously attractive theme to novelists, playwrights and film makers; they have attacked it whimsically, patronisingly, grimly, comically, but seldom with the sincerity of *Brief Encounter*. It is because of this sincerity and its infallible evocation of *High Suburbia* that I rank this as the best of the Noël Coward-David Lean-Havelock Allen-Ronald Neame productions, and forgive its disturbing patches of violent light relief with synthetic cockneys in the station buffet.

How simple, commonplace, uncomfortably true and fascinating is this story of not-so-young, not-so-illicit love between two respectably married and nice people

48

conducted furtively and unhappily and exultantly in Kardomah cafés and railway buffets and super cinemas until lies and small deceits so tarnish their joy that they tear themselves asunder.

Much of the power of the love passages is due to the acting of Celia Johnson, who, without manufactured glamour or conventional good looks, magnificently portrays the wife and mother meeting passion for the first time; who wants to die because of it and goes back to her husband and the books of Kate O'Brien, knowing that this golden brief encounter will die in her memory. This is perhaps the real twist of its everyday tragedy. Trevor Howard as the lover, more than good, is outshone by such a performance.

Polished as is this film, its strength does not lie in movie technique, of which there is plenty, so much as in the tight realism of its detail which enlarges the one-act Coward play from which it was taken without loss of flavour or increase of volume.

LOVE ETERNAL : *Directed by* JEAN DELANNOY: *16 February 1946*

When I saw *Love Eternal* fresh from France (it was made during the German occupation under the more potent title of *L'Eternel Retour*) I got a mixed reaction of pleasure and repulsion which sharpened on the second viewing.

Pleasure because, for the first half hour at least, the film has a filmic logic which flows serenely over words and music. (The words are by Jean Cocteau, who conceived and wrote the film, the music is by Georges Auric.) Repulsion because the trance-like atmosphere of doom and despair swept me into a nightmare of Teutonic mysticism in which the only missing element was Wagner's music.

The choice by Jean Cocteau of the Arthurian legend of Tristan and Isolde, of which every detail of event has been held to in the modernisation, is characteristic and therefore to be taken as it comes. But the pervading mood of defeatism sublimating itself in death and the pristine blondness and humourlessness of the two leading actors must, though, have made it a pleasure for the Nazis to give permis-

Dead and happy at last — Madeleine Sologne, Jean Marais and Pieral in *Love Eternal*

sion for the production as well as to view the picture. It is right up the Nordic street.

These two woodenly beautiful creatures, Madeleine Sologne (a marbled Veronica Lake) and Jean Marais (his knighthood symbolised by windswept hair and open-necked shirt and riding boots), are rendered even more remote from life by M. Pieral's ugly, evil but utterly vivid dwarf, their mortal enemy, the encompasser of their gorgeous mutual death, the representative of all that is earthy and wicked, dark-haired and (could it be?) Gallic. It is he who gives balance to the masochistic monotony of love eternal.

Well, there it is, the whole dolorous bag of tricks, the island, the love potion, the scarf on the mast, the dark tower, the aching rejection of life, valid according to its intentions, often superbly beautiful in its execution, but rotted.

A SLIGHT CASE OF MURDER: (LE JOUR SE LEVE)
Directed by MARCEL CARNE: *11 May 1946*

This week has given me the most saddening experience of all my years of cinema going. It was to see, probably for the last time, a fine and rare film that has been sentenced to death by Hollywood.

An unnamed American company, trading on France's urgent need of dollars, has bought up the French film, *Le Jour Se Lève* in order to remake it. We know what that means — every copy will be withdrawn or destroyed and put out of the reach even of film societies and private clubs. *Pépé-le Moko* and *Gaslight* were murdered and then mocked by remakes.

M.G.M. have just acquired that charming if not great, picture *La Mort du Cygne*. Let M.G.M. back up the self-confidence of their own publicity and face the world with their version and the original.

For what purpose does Hollywood want *Le Jour Se Lève?* The bare plot has nothing to distinguish it from a dozen others they could have got from the files. A young workman murders at dusk the ageing seducer of his sweetheart, barricades himself against the police in his room through the night and shoots himself as the dawn breaks. Flashbacks give you the events that lead to the tragedy.

All the things that make *Le Jour Se Lève* a bright confirmation of one's sorely tried faith in the cinema are not to be imitated, certainly not in Hollywood. There's the wonderfully evoked atmosphere of an ugly Parisian industrial quarter, built up with loving and bitter observation by Marcel Carné, the one director of all European film makers who has got to the heart of the proletarian film.

There's the workman of Jean Gabin, self-contained and silent in his frustrated search for peace and love, for whom life in the cities has been 'unemployment and toil, always different and always the same'. This contemporary mature figure of tragedy and disillusionment in whom the instincts of a poet are choked is played with depth by Gabin. There's the complex and strangely sympathetic portrait of the seducer by Jules Berry.

There's the murmured movement and sympathy with the hunted man from the crowds below as Gabin in his top room smokes his last cigarette and rejects everything, rejects life. There's the sharply sensed stirring and transitory gaiety of a sunny Sunday morning which brings a pang every time I recall it. There's the poetry and realism of the love passages, sacred and profane (Jacqueline Laurent and Arletty). There's a fluid perfection of visual and sound-track.

I have written of this film in superlatives before. I have seen it four times and it still seems to have no flaw. It's absolutely national and absolutely universal. Hollywood must hate it a lot.

THE STRANGE LOVE OF MARTHA IVERS:
Directed by LEWIS MILESTONE: *15 June 1946*

In this film Martha (Barbara Stanwyck) murders her aunt as a child, implicates the son of her tutor (Kirk Douglas), sends an innocent man to the gallows, grows up, marries and drives to drink the tutor's son, trebles the family fortune and then meets and falls in love with an old childish playmate (Van Heflin). This is her undoing, for Van Heflin (one of those tough, hurt, resentful, wise-cracking anti-social young heroes) is in love with a nice non-murdering girl just out of five years' stretch in gaol (Lizabeth 'The Threat' Scott). Barbara Stanwyck gets the bullet as once before in the stomach and the gambler and the probationer go off hand-in-hand to that golden joint in the distance. Not even a Quarter Indemnity.

A NIGHT IN CASABLANCA: *Directed by* ARCHIE MAYO: *6 July 1946*

I estimate that I've spent sixty solid hours of my life looking at Marx Brothers' films, cosseting thereby a deep-seated anarchism. Prepared to subsist to the end on existing stocks of Marxiana I faced their new film with fingers crossed. One beautiful gag from Harpo — not quite equalled thereafter — had them uncrossed in three minutes. Whatever the failings of the film you can take it that the Marx Brothers are still, after five years, with the angels of disruption and disrespect.

A Night in Casablanca is half as good, because half as disruptive as *Night at the Opera* and twice as good as any film made since then.

The united front of Groucho, Harpo and Chico against the evils of law and order has been bent but not broken by enlistment in the Service of Patriotism. As with a cartoonist in war-time their range is restricted. Their victims have to be those poor old slow-thinking, sabre-scarred, guttural Nazis: the Chief of Police and hotel proprietor receive no Marxist conditioning.

The new film might- put to a merciful end the Near-Eastern spy-thriller inaugurated by *Casablanca*, which it burlesques. It has everything — the Nazi agents, the beautiful spy who croons in the luxury hotel, the plots and counterplots. Into this hotel bustles Groucho indomitably lecherous and jocund in tropical suit and fez, as the new manager unaware of the high mortality rate of his predecessors or of the hidden Nazi loot which caused it. He is laid for by the beautiful spy with the slinky accent. 'I am Beatrice,' she says. 'I stop at the hotel.' 'I'm Kornblow,' he replies; 'I stop at nothing.'

He does not exactly fulfil that promise but there are three scenes of vintage Marx in a film that is otherwise over logical and sedate, more clear in its mechanics than nine out of ten straight spy films. For those scenes I shall return to *A Night in Casablanca*. Never did I need the Marx Brothers as much as now.

MEN OF TWO WORLDS: *Directed by* THOROLD DICKINSON: *29 July 1946*

I have been trying to determine for three days why an expensive and ambitious British film, starting with every possible advantage, should turn out to be just a well-meaning bore. The answer is that it could never have looked like a good film at any stage.

For *Men of Two Worlds* Joyce Cary wrote the story and dialogue. E. Arnot Robertson supplied the original idea, Arthur Bliss composed the music, Eileen Joyce and the National Symphony Orchestra played it, and Tom Morahan composed the colour. The film was directed by Thorold Dickinson (*The Prime Minister, Next of Kin, Gaslight*) for Two Cities, took three years to make and cost £400,000. The weight of talent, you'll agree, is formidable.

It has all gone in to telling the story of a negro composer of music, Kisenga (Robert Adams) who leaves England at the moment of his first triumph to return to his native tribe in Africa at the behest of the British Government. This is because his tribe, the Litu, influenced by the wicked witch doctor Magole (Orlando Martins) won't go to the nice hygienic clearing the Government have prepared for

Hebridean live story — Wendy Hiller and Roger Livesey in
I Know Where I'm Going

them, but insist on staying in their tsetse-infested bush with their superstition and sleeping sickness.

His tribe rejected Kisenga as a 'white man with a black skin' and the thing resolves itself into a struggle between Kisenga and Magole (science v. witchcraft), with the white district commissioner, Eric Portman, and the priggish, humourless female doctor (Phyllis Calvert) backing Kisenga. Dr Calvert, in the smartest tropical kit ever, is all for thrusting progress down the natives' throats, D. C. Portman is all for caution and caginess. Neither of them looks anything but utterly unhappy in the African bush. Their melancholia is unrelieved, even when their pent up passion for each other, or so we gather, finds fulfilment at long last in a hand clasp, as Kisenga beats death and the wiles of Magole (by far the best player of the lot of them).

Seriously, this lengthy film on that old favourite Superstition v. Progress fails, as a documentary, to come within a thousand miles of *The Forgotten Village*, and *Children of the Arctic North*, because its settings being mostly fake, though amazingly good fake, are unable to compete with the excitement and beauty of the actual, and the story is not strong enough to compensate. The exterior shots, taken in two expeditions to Africa, form a minute part of the film. The main action takes place in Denham Studios.

And as a fiction film it is thin, hackneyed, over simplified and naive, thinly and naively played by all (black and white), except Orlando Martins and Cathleen Nesbitt as a delicious anti-progressive negrophile. The passage between her and the others is the one intrusion of maturity into the dialogue. Yes, the two reactionaries had my money. And therein surely lies part of the film's lack.

To be praised without qualification are the musical score of Arthur Bliss, the colour manipulation of Tom Morahan, and an outstanding short dream sequence. Here is solid progress in British technique — the film's salvage.

RANK v. RANK
THE WAY WE LIVE: *Directed by* JILL CRAIGIE: *27 July 1946*

Last year Two Cities Films with the consent of Mr Rank, produced a very good documentary film on the Abercrombie-Paton-Watson Plan for the rebuilding of blitzed Plymouth.

For a fiction-film producing concern this was a bold step, the general aim being to replace with intelligent British celluloid on British screens some of the wilder nonsense of American B films.

The completed film, *The Way We Live* (directed by Jill Craigie), then went into the hands of General Film Distributors (the Rank distributing company) and was shown to the exhibitors. Fortunately for the Press and the public and Two Cities Films and the citizens of Plymouth, my distinguished colleague Miss C. A. Lejeune smuggled herself into the trade show. She was thus able, by making a fuss, to prevent the sidetracking and suffocation of an important British film.

For the exhibitors were so disdainful and the distributors so apprehensive that it had been decided not to show the film to the Press at all until the critics raised their voices and were allowed to see it.

'We're not monopolists, are we!' — J. Arthur Rank to Joseph A. Rank

The Trade Press reviews, written for exhibitors, praise it as 'intelligent, thoughtful, comprehensive', and sound the warning note, 'its wider appeal will be restricted to thinking audiences'.

This interesting sequence of events at once displays two truths. First the irreconcilability of Rank the producer of British films with Rank the exhibitor of Hollywood's films (through two of Britain's largest circuits), a contradiction that forces Mr Rank to reject with the right hand what he has made with the left hand.

And second, that the critics are not, as Mr Rank would have it, entirely useless and destructive.

The Way We Live has had two public showings at Warrington and Coventry and on Monday it will have its première at Plymouth. It has not yet been booked for exhibition.

Now let me say that this stimulating 64-minute film has far more of the attributes of entertainment, such as speed, tension, humour and humanity, than a dozen recent A films. It is not a political tract — all parties and interests involved in the argument are allowed their spokesmen — although it is a vivid social commentary.

Nor is it an impassioned, emotional play for our sympathies or an illustrated lecture, though it perfectly explains the Plan and the obstructions that beset its fulfilment.

It is all that the London Plan film should have been and wasn't, and its faults are so slight and so obvious that they can be ignored. I think it represents the mature British social-fiction film, and I think, properly exploited, that it would succeed with almost any audience.

Thirty-year-old Jill Craigie, who wrote and directed *The Way We Live*, has a valuable flair for characterisation and satire. The non-professional cast — councillors, sailors, engineers, mothers, fishermen, Sir Patrick Abercrombie, James Paton-Watson, Lady Astor, Michael Foot, M.P., the Lord Mayor and Corporation of Plymouth — have all a quick veracity.

In the fictional kernel to the film she has drawn an evacuated British working-class family without an atom of condescension or caricature. The adolescent daughter, restless and stirring, the father, sceptical and indomitable, the harassed mother and the mother-in-law are portrayed with a warmth of honesty not equalled in any film since *Millions Like Us*.

Praise must be given to the acting of Francis Lunt, as the father, and to 17-year-old Patsy Scantlebury, as the daughter. She has already signed a contract with the Rank Organisation.

You will, by the grace of Mr Rank, be stirred and moved by this film, which is wholly of the cinema and of Britain and of our times, which is lucid and hopeful and clear-eyed. And you will note once again, hearing the musical score of Gordon Jacob, that British sound tracks are ahead of any others.

If the topicality and intelligence of *The Way We Live* is considered by exhibitors too heavy a burden for your unthinking minds, then protest with all you have got.

COURAGE OF LASSIE: *Directed by* FRED M. WILCOX: *1946*

The gorgeous fun of the Lassie films has gone. In *Courage of Lassie* they have taken her from the beautiful unbelievable Britain and her Duke and grooms and Brooklyn-accented Duchesses, changed her sex, and made her into a G.I.

She is now a male collie in America torn from the side of her doting little owner (Elizabeth Taylor), enlisted into the Dog's Army Corps and sent to the Aleutians. She rescues a company of men, is cited for gallantry, gets shell shock, goes savage and kills sheep, is sentenced to death, rescued, and rehabilitated. She might be Sonny Tufts.

'Men go to Church to pray to a God they can't see. Bill worships a God he can see. You're his God,' says Uncle Frank Morgan to little Kathie in a transport of Dog worship. Later on she observes in that bated wonder-stricken voice. 'It's an odd feeling to be a God.' I'll say.

LONDON TOWN: *Directed by* WESLEY RUGGLES: *31 August 1946*

For over a year streams of publicity bulletins have kept us informed about the progress of Britain's first giant musical in Technicolor (started on two years ago), designed to rival the glories of Grable.

To ensure that the film was strictly to Hollywood pattern, Mr Rank engaged an 'ace' American director Wesley Ruggles and gave him full control over the story, production, and direction. There was to be no experimenting to find the elusive form of the British musical: it was to be a challenge to Hollywood in a field that was and still is, enviably or unenviably, Hollywood's own. We thought all along that Mr Rank was wrong and now we know he was wrong.

The finished work 'London Town' is a flaccid, ugly, ill-assembled film running for two hours and yielding a total thirty minutes of fun (for which you have to wait an hour) and a couple of numbers that will be whistled, played and hummed around. The fun consists of Sid Field being his inimitable and brilliant self in his established stage turns. Elsewhere he is lost, with Sonnie Hale and Claude Hulbert, in a film that distresses by its poor continuity, shoddy dialogue and general ineptitude.

55

Breaking in on our ennui are the London Town Dozen and One Girls, whose uniform hardness of expression and voice is balanced by a wilting male chorus. Their (the girls) ballet number in a field of daffodils reaches a high pitch of idiotic pruriency, and their dancing never comes near the normal Hollywood standard for musicals.

Mr Ruggles's London is evoked by a few shots on the Thames, Cockney land-ladies, pearly kings and queens and the inescapable Dozen and One. In that respect the film is the purest Hollywood, which is, I take it, what Mr Rank wanted. But they cannot generate the essential spark that animates the most banal back-stage musicals from 20th Century or M.G.M., that unshakable belief in and courage of their own vulgarity.

But I still can't see the point of importing an American director and giving him all the time and money in the world to play with when we can make bad musicals on our own, and quicker.

THE OVERLANDERS: *Directed by* HARRY WATT: *September 1946*

The achievement of Harry Watt's refreshing little Australian film (I use the word 'little' without referring to celluloid length and without derogatory intent) is to give you and me a large slice of the wide open spaces of a comparatively unknown Dominion. It was a formidable task that he undertook when he went to Australia on behalf of Ealing Studios, and it was a formidable result to have brought back a film that will sell in the open markets of commercial cinema, without departing from his austere documentary principle that the theme is greater than its parts.

The open-air movie up to now has belonged exclusively to America, who has exploited the western areas of her continent for twenty-five years with astonishing variations and permutations on a single theme. The well has now run dry.

India, Africa, Australia, the Federated Malay States, Honduras, and what have you, lie in front of British cameras and writers with a thousand strange conflicts and eccentric adventures to record.

Working under immense technical difficulties, Harry Watt has produced a real open-air movie, with a lot of space to move in. It is apparent from the finished film that it was shot in Australia with a rough general idea of the story and then given its finished form in the cutting rooms of Ealing. This is evidenced by the broken movement of a narrative, cut into too many chatty incidents.

I felt that the film should have defined itself into a deliberate momentum convey-ing a feeling of vast tracts of country being fought over by furious endeavour. I wanted more heat and more struggle. The materials were inherent in the story and abundant.

There surely was no need to be so naive in characterisation or in telling the dear little refined love story. If we had to have this it might have been a little violent or a little poetic or a little real. During a back-breaking adventure, such as the trek over thousands of miles of hellish country, Boy and Girl would not talk and act as if they were on the verandah of the tennis club. But would that sort of boy and girl be found in the outbush?

56

Sid Field in *London Town*

All the way through there are hints of Harry Watt's grasp of the potentials in his story; the night scene for instance with the cockatoos clustering on the trees and the Southern Cross glittering in the sky. And in the sequences with wild horses, which were fluidly beautiful. And the jamming of the cattle on the mountain-side. And let us congratulate Harry Watt on the absence of kangaroos and camp-fire songs, items which few directors could have resisted.

The restraints of the picture and the superb control of the cattle through the long months on location helped considerably to atone for the over-simplification that could only have been justified by a grand sweep. I think Harry Watt has found something though, and I trust Sir Michael Balcon will pick, from among a large choice of Australian writers, one who will give Harry Watt the sort of script that will make his second journey really necessary.

ZERO DE CONDUITE: *Directed by* JEAN VIGO: *7 September 1946*

There is showing at the Academy a remarkable French film *Zéro De Conduite* the first full length work of Jean Vigo, who died in his early thirties to the loss of world cinema. It is a surrealist fantasy about boys and masters at a French school, witty, intelligent, vital and original. It has already been condemned as highbrow.

The story, which ends with a triumphant revolt by the boys against the masters has, it is true, a dreamlike inconsequence and an apparent vagueness which might be found disconcerting after the simple logic of the Hollywood musical. It makes demands upon you, which is unusual in a film, but when you've met it halfway handsomely rewards you.

For it gives you a startling picture of a community of boys, savage, ritualistic and remote from the normally levelled adult eye and understanding. And it gives you a boy's eye view of the masters, too, with all their deficiencies, absurdities, madnesses and indecencies thrown into necessary caricature. It gathers lucidity with each viewing.

CHILDREN ON TRIAL: *Directed by* JACK LEE: *7 September 1946*

A good programme balance is given to *Zéro de Conduite* by Crown Film Unit's *Children on Trial*, a 60-minute film about juvenile delinquency.

The narrative takes two delinquents, a boy and girl, follows them from their hopeless homes through arrest and sentence into the approved schools, through their three years of rehabilitation to the threshold of the new life: brings them back, in fact, to the social swamps which bred them. The film ends with them facing the hardest test of their lives by no means certainly.

Children on Trial is a well-made film in every respect — acting, cutting, dialogue, music, photography, script; one that can hold its own as entertainment with any fiction film. Ministerial primness had obviously to be negotiated, particularly in the female school, where aberration is mainly sexual and treatment more hopeful than efficacious (the teen-year old girls are women, the boys adolescents). All this is no more than hinted at.

This film represents the new down to earth style of British documentary, relying as *The Way We Live* relies, on a central narrative and a stressing of human values and relations rather than on a series of images for their own sakes related to each other by montage and cutting (the old fancy style of documentary) and it should soon be apparent to British audiences that films like *Children on Trial* and *The Way We Live* (which incidentally locate some first rate natural acting material) are better value, in all ways, than any 'B' film, and a good proportion of 'A' films.

THE BIG SLEEP: *Directed by* HOWARD HAWKS: *21 September 1946*

There are some big names in *The Big Sleep* — Raymond Chandler wrote the original book, William Faulkner and Leigh Blackett wrote the screen play, Howard Hawks directed the film, and Humphrey Bogart and Lauren Bacall permeate it. This combination guarantees you anything but a sleep, big or small. The term incidentally signifies Death: who takes first lead in the film.

The Wild West hero is out, rendered flabby and effete by song and cabaret, the Thin Man has put on weight and taken to religion, the gangster is forbidden, the Odysseus of the new world is now the shamus (private dick or eye) put into dour and classical prototype by Humphrey Bogart.

He operates with blasé acumen in a ferocious heavy lidded milieu of gamblers, murderers, loose lovelies and aristocratic rakes, biting out with the speed of a machine gun his words of wooing and warning.

He is in unexpected possesion of a corpse, he dials the police: 'I've got some cold meat lying about.' He has no reverences, no fears, no love — until he meets his female counterpart in sourness and cynicism and clasps her to him as the sirens shriek and his enemies die on the ground.

A sullen atmosphere of sex saturates the film, which is so fast and complicated you can hardly catch it. I found these dowdy heroics fascinating and I recommend the film whole-heartedly both as entertainment and as a study in social sadism.

DAY OF WRATH: *Directed by* CARL DREYER: *23 November 1946*

Wardour Street would do well to study the effect on the war-isolated stranger from Europe of the standard cinema programmes enjoyed by British and American audiences.

Such a visitor is stunned by the monotonous triviality of the programmes. More sharply than the critic he perceives the degradation of the Hollywood movie; more sensitively than British film chiefs he sees the way the British film should move.

Carl Dreyer, Danish director of the French classic, *Passion de Jeanne d'Arc*, has been catching up on six years of missed films. His comment is succinct! 'They all look alike,' he says.

Carl Dreyer is here for the opening of his new film, *Day of Wrath* made in Denmark in 1942. It does not look like anything less than a masterpiece.

Day of Wrath will ravage you with its power of horror and pity and will haunt you with its beauty. Dreyer, as in *Jeanne d'Arc* is obsessed by pictorial image, by lighting of face and composition of groups, that will inevitably produce and possibly deserve the description 'Rembrandtesque'.

He is also obsessed with the horrors of superstition and witch-hunting in 17th-century Denmark and his story is of the dreadful tragedy that followed the denunciation and burning of an old woman for witchcraft after confession extracted by torture. In her death agonies she curses the pastor, his young wife, the inquisitor. The credulous fears and guilt sense of this trio and the witch-ridden village community propel them into a self-instituted accomplishment of the curse.

The development of the tragedy is slow, sombre and majestic. Its real victim is the young wife of the pastor (Lisbeth Movin). Childlike, unfulfilled and superstitious, she meets and loves her stepson. To see her suddenly glow and grow smug and gay with fulfilment is to watch something that Hollywood doesn't understand — grown-up sex. Deserted by her lover, defeated and hopeless, she readily confesses to witchcraft and faces the stake.

The acting, especially with the old woman (Anna Svierkier), the pastor's mother (Sigrid Neiiendam) and the young wife, has an unusual quality as of emanation from an inner force of emotion: it does not depend on normal acting technique. None of the characters wears make-up.

The savage strength of the film, its fragile pastorals and deep shadowed interiors, the costume and *décor*, and the exquisite and sensitive sound track make *Day of Wrath* one of the great experiences of the frustrated cinema enthusiast.

GREAT EXPECTATIONS: *Directed by* DAVID LEAN: *11 December 1946*
(*See also pages 171, 172*)

For some time now I've been troubled by an uncomfortable urge to overpraise British films, to wish them, almost, into realms of thought and feeling they inherit but never fully enter. It is not enough that they overtop the normal Hollywood production — and they have done that since 1942 — in discretion and discrimination and taste. It is, I think, their heritage to freshen the whole business of film making. Britain has the biggest start of all countries on the new paths of the cinema with lots of stories to tell in celluloid, and the ability to tell them and the places to tell them in.

As proof of this, I ask you to note a definite break from discreet miniature and delicate water-colour into full canvas. I ask you to pay attention to the first big British film to have been made, a film that confidently sweeps our cloistered virtues into the open. The best, I think, of Dickens's novels comes to the screen with all the magical thrill it gave you on the first reading.

Dickens has never before been rendered effectively into cinema terms: now the acceptable adjustment between the realism of the camera and Dickens' robustious enlargement of character is made. The original dialogue, left largely intact, comes out fresh and vivid. Behind this proud achievement is some of the finest and most nervous talent of the British cinema.

Ingrid Bergman and Bing Crosby in *The Bells of St Mary's*

David Lean (co-writer and director), Ronald Neame (co-writer and producer), Anthony Havelock-Allan (producer-in-chief) are the team who made *In Which We Serve*, *Blithe Spirit* and *Brief Encounter*. They have given *Great Expectations* an increasingly technical finesse and a large sweep. It is their first break from Noël Coward.

The casting on which so much depends is nearly perfect. Jaggers (Francis L. Sullivan), Magwitch (Finlay Currie), Wemmick (Alec Guinness) The Aged Parent (O. B. Clarence), Joe and Mrs Gargery (Bernard Miles and Freda Jackson) and the rest are kept on a tight rope balance. They are never allowed to lapse into Coloured Christmas Supplement portraits.

Pip, the boy (Anthony Wager), and Pip, the man (John Mills), bring to necessary life the off-stage narrator of the book (it is John Mills' best and most sensitive performance in films). But it is the young Estella of Jean Simmons and Martita Hunt's Miss Havisham who give the film an extra and inimitable cachet and revive most potently the dreams of the book.

A turn of speed attained by cutting that is ingenious enough to hide its brilliance, rebukes the pedestrianism into which most contemporary British films have fallen. This film could only have been made in England, and a large amount of its visual pleasure is derived from the superlative photography of the Medway Saltings, and a recognition of mordant beauty of English 'weather'.

Great Expectations is a lavish, unostentatious film, romantic, exciting and English to the core. It will have, I venture to prophesy, the best of all Box-Office worlds.

BOOMERANG: *Directed by* ELIA KAZAN: *25 January 1947*

Three times, in three years, at the Tivoli cinema I have been given the critic's most special treat: the pleasure of recognising in an unknown unadvertised Cinderella of a film elements of character and distinction that stamp it instantly as an event.

Such films were *Phantom Lady* and *Sunday Dinner for a Soldier* and such in a more significant way is *Boomerang*. Produced by Louis de Rochemont.

Boomerang is a reconstruction of an actual unsolved murder committed in a Connecticut town — a case that is still open on the files of the U.S. Courts of Justice. The victim, inexplicably shot on the main street, was the town's well-loved priest of the High Episcopal church. The crime was used as a political lever and mass hysteria was so stimulated that an arrest had to be made at all costs. A young man was arrested, tried and acquitted.

The central figure in the film is the State Attorney whose whole future, as well as his party's, depends on a conviction. As he seeks to confirm the strong evidence against the accused man he becomes uncertain of it and finds himself destroying, piece by piece, his own case and his own political party.

The film is a study of integrity, beautifully developed by Dana Andrews (the only well-known player in the flawless cast) against a background of political corruption and chicanery that is doubly shocking because of its documentary understatement.

This is not the pleasant Lullaby of Democracy we normally receive from Hollywood; but a much prouder work, ruthless and revelatory. It will disquiet you less.

Leading Hollywood Heart Throbs, 1946: William Blythe, Cornel Wilde and Van Johnson

Because de Rochemont and Kazan tell a story as a story should be told on the screen the film is absorbing for every second of its 86 minutes.

They give you the whole flavour of this small town, its normal horrors and normal hopes. The cutting is dramatic and sure and the sound track minimises background music and uses silence and the muted sounds of life to heighten the realism and, as most producers wouldn't know, the emotional power of the film.

ODD MAN OUT : *Directed by* CAROL REED : *1 February 1947*

Odd Man Out is ostensibly the story of a doomed man on the run from the police. It spans eight hours from 4.0 p.m. when the chase starts, until midnight, when he is killed. He is the leader of an illegal organisation (undefined) and it is in pulling off a robbery for party funds that he shoots a man and is himself mortally wounded. The scene is Belfast in mid-winter.

Through rain and snow, his strength slipping with each hour, he performs a harrowing *danse macabre*, in air raid shelters, junk-yards and pubs. And the people he desperately turns to — a cabman, a disreputable old police nark, a housewife, a publican, a drunken insane artist — rise round him in a sort of ballet of lost souls.

Jostled in his agony, from one to another, he is the pivot of their reactions, the illumination of their cowardices, terrors and unwilling goodnesses.

Always the city and its noises dominate. Reed has wrought this sound track as brilliantly as he has caught poetry in the sideways and alleys of a shabby city. The shouts and laughter of children coming out of school merge into the more strident, grimmer notes of the slum children in the dark until there are no children, only the murmured clamour of pubs, ships' sirens, and trams. The fine musical score of William Alwyn has been woven into the rhythm of the film.

The acting is mostly without flaw, being chiefly from the Abbey Players of Dublin; in the case of F. J. McCormick and Cyril Cusack, it has something of inspiration. The latter reflects most subtly the pathetic nervousness and inefficiency that have wrecked so many projects of fanatical terrorists. Robert Newton is the core of an interlude of sombre fantasy placed in a beautiful decayed rococo setting.

There are minute and close packed subsidiary portraits — the stool pigeon shebeen keeper (Maureen Delany), the head constable (Denis O'Dea) and the publican (William Hartnell). James Mason as the hunted man plays with credit a most thankless and difficult part.

The film, for all its meticulousness and shaping, would improve by some cutting. I could willingly have been deprived of some of the passages between Father Tom and the girl (Kathleen Ryan); and one or two other short sequences, notably that wherein Mason, in his delirium, quotes from the New Testament, jarred.

But these are afterthoughts. *Odd Man Out* is a brilliant film, with a feeling for the beauty of city streets and places of habitation that I would like to see dedicated to some of the aspects of London.

Nocturne, Belfast — James Mason, Kathleen Ryan and Robert Newton in *Odd Man Out*

Merle Oberon in *The Lodger*

PARTIE DE CAMPAGNE: *Directed by* JEAN RENOIR: *11 October 1947*

In the seven months that have creaked by since I was absent from the films the scene has radically changed. While the unremitting mediocrity of the new films was inducing a widespread critics' cafard and the spectre of Dalton was haunting Wardour Street, an era died. Hollywood unspectacularly lost dominion over the world's screen. [. . .]

It was fortunate that I was able to see this week a film that by having a simple, poignant and absolutely filmic eloquence allows me to praise nearly without stint and thus exonerates me from a possible charge of returning with an intolerably harsh critical approach. It is *Partie de Campagne* a fragmentary film made (and not quite completed, although it makes sense, perhaps more sense because of an almost inspired hiatus) by Jean Renoir just before the war, from a short story by Maupassant.

The story is of the first amorous experience of a young Parisienne on a country outing, from which she returns to a drab marriage. Years later she meets her fascinating seducer in the same place and they both know they have lost something precious and beautiful. Two of the minor parts are overplayed, the sub-titles weigh heavy, but nothing can tarnish the intense lyrical simplicity underlaid with an aching irony and made almost unbearable by the yearning musical score of Kosma. This is everybody's lost love.

FAME IS THE SPUR: *Directed by* JOHN BOULTING: *11 October 1947*

I cannot take calmly the inadequacies of *Fame is The Spur* (Produced by Roy Boulting, and contributed to by Nigel Balchin), they go in so many directions.

It would have been possible to have sorted out of a long unwieldy book a biting, haunting portrait of that unhappily characteristic British figure — the chauvinistic power-bought, vain, obfuscating Labour demagogue. It might have been lit as *Citizen Kane* was lit by diverse spotlights, emerging as a loved empty creature of horror and pity and charm.

The MacDonaldesque effigy supplied by Michael Redgrave is the film's central and incurable flaw, though in its sole moment of compulsion (when he is rejected contemptuously by the Welsh miners he had betrayed) even he is rocked into brief living.

The period dressing is careful and intractably modern looking and much more glossily finished, of course, than *Partie de Campagne*. Almost any Russian and lots of French period films have the trick of both creating the nostalgia of the past and making us live in it. Here the illusion utterly fails.

The dramatic technique is slow and trite and considering its length and the length of time it spans and its theme, curiously uneventful. Rosamund John as the disillusioned but still ever-loving spouse would, I should say, have lived up to any demands made on her. There were not many. But the film had its small integrity in the ending, which would not have discredited the work it might have been.

VIVERE IN PACE: *Directed by* LUIGI ZAMPA: *25 October 1947*

There is nothing from Hollywood this week, except the great tragi-farce in which Menjou, Taylor, Montgomery and Cooper have been participating — the Inquiry of the House Committee on Un-American Activities. This is the efflorescence of a ridiculous and savage persecution that has been going on a long time to the steady detriment of American films.

The hunted are those who dare to express any sort of liberal approach to politics or their craft, who have an inkling of its power and the talent and the wish to advance it: the hunters are the safely contracted has-beens, the fanatical Russian haters, the hamburger manufacturers, the boys who make us welcome the 75 per cent tax.

If only America could realise the effect on Europe of the evidence on Communism in the studios by Mr Robert Taylor, a star who, according to his wife, is constitutionally unwilling to read a line of print, she would bring in Mr Deeds for a quick clean up of the Committee.

To balance this insanity Italy has given us the first really detached and therefore the most interesting and mature film of the last war. *Vivere in Pace* deals with the resistance of men and women to the contagion of war. The peculiar position of Italy in the war and what may be described as a national allergy to warfare does not belittle the achievement, although it may explain it. *Vivere in Pace* goes into the pacifist gallery of honour with *Westfront 1918*, *All Quiet on the Western Front* and *La Grande Illusion*.

The scene is a village in the central mountains of Italy, left, because of its remoteness, in the charge of a single German non-commissioned officer and the local Fascist secretary. They, all of them, including the German, want only to live in peace while the war rages round them; the German collecting his tribute, the Fascist extorting his graft, the peasants working the land. They are all uneasy and uncertain. There isn't a hero among them. The artless-appearing technique gets round and models with a perfection of portraiture each one of these adorable escapists. Their landscape and homes, their habits and their talk grow upon you with the surprising familiarity of truth.

The end to all this illusion comes with the sheltering of two escaped American prisoners (one of them a Negro impossible to disguise) by Uncle Tigna, fearfully, protestingly, unhappily but unquestioningly. The German calls. The Negro is thrust into the cellar where he proceeds to get drunk and roister. Upstairs they ply the German with wine to drown the noise, but the Negro breaks out and confronts the German.

This is a moment when the film hangs poised. Then they, the German and the Negro, become brothers in drink and go out on a wild jag in the village, shooting

All bores together — Joan Blondell, Clark Gable, Thomas Mitchell's soul, Greer Garson and Thomas Mitchell in *Adventure*

out the lamps and shouting that the war is over and inciting the villagers to help themselves to the German stocks of confiscated food. After which the German collapses in a stupor. Will he remember in the morning? The whole village is at the mercy of one man's hangover.

Such is the core of the film, further embroidered by a limpish love idyll between Tigna's niece (Mirella Monti) and the white soldier (Gar Moore) and a conventional death bed finale. The playing from Fabrizi (Tigna) down to the smallest part has the hard warmth that distinguished I am told, *Open City*. I particularly recommend the Fascist trying to convince himself, and not succeeding, that the Germans will win.

The film is always lovely to look at, even if it fails as drastically as Hollywood or Britain to make love (or sex) on the screen something to watch without restlessness and even if it does touch slapstick in the drunk scenes *Vivere in Pace* establishes that insufficiently appreciated truth that normal cowards are as film material more interesting, more stimulating and braver than abnormal heroes.

MONSIEUR VERDOUX: *Directed by* CHARLES CHAPLIN: *8 November 1947*

Let's not make any mistake! Chaplin's *Monsieur Verdoux* is the most exciting thing that has happened to the screen for years; very probably it is his greatest film. At the cost of comfortable popularity this inviolate artist has pursued the logic of his own nature. He has given us a work that in all its power and weakness is the emanation of a single and matured mind. He has paid a heavy price for this in America and already in Britain the yahoos have raised their voices.

The figure of pathos and defeat of his previous films now hits back in protest. To do this he has discarded the baggy trousers and bowler hat. He has become a dapper Latin mass-murderer in the Landru-Wainwright tradition, seeking out wealthy women victims and on the profits maintaining a rosy little bourgeois home with crippled wife, young son and domestic pets. He has been driven to this exacting career by unemployment after thirty years service as a bank clerk. In the pursuit of it he is meticulous, hardworking, harassed. The scene is ostensibly France, but it is more than ever the bright, twisted, super-realist world of Chaplin. The strange thing is that you don't for an instant miss the beloved properties of Charlie Chaplin. He is perhaps freer for their surrender to make his protest.

There are five ladies, including an uproariously murder-proof Martha Raye and the inevitable dewy protégée (Marilyn Nash). You may find it hard to credit, but the dispatching of these women is a consistently funny business, packed with comic inventiveness. Through relaxing the hard ethics of his trade and sentimentally allowing the girl to go free M. Verdoux undoes himself and the film fades out classically with his walk away from the camera towards the guillotine. The anarchist has been beaten again. Before his extinction M. Verdoux delivers the 'message' that has caused so much fury and abuse — that he had merely been practising on his own, what, on a scale involving millions, is sanctified by Commerce, the Church and the State; that the world needs more love, etc. etc. 'May God have mercy on your soul,' says the chaplain before the last walk. 'Why not,' says Verdoux, 'it belongs to Him.'

Platitudinous? Of course. But who else would chase such a platitude to the bitter end? It is Chaplin as much as the suffocating sentimentality with the young girl is Chaplin and the unmatchable sense of irony and horror and of pathos and comedy and slapstick is Chaplin. Who else could compel you to watch every movement and flicker of expression as he rushes up the stairs and makes an elaborate telephone call that has no apparent relevance? And to do it several times and add to your apprehension of the figure he is creating. In his cutting, Chaplin is individual and rhythmic; only those who are blind to the immense virtuosity of his playing could call the film slow. There is no trace of visual platitude. The flaws are emotional and rhetorical, and, let it be confessed, occasionally aural, for his score has its vulgarities. I will not enumerate any of the exquisite pantomimic subtleties that decorate the sustained irony of *Monsieur Verdoux*. Go for yourself and see a film that is refreshing in its moral courage and pacifist assertion of human dignity. And then, as I will do, go again.

MINE OWN EXECUTIONER: *Directed by* ANTHONY KIMMINS: *22 November 1947*

Korda has broken the ice at last and can be said to have contributed the fourth noteworthy British post-war film in *Mine Own Executioner*. *Great Expectations* had romantic breadth, *Brief Encounter* its sad music, *Odd Man Out*, its poetic slant on the human plight; all had technical brilliance. *Mine Own Executioner* does not experiment in the sense these films did; there is no angling of the camera or manipulation of focus. There is missing in the film, as in the book from which it was taken, an overriding poetry. What it does is to deliver an intelligent translation of an intelligent contemporary novel, a below-the-surface novel of implication and inference. And that, as we know screen practice, is plenty.

The book's author, Nigel Balchin, also wrote the screenplay. And the director, Anthony Kimmins has nearly everywhere placed the right emphasis in a story that moves ruthlessly on more than one level. *Mine Own Executioner* is also the first psycho-analytical film that a grown-up person can sit through without squirming.

The central figure is the alienist himself, the self-destroyer who can sometimes cure others but must torture and maim his wife, who he loves, through his own incurable neurosis. Burgess Meredith plays this part with a nervous power he has not equalled since his first appearance in *Winterset*.

The accumulation of professional frustrations as a lay practitioner, his nagging self-disgust, his perverse adolescent inclination for shop girls as an escape, build up into a terrifying migraine which hits you from the screen. At the lowest ebb of his resistance and at the most delicate and dangerous point of the treatment he lets loose a schizoid patient (Kieron Moore). The patient murders his wife and commits suicide, as the alienist knew he would. There is a post-mortem and the alienist just about scrapes through. The coroner's inquest is one of the best observed court scenes ever.

The integrating into a whole of the surface story of the schizophrenic airman, the dominating undercurrent between the alienist and his wife and the clinical clashes

Suffering psychiatrist — Christine Norden, Kieron Moore, Burgess Meredith and Dulcie Gray in *Mine Own Executioner*

in the background is a startling achievement of scripting. The smooth conviction of the film must be equally accredited to the intuitive brilliance and experience of Burgess Meredith, the unobvious craftsmanship of Kimmins, and the inherently cinematic quality of Balchin's narrative and dialogue. The concessions are, as I said, small — a slight lifting at the end by a kiss and a half-promise of happiness (not in the book), a failure to define the root cause of the airman's *malaise*.

The playing is generally first rate, with the deep exception of the two women, Dulcie Gray (the wife) and Christine Norden (the light o'love), who, in common with most British women of the screen, are suburbanised and simplified into non-entity. There is, too, an obtrusive and unnecessary underlining by music of the moments of dramatic tension.

It is a pity the publicity boys don't understand their own film. The posters indicate that something forced Kieron Moore to kill himself. Perhaps they know by now that it is Burgess Meredith who symbolises all of us who, self executed, still go on living and looking the same.

GOODBYE TO ALL THAT: *27 December 1947*

In respect of everything but films the cinema's year has been revolutionary. Our supply of Hollywood culture has all but dried up, Mr Rank has lost £2,000,000 on production, the studios of France are in thrall to the dollar, Italy leads the world. A few words will cover the customary New Year's Eve survey of the Old Year's films. There were I think, five: *Boomerang, Open City, Vivere in Pace, Monsieur Verdoux,*

69

Odd Man Out. These alone had individuality, stature. There is no gain in recollecting the mundane virtues and vices of the rest. Now is the time, I think, finally to assess J. Arthur Rank as a benefactor of the British film.

The film critic cannot look at a film as if it came spontaneously from nowhere, a finished creative work. He must take in economic and political factors that govern the making, marketing and exhibition, factors that often divert or destroy ideas and soil talent. He must identify the many separate elements that flow into a film. And he must very soon recognise that the hucksters of the cinema, the middlemen and monopolists, have a lower set of values than the public whose pulse and pocket they have their fingers on and in.

To the critic thus aware the apparently illogical shifting from one country to another of the inspirational force of the cinema is no mystery. It can be seen and understood while it is happening. Mr Rank came on the scene when it looked as if Britain might be the inheritor after Russia, Germany, France and America had variously held it, of the custodianship of the fragile art of the film. Mr Rank entered a field he still doesn't understand the first thing about with mystic notions of profit, uplift, prestige and sheer boyish monopolising.

Mr Rank made the British industry big and vertical when it should have been small and horizontal. Mr Rank's advisers did not grasp, as the conscious critic grasped and protested that financial success lay in a direction contrary to the Hollywood path of lavishness and extravagance, that it was parallel to the utmost development of the poetic realism Britain had forged in documentaries and near documentaries. But neither Mr Rank nor his advisers had a clue to the later world scene that was obvious to the most modest observer of historic events.

They were taken for buggy rides by slick transatlantic executives in a futile chase of the dollar. They harnessed the half-developed power of the British film industry to a gamble that has failed financially and aesthetically.

Mr Rank has already made his defence. He has lost money, it seems, by making 'artistic and cultural' pictures for the sake of British prestige and in doing so has put British directors and stars in the top flight. What are these triumphs of art before profit? *Caesar and Cleopatra, Colonel Blimp, A Matter of Life and Death, Henry V, Men of Two Worlds, Odd Man Out, Brief Encounter, In Which We Serve, This Happy Breed, Great Expectations, The Way Ahead, A Canterbury Tale.* These and scores of ridiculously expensive minor films.

Of them, five (less than one a year) can hold their own with half a dozen cheaply made post-war Italian pictures. The others are stillborn epics conceived and made in the sort of individualistic romp Mr Rank was led to encourage in the name of Prestige. Actually they were neither box-office nor prestige, not honestly high, low or middlebrow. The two directors who have come through with distinction, David Lean and Carol Reed, owe nothing to the Rank Organisation. They are dedicated characters who would have made films anyway. Without the time and resource to become prima donnas they would have made rougher and possibly better films, certainly more.

The biggest romp of all — the Rank Organisation — is now being drastically curtailed, production expenses are being cut and austerity lies ahead. It looks as if the slogan will be 'Box Office at all costs'. This is a bad outlook when it is considered that Rank proposes to integrate even more closely the distributing and producing ends of his empire. It means that the Wardour Street boys will have more say than ever as to what you will see in two-thirds of the big cinemas of Britain. And I'll leave you to guess where that will take the British film.

QUAI DES ORFEVRES: *Directed by* HENRI-GEORGES CLOUZOT: *3 January 1948*

In the course of a quarrel in this week's new French film the wife says, 'Go on, blame the capitalist system. Me, I'm a Royalist.' 'You're a Royalist and you come from two rooms in a back street,' sneers the husband. Now this is not only the language of love; it is the human idiom in French, English or Turkish, a live voice almost never used on the English-speaking screen.

Nearly all the characters in *Quai Des Orfèvres* connect with life outside the bounds of a far from well organised or savoury murder story. The detective (Louis Jouvet) has an African Service background and a half-caste son on whom he dotes. He has a sardonic disrespect for his chief and the illusionless wisdom of an ordinary man who has lived hard.

He is fascinating not because of what he does, but because of what he is. And so is the lovers' friend (Simone Renant) with her unmentionable and so delicately conveyed passionate obsession. And the lovers (Bernard Blier and Suzy Delair), sensual, jealous, cruel like any one of us, have, without recourse to petrified endearments, more love in their little fingers than the whole content of the last five years of British pictures, specifically dedicated to sacred and profane variations on the theme. In addition to this stereoscopic knack with character Clouzot is infallible with background — here the hinterland of Parisian variety, teeming with the sort of veracity we never saw in any American backstage film. On the strength of this minor film Clouzot appears as the most interesting manifestation of the post-war French cinema.

Clouzot appears to have a weakness for the thriller form. Intricacies of plot and the tying and untying of knots conflict with the subtler conflicts within these un-resilient self-imposed bonds. He has more than an affinity of viewpoint with Georges Simenon. Is he a mere thriller-maker with unusual endowments? Or a truly creative director temporarily handicapped by commercial necessities or instincts?

CROSSFIRE: *Directed by* EDWARD DMYTRYK: *3 January 1948*

Again we salute, as we saluted *Boomerang* this time last year, a small (in the trade sense of cost and settings) and courageous American picture. *Crossfire* is another murder story that holds its own with any on the basis of suspense and speed. The courage lies in motivating the murder with something that is dreadfully real and practically unmentionable in films unless in connection with the safely villainous Nazi — anti-Semitism.

Several American soldiers, in pub-crawling transition from Service to civilian life, get drinking with an amiable Jew. He is beaten up and dies. It becomes rapidly clear that he died because he was a 'Jew-boy' at the hands of a typical dupe of racial consciousness, although the trail points in other directions.

Fastening the crime on this man (Robert Ryan) is the main business of the film, but it allows the detective (Robert Young) to diagnose the fear that leads to hatred and then violence — to detect the mainspring of anti-Semitism. It also allows Robert Ryan to perfect a portrait of the universal recruit to the lower ranks of Fascism — the resentful bully with his catch-phrases, ignorance and fear. And he is, because he still threatens us all round, more spine-chilling than a dozen oily emanations of Greenstreet or all the boyish horrors of Karloff.

Crossfire is not an anti-anti-Semitic tract nor a definitive study of the disease. It is a thriller that insists on being more than just a fairy tale. And this realistic slanting somehow adds to the consciousness of the actors. Robert Mitchum has never been so good since *Ernie Pyle*, Ryan is first rate, Robert Young never happier than when pinning down anti-Semitism as un-American. Gloria Graham persists in remaining my favourite cutie. Admiring the restraint in the handling and playing of the Jew I yet feel that he need not have turned out to be a war-hero. He did not have to be glamorised to point the thing's horror.

BRIGHTON ROCK: *Directed by* JOHN BOULTING: *10 January 1948*

Had I been a film-maker that relentless and terrible book *Brighton Rock* would have tempted me from the moment of its publication. It is the most filmically written book of Britain's most filmic writer. It is also the clearest exposition of his view of humanity. Because of that I should have resisted. To make the film truly — and what is the point of doing otherwise — would be to circulate a drab and nihilistic Roman Catholic conception which I hate. To bowdlerise and sweeten the book for censor and box office purposes is an alternative.

It has been chosen by the Boulting Brothers with the approval and scripting collaboration of Graham Greene, the author. *Brighton Rock* has been dexterously packed with most of the detail of the book's superficial excitement.

The opening murder, the gathering of the seedy razor gang under the leadership of the immature, life-hating Pinkie Brown, the distrust and murder within the gang, the horrible wooing by Pinkie of the girl to silence her, the hunting down of Pinkie by Ida, the cheerful promiscuous stout drinking believer in Right and Justice — are in faithful sequence.

But what will a person, untutored as to the book and Graham Greene's pre-occupation with cosmic Evil, make of these characters? They come from nowhere to flit motiveless before us. Pinkie is not explained. The hell that lay round him in his infancy and drives him from horror to horror is undisclosed. A few hints for the knowing are not enough to lift the film out of the sadistic norm of British gangster films. Films have been made that said forbidden things and got by. *Brighton Rock* falls over itself to placate by steady dilution and makes a final surrender with a trick ending that M.G.M. might well envy and that we have been politely asked not to disclose.

72

Child's guide to Graham Greene — William Hartnell, Carol Marsh,
Richard Attenborough and Hermione Baddeley in *Brighton Rock*

It is an ending concerned with Mortal Sin and Divine Forgiveness that is reported
to please both Graham Greene and John Boulting as pro- and anti-Roman Catholic
respectively. As one of the most unscrupulous tamperings with a book I have yet
encountered it displeases me intensely. But I am no sword swallower.

The playing of Richard Attenborough, Hermione Baddeley, William Hartnell
and Harcourt Williams is as good as it could be without touching any sort of
magnetism. The girl (Carol Marsh), plump and nice instead of peaked and
tortured, scrapes by except in moments of grief when suburbia breaks relentlessly
through her voice. *Brighton Rock* the film is slower, much less compelling and, if
you get me, much less cinematic than the book, as a child's guide to which I
hereby offer it.

OLYMPIAD FESTIVAL OF THE NATIONS: *Directed by*
LENI RIEFENSTAHL: *7 February 1948*

The film famine has also evoked the four-hour German epic, *Olympiad Festival of
the Nations*, a brilliant and intermittently repulsive work. Leni Riefenstahl,
commissioned by Goebbels to produce the film, fulfilled every demand. An
impeccable and ingenious coverage of the Olympic Games in Berlin 1936 is inter-
larded with *Kraft durch Freude*, with Teutonic Mystic and idealisation of the young
male body, with fanfare and ceremonial, ugly neo-classic sequences and happy
laughing aspects of the Fuehrer.

These odious infringements apart, the film is a triumph, a complete use of the
movie to describe a great event. The omnipresent cameras work at every speed
from slow motion to normal and from every angle and distance to induce a feeling

of closeness to the personality of each competitor. Style and character astonishingly come through. Repetition is eschewed.

Olympiad is eminently capable of being deloused. Put into convenient size and shape (60 minutes) it would stand as a standard piece of imaginative reportage — a lesson not only to the Rank Organisation, who will cover the Olympic Games in Britain this year, but to the authorities on whom they depend for facilities.

THE WORLD IS RICH: *Directed by* PAUL ROTHA: *14 February 1948*

In April 1946, the Government commissioned Paul Rotha to make a film on the subject of international food. He completed it by August 1947. Since then its fate has balanced delicately between trade opposition and C.O.I. tardiness.

Tomorrow it will be shown at the New Gallery and Tivoli cinemas. Its chances in the matter of distribution are uncertain.

Men in Wardour Street may decide that you are too light-minded to endure for 35 minutes an able and sincere document on a vital theme that you yourself have paid for.

Rotha in *World of Plenty* and *Land of Promise* developed a platform technique that some found overbearing, some irresistible and none could ignore. *World of Plenty* was disconcertingly box-office.

In *The World is Rich* Rotha has cut down on the Isotypes with their abstract and, to me, chilling authoritarianism. And equally happily he has lost the gormless man-and-woman-in-the-street and their smart Aleck interlocutor.

Seven voices toss the argument about as scenes of starvation and plenty from the world's archives, some familiar, others new, pound at our propaganda-drunk consciences. And it is an argument.

A bit diffused in tense and geography, a bit specious in the fictitious black market gorgings, a bit jejune, it is in the main exposition irrefutable, impassioned and timely.

The World is Rich closes the didactic phase of documentary on themes of contemporary life. The individual, contrary to the Grierson tenet, becomes more and more important. He will be the core of the new documentary, whose aim will be to reach your mind not by giving a lecture but by telling a story.

BLANCHE FURY: *Directed by* MARC ALLEGRET: *21 February 1948*

A long time ago I fell in love with a house in Staffordshire. A circular drive and an amazing flight of steps swept the eye to a soaring perfection of line.

It could be seen from a half-mile away dove grey sedate and absolutely pure Elizabethan. It blended with and completed a stretch of unhampered landscape.

This week a British film started off with some atmosphere and speed and brought up suddenly at this house — Wootton Lodge. The shock of this revolutionary economy was intense.

And then a few shots of unexploited English scenery in notable Technicolor induced a palpitation of hope that could only be dissipated by a couple of reels of

Stewart Granger and Valerie Hobson assisting British costume melodrama on its predestined course.

Though *Blanche Fury* betrays Wootton Lodge it does get away from the Home Counties and Devonshire and it does effect some interior decor that very nearly approaches that of the American film *Kitty*. As much technical assurance as can be is injected into a third-rate story by the most efficient studio in Britain.

This is all about murder, mayhem and seduction among the Furies in 1860. Our interest in them is not enhanced by the necessity of watching Miss Hobson pose against fulsome backgrounds for long stretches, though she is very beautifully coloured and they are very beautifully decorated.

All four Furies die violently. Miss Hobson in giving birth to the son of the illegitimate but rightful heir (Stewart Granger) who had murdered her husband and her father-in-law and is hanged. Thus the heir comes to Clare Hall and the sun shines. By the smirks of the expiring lovers this is assumed to be a happy ending. Mr Granger, by virtue of scowling through the film is assumed to be giving us the 'acting' we are always being promised.

I asked Anthony Havelock-Allan, the producer, why he didn't use some of the interiors of Wootton Lodge. The expected reply was that the rooms were too low for lighting. My reply to this is: Let's have some bad lighting and some bad photography and perhaps a bit of good movie.

In acquiring perfection the movie camera has lost range and adventurousness. Technicians adore studio sets where they have domination over weather and lighting and time to give art paper finish and gloss to their pictures. But as they get glossier British films get emptier and sillier.

House steals picture — Valerie Hobson, Stewart Granger, Walter Fitzgerald, Michael Gough and Wootton Lodge in *Blanche Fury*

FARREBIQUE: *Directed by* GEORGES ROUQUIER: *13 March 1948*

So free of uplift and mock-simple, of sermonising or instruction is *Farrébique* that to introduce it as a documentary, with the present sad associations of the word, is somehow unfair. *Farrébique* is documentary in the best and truest sense. It details a way of life that is remote — that of a French peasant in the centre of France. It compels us momentarily to participate in a cramped existence, guided by toil and avarice, in very beautiful country. As often in French films one senses in the director the instincts of a painter, which is in part an explanation of how so much is done with so little.

A year's existence on a farm kept by miserliness and the law of primogeniture (which gives all to the eldest son, who has to indemnify the rest), sowing and harvesting, the family meeting and bickering about the share out, the death of the grandfather, the going away of the second son, the long debated installation of electricity, the birth of a grandson. That is *Farrébique*.

But it is revealed to us by an artist who filches the essential detail out of each small scene and thereby gives the film tempo. He adds to its power by a perfect sound track. He has also worked a miracle with the peasant family whose untutored playing goes as deep as that of Russian peasants in the great days of Russian documentary.

It is a pity that a man of such intense power of scrutiny should have intruded all those ecstatic documentary tricks of vernal wooing and mating. Such false and unwanted scenes spoil an otherwise perfect narrative of the simple life that does not glamorise its narrow monotony and makes us grateful for the shabby urbanities of our austerity existence in London.

FOUR STEPS IN THE CLOUDS: *Directed by* ALESSANDRO BLASETTI:
29 March 1948

The choice this week is wider than usual — American, British, Anglo-American, Argentinian and Italian. The Italian film, *Four Steps in the Clouds* (*Quattro Passi Fra le Nuvole*) is the only one to make contact with the living world. The rest condemn us to the ritualistic dimness of the studios.

Four Steps in the Clouds is a gay tender ironic story of a brief encounter; a small film with an effervescent belief in life. The hero (Gino Cervi) is a commercial traveller in a shabby creased suit, coping with the small miseries of family and commercial life. On a two-day sales trip in the country (the outward journey is the merriest thing in recent films) he meets and befriends a girl (Adriana Benetti) who has been betrayed.

He unwillingly masquerades as her husband to placate her family who have all the narrow intolerance of small farmers. After some embarrassments he succeeds in winning their acceptance of the girl's plight and returns home to a nagging wife always to be haunted thereafter by the dewy yielding beauty of the girl. The quality of this film derives from some very good script writing (necessitated by small resources) and from the superb acting of the players, who wear their parts as naturally as they wear their clothes. *Four Steps in the Clouds* evading bathos by hairbreadths has caught enchantment.

THE FIGHTING LADY: *Supervised and edited by* LOUIS DE ROCHEMONT: *March, 1948*

This truly inspired record of a single U.S. aircraft-carrier in the Pacific is probably the war's best documentary.

From the *Fighting Lady's* decks, from her fighters and bombers an apparently ubiquitous camera keeps an endless observation of every phase of her two years of widespread and devastating offensive.

It has captured a fantastic panorama of fantastic warfare and has at the same time wrought an amazing group-portrait of a floating community of 3,000 souls.

It was done by U.S. Navy photographers in Technicolor on 16 mm. film, which was then blown up to 35 mm. The colour not unnaturally varies in quality, but these vistas of blue seas and green-brown tropic islands shot with the red glare of explosives, of sunset and sunrise, clamour with colour. The film would have lost more than half its force in black and white.

War has never before been so intimately reproduced. Cameras in the guns of fighters plunge us into the thick of air battles, Zeros buzz around us in swarms and are shot down in scores. The lens swoops down with dive-bombers and as the incongruous loveliness of Truk, Marcus Island, Guam or Kwajalein reels sickeningly away with the plane's climb the screen shivers with the jolt of the explosion. On the decks returning planes give moments of paralysing anxiety to the crew as they did to me and the audience. A plane comes down without steering control, chases the signalling officer across the deck and pins him against the island whilst a watching pilot unable to bear it hides his eyes and turns away. Others come down on fire and are extinguished or jettisoned in minutes. And always there is that tense business of taking off and landing to the complicated and fascinating ballet movements of the signalling officer.

Ingenious cutting and editing have crowded all this into one hour and have given the film continuity. Narrative is well delivered by Lieut. Robert Taylor, U.S.N.R., written with imagination and used without obtrusiveness.

It is good to note that distributors have decided that this fine and exciting film is not above the heads of audiences, nor beyond their patience. The public, in fact, will be permitted to see it.

But a sad thought stole in at the end of this revitalising experience. Britain was the pioneer in this new technique of warfare. British carriers, ill-equipped as they were, played a terrific and adventurous part in the early days of the war when America had but one such ship.

Worse than that I am informed that in the whole of the British Pacific Fleet there is not one film unit at work to record in the finest conditions of light and weather the achievements of the British Navy. And the Admiralty so far as I can discover have not even officially seen this great American documentary.

The melancholia is increased when we remember that Britain, once the pioneer of and leader in documentary films, is being rapidly outstripped by America in that field of cinema.

THE MURDERERS ARE AMONGST US: *Directed by* WOLFGANG STAUDTE: *7 April 1948*

For arrogant drivelling I recommend a piece by Tatler, editorial voice of *The Daily Film Renter*. Protesting against the first exhibition in London of a post-war German film he had not seen, he advises his readers not to touch this 'precious' picture with a 'barge-pole' and concludes with 'At the risk of being monotonous, I will again repeat — to me, every German film, no matter who makes it, stinks.' This sort of attitude and style is familiar in Tatler's column, whose readers are the men who rent films. It is the Trade articulate and conveys something of its hard opposition to any infiltration of enlightenment and artistry into the cinemas of Britain and America.

The film in question, *The Murderers Are Amongst Us*, enlightens and has artistry.

Beware of self-pity — Alexis Smith, Paul Henreid and Eleanor Parker in *Of Human Bondage*

It is in the real sense of the word post-war and that can be said of few films to-day. It is German and reflects German consciousness into which it is surely incumbent on us to gain every form of insight.

The scene is Berlin immediately after defeat; the theme is the rehabilitation of a young German Army surgeon neurotically obsessed by guilt and self pity through involuntary participation in a Polish mass execution.

He sees salvation in an individual act of retribution against the captain who gave the order, is prevented from putting this into effect by the love of a woman and delivers the captain to official justice. Ernst Borchet playing the doctor with a tremendous sincerity crystallises the national Weltschmerz raised to unbearable intensity by defeat. Hildegarde Knef, the girl from the concentration camp, who loves him, is beautiful enough to be already in Hollywood.

But the essence of the film is its whole anguished mood of helpless self-pity in a condition of blind chaos and its most memorable creation is Captain Bruckner, acted by Arno Paulsen. He is, in looks and deeds, a microcosm of all the big and little Himmlers, smug, pompous, sentimental, bourgeois, implacably and perfunctorily destructive. We have seen the German criminal portrayed by everybody except the Germans. Here he is and it is the most harrowing portrait of them all.

The Murderers are Amongst Us carries a Ufa heritage of camera angles, heaviness, neurosis, sentimentality and deviations into dim and fleshy cabarets. It is sombre, slow, intense, tragically moving and in common with the post-war Italian films as true as it can be to the surrounding reality. It would seem that only the impoverished and the defeated can focus the camera lens on life.

The sound track with its rediscovery (for us) of silence and the spare and apt music of Ernst Roters is a joy and a relief.

GERMANY, YEAR ZERO: *Directed by* ROBERTO ROSSELLINI:
24 April 1948 (see also page 94)

This week, as one of a small audience containing several leading British film directors and technicians, I saw the third film of the Italian Roberto Rossellini — *Germany, Year Zero* — to be shown in Britain. Rossellini himself was present.

It became patent to some of us, if we had not known it before, that Rossellini is the brightest thing that has happened to cinematography in perhaps two decades.

It became clear to me, after some hours of subsequent talking with him, that I had encountered a rare and intact person, an affirmer of life whose technical originality is the complement of a passionate humanitarian conviction.

Germany, Year Zero, made from scratch, was shot last year in the Russian, British and American zones of Berlin. Written, directed and produced by Rossellini it is acted, with one exception, by German amateurs. The theme is German destitution and despair mirrored in the tortured being of a boy of 12.

This film delineates Berlin today physically and mentally as nothing else has done. Its tragedy is sublimely conceived and wrought with an uninterrupted flow of unique camera logic. The camera moves continuously; the cuts are made from action, a notable achievement of control over medium. This mastery gained with a minimum of equipment struck David Lean, Britain's best cutter and camera manipulator, into a condition of dumb ecstasy and envy on that memorable night.

The secret lies in the approach and spirit of Rossellini, who refutes if necessary every canon of established film making and repudiates its monumental elaboration. He affirms the cinema, as well as life. His realisation is that if you look closely enough into a person you discover his world; his dedicated purpose is to document the individual and his method is ceaselessly to reveal that individual in his own environment by an ever-moving camera.

Rossellini, like some of us, is astounded at the failure of British films to document or even touch a climactic period of British history.

HAMLET: *Directed by* LAURENCE OLIVIER: *May 1948*

The thing to say of Olivier's *Hamlet* is that it will enhance British 'prestige'. Another dominant claim is that it will painlessly inculcate in the unconscious millions an appetite for the works of William Shakespeare. These expressions by implication defend the glamorisation, pruning and simplification of the original text and plot and the de luxe style of the production.

Could anything be more ironic or futile than the advent of a 'prestige' film on behalf of British cinema, at a time when British cinema has wilfully surrendered the brightest prospects it has ever had or is likely to have for a long time to come? Can one believe that, any more than *Henry V*, *Hamlet* will make cultural inroads on mass consciousness? Most will miss the deeper meanings of the soliloquies and speeches, instinctively resist blank verse and fail to grasp a plot that however simplified is still more complex than a dozen of the obscurest whodunits.

Olivier's *Hamlet* puts the film critic on the spot. To deflect his true evaluation, admiration for the gallantry and dynamism of Sir Laurence Oliver (producing, acting, directing, evolving) combines with the publicity fanfares and the patriotic angle.

Hamlet is for the film critic an absorbing experience outside the run of his critical regimen. But he will admit in all honesty that Olivier has made in *Hamlet* no contribution to the evolution of the cinema or to appreciation of Shakespeare. The insuperably difficult task of transposing a great tragedy, depicted in sublime and intricate flights of verbal shades of meaning, into a medium predominantly visual has been essayed. It must be said that in all its boldness the attempt has failed.

It is precisely when Olivier is most enthusiastically cinemising that we lose contact with tragedy and pathos and become conscious of ingenuity and technique; the assertive lighting, the glossy art photography, the pointless meanderings of the camera, the self-conscious *décor* inhibit a full surrender. This is not to say that at times he does not consummately fuse image, word and meaning, as in the first and in the *To be or not to be* soliloquies, in the closet scene with Eileen Herlie in' the impeccable graveyard sequence (that tawdry backcloth effects cannot tarnish) and in the terrific duel and finale of slaughter that are perfect as cinema and Shakespeare.

All the more obtrusive and boring then are the innumerable tracking shots that leave no stone unturned in Roger Furse's mediocre conceptions of Elsinore. It cannot be denied that the camera has got completely out of hand through large sections of the film, has been enlisted in the service of Gilbertian 'compositions' that make great play for and look utterly at home in shiny magazines. It could be that by these extravagances Olivier designed to woo the middlebrow on mutual ground. Such excursions are aesthetically fatal.

The extra illustrations — Ophelia's death, the fight at sea, the murder of the King — not only fail but add an unwelcome flavour of Hollywood. In these surely, and in the 'Ghost' scene, the cinema should make triumphant and inimitable effect, yet the former merit the description 'cheap' and the latter is sheer travesty and nearly inaudible.

The standard of acting in *Hamlet* is sufficiently high to make me resent all the elaborate interferences with my proper enjoyment of it. Given the existing talent and the score of William Walton I could dispense with the deep focus effects and all the extraneous trickery. In fact, an altogether simpler recording of the play, as in the television version, would have established a closer contact between audiences and Shakespeare and could have admitted those excisions that are germane to a full comprehension of *Hamlet* without extending the film beyond two and a half hours.

Critical reception of *Hamlet* has staggered me. The word genius has been plentifully applied to Olivier, the producer and director. I stake all my instincts for cinemaphotography that this is nonsense. If he intends to go on making Shakespearean films let him discover a director with something new to say in cinema terms, for Olivier clearly does not know how to make a film flow visually. My predilection is for the straight unvarnished photographed play in lieu of a revolutionary, unliteral assault on Shakespeare by the movie camera.

It is highly debatable. Shakespeare is for me primarily a shaper of words, for all that may be said by my colleague Dr Manvell and others, to the effect that had he (Shakespeare) lived today he would probably be leading script-writer for M.G.M.

OLIVER TWIST: *Directed by* DAVID LEAN: *23 June 1948*

David Lean's second Dickens film *Oliver Twist* is, as one anticipated, a thoroughly expert piece of movie entertainment. As such I can guarantee it. In any deeper aspect the film profoundly disappoints. *Great Expectations*, a far more uneven film, touched higher levels of poetry and drama. My impression is that Lean has become imprisoned by technique.

First, I must say that Lean's telescoping and simplifying of the plot should not incense the most rabid Dickensian. I personally rejoice in the liquidation of Mrs Maylie, Rose and other bores from the happy sections of the novel.

But Lean and Stanley Haynes (his co-writer) have jollied and to a large extent lost Bumble, the real and memorable villain of the piece. They have tempered the savage hatred that raged throughout the novel, ironed down the squalor and degradation, filled the film with *Beggar's Opera* musical interludes, and built up the whole action to a Cops and Robbers climax. Lean has done credit neither to himself nor Dickens.

Is it not ridiculous that descriptive passages of Dickens should be far more

To
John Howard Davies
from
his fan
Richard Winnington
January 1949

John Howard Davies and Francis L. Sullivan in *Oliver Twist*
(inscribed on the flyleaf of a copy of *Drawn and Quartered*)

visually effective, far more filmic, than their equivalents in the film? Oliver's terrifying march with Bumble to the undertakers, for instance, becomes an almost gay affair, with the help of some facetious music from Arnold Bax. Dickens pursued Bumble to his ignoble end with a hatred that never wavered. Francis L. Sullivan renders him — on his limited appearances — comic, likeable, even pathetic. And Robert Newton, inveterately himself, reduced to commonplace the oddly human figure of depraved cruelty that was Bill Sykes.

Three alone in the cast have the power to affect the images we have carried in our minds through a lifetime: Alec Guinness, who consummately lives up to every terrible aspect of the Fagin of Dickens and Cruikshank. Anthony Newley, who as the Artful Dodger, could have reached an equal perfection had Fagin's thieves' kitchen not been cleaned up to make of him and his confederates repentant Dead-End-Kids. And young John Howard Davies's Oliver, the quintessence of sensitive, abused, deprived and spirited boyishness.

Oliver Twist is, of course, beautifully cut and photographed. On its own crisp level of simplified entertainment nobody in Hollywood or Britain, except perhaps an unevasive David Lean, could have bettered it.

But Lean in failing to develop the purpose, passion and atmosphere of Dickens's great tract has also failed for the first time in his career as a director to move forward with a new film. And Lean is of all directors in England the most favoured and the most free, the most answerable to himself.

THE IRON CURTAIN · *Directed by* WILLIAM WELLMAN: *12 July 1948*

In New York Communists picketed the cinemas showing Hollywood's first anti-Soviet film, *The Iron Curtain.*

I suggest British Communists might easily welcome a film whose propaganda is so naive as, in effect, to reverse itself.

The Iron Curtain purports to document the events leading to the Canadian spy trials. A commentator using March of Time style and a few location shots in Canada gives a spurious documentary air to a blatantly fictitious build up of the Russian traitor Gouzenko as a hero. It is to be credited to the Canadian Government that it would not allow interiors of the Parliament building to be photographed for the film.

It is, of course, possible for a man to be a traitor and not a villain. In a situation where Allies distrust and spy on each other whilst still fighting a common enemy peculiar disillusionments can descend upon men engaged in dishonourable work for honourable patriotic ends. This might apply to British and Americans too in certain circumstances.

But Darryl F. Zanuck is not concerned with such adult complexities. Gouzenko's betrayal must be because his Russian colleagues in Canada are sinister figures of destruction, neurotic drunks or nymphomaniacs and because his month-old son already shows a predilection for the Canadian Way of Life. And, of course, because only the Russians are so wicked as to employ secret service agents and military attachés in their embassies for the purpose of collecting military information.

Remember those over-simplified grotesque Nazis we got so tired of in American, British and Russian war films? Well, we've inherited them again as Russians: simple, dehumanised and easily hoodwinked by the handsome Mr and Mrs Gouzenko (Dana Andrews and Gene Tierney) plus, of course, the Royal Canadian Mounted Police.

As spy entertainment *The Iron Curtain* is muddled and slow, a vastly inferior film to *Confessions of a Nazi Spy*, the superficial resemblance to which adds a melancholy comment to this review. Its biggest condemnation perhaps lies in its reduction to mediocrity of the brilliant director of *Public Enemy, Nothing Sacred* and *The Oxbow Incident.*

THE RED SHOES: *Directed by* MICHAEL POWELL: *26 July 1948*

The new British heavyweight, *The Red Shoes,* is an ambitious attempt on a great filmic subject — the tragedy of Diaghilev and Nijinsky — that falters into trivial Technicolored magnificence.

At first the film partakes of the authentic fantasy of backstage ballet life: then the interpolated specially devised ballet occupies the screen for 20 minutes and clears it for a hackneyed plot to wind its way to a sticky end.

We open with shots of clean-swept Covent Garden, its ruddy porters singing Old London Street Cries, and move into the gallery of Covent Garden Opera House, where the famous Ballet Lermontov is performing. It can be noted that the Archers (Michael Powell and Emeric Pressburger) have quite failed to hit off the constitution and character, predominantly suburban, of the ecstatics who inhabit the ballet galleries of London.

Thence into the story of an ambitious little rich girl (Moira Shearer) who craves to be a ballerina, of her discovery by the great impresario Boris Lermontov (Anton Walbrook), which coincides with his discovery of a young student composer (Marius Goring).

And into the flurries, flounces, turmoils and sweat of that esoteric life behind the curtains of the ballet in their portrayal of which, owing it cannot be imagined how much to the presences of Massine and Helpmann Messrs Powell and Pressburger touch better cinematography and better realism than in any other of their films.

The colour in these passages is excellent, the material, feverish and photogenic, lends itself to all the Archers' little tricks of filmic whimsy. You almost accept the Svengali-Diaghilev of Anton Walbrook, bending the girl to his sublimated purpose and inspiring the composer to write just the ballet for her, out of gratitude for the Mercury Theatre scene, the long shots of practising dancers, the snippets of dancing, the wit of Massine, the general truth of atmosphere.

But when the curtain goes up on the film's *pièce de résistance* — the Red Shoes ballet, composed by Brian Easdale, designed by Hein Heckroth, choreographed by Helpmann and Massine and based on the Hans Andersen fairy tale — you have had nearly all of such enjoyments.

This ballet is certain to be acclaimed as a cinematic masterpiece on the ground that it departs entirely from realism. But its escape is into the realms of Disney and the Hollywood dream sequence. Far from gaining by such licence it becomes blurred by Technicolor, overpowered by *décor* and confused by its own fantasy. The Red Shoes ballet is an essay in complicated camera trickery for its own sake, assisted by some no more than adequate music and dancing.

And after the ballet — the old nag between Art and Love. For the composer and the ballerina fall in love, marry and are thrown out by Lermontov, who mopes either on behalf of his own unrequited love or on behalf of unrequited art. It is not made clear.

But when she comes back to Monte Carlo pursued by the husband who should be conducting at the début of his opera in London, puts on her red shoes and throws herself from the balcony in front of a train, you have a sort of suspicion that Messrs P. & P. are getting vaguely allegorical and that the story of the ballerina is meant to be a larger version of the Hans Andersen story of the little girl whose red shoes danced her to death.

And a long, exhausting pretentious film ends morbidly and in bathos with anatomical close-up details in full colour of the cuts, bruises, lacerations and blood on the legs and body of Miss Moira Shearer, who it should be mentioned is an undeniably photogenic dancer with as much chance as any other girl of becoming a good screen actress if she wants to.

A FOREIGN AFFAIR: *Directed by* BILLY WILDER: *3 August 1948*

I put this week on record as containing four commercial films that leave the customer with an unfamiliar sense of some value received.

Satirically, cynically, sentimentally or melodramatically they connect somewhere with reality.

Accusations of bad taste have been and doubtless will be made against Charles Brackett (writer-producer) and Billy Wilder (writer-director) because they have made a comedy out of occupation life in Berlin. Such complaints can be ignored.

Their joke comes off: an acrid, back-firing sort of joke if you like, but a joke that, as all good jokes should, illumines while it stings.

A Foreign Affair is very much the other side of the Berlin picture presented by *Germany, Year Zero* and *The Murderers are Amongst Us*, and the best satiric comedy from Hollywood since *Hail the Conquering Hero*. It owes its speed to hard, brilliant writing as much as to direction.

The effect is of a film made in Berlin, though only the outside scenes, which are excellent, were photographed there. Billy Wilder can be congratulated on the realism of his back projection.

The merging demoralisation of victors and vanquished in a conquered city is a theme that harks back beyond Hannibal and loses none of its implications by being handled as racy, idiomatic comedy. The satire here is at the expense of the Americans — occupying and snooping on Congressional missions.

The plot is classic Hollywood — frigid, puritanical, sin-hunting Congresswoman (Jean Arthur) being softened, broken down, compromised, humanised and beautified by love and the black market.

Her rival is Marlene Dietrich, singer at the Lorelei Night Club, ex-girl friend of a high-up Nazi and shameless camp follower. Perennially alluring and beautiful, she sings the wry acid sexy songs of Frederic Holländer, the composer who helped to make her famous in *The Blue Angel*, and who is seen accompanying her on the piano.

The man between the girls is John Lund, a newcomer whose nonentity is given no time to weigh on us.

The love-clash put over with expert lightness by Dietrich and Arthur, is regarded with no seriousness at all by Brackett-Wilder, who mock it to the end. The real hero is the Colonel of Millard Mitchell (remember his brilliant reporter in *A Double Life*), who steadily sidelights the backwash of Victory with cynical-tolerant wisecracks.

I recommend *A Foreign Affair* as a film without a bore to its name, as American comedy in the tradition of Lubitsch and Wellman, as an example of how to get by the Hays Office with tongue in cheek.

LOUISIANA STORY: *Directed by* ROBERT J. FLAHERTY: *23 August 1948*

The enterprise of the Edinburgh Film Guild — a body of film devotees unique in Britain or for that matter in the world — procured for the festival the first view in Britain of Robert Flaherty's new film, *Louisiana Story*.

The enterprise of Robert Flaherty procured the backing for his film — to the tune of £250,000 — from the Standard Oil Co.

Since 1922, when he made the first documentary film to hit the box-office, *Nanook of the North*, Flaherty has successfully pursued and developed a style of film-making that quite ignores the outside world of cinema or the nagging pressure of contemporary life.

He is a story-teller of remote and simple ways of life. His favourite protagonist is the wandering, dreaming, unlettered boy in tune with nature.

In *Louisiana Story*, he is a Cajun (Acadian) boy of 13 (Joseph Boudreaux) called in the film Alexander Napoleon Ulysses Latour.

With a bag of salt as a mascot and a pet racoon he wanders through the bayous of Louisiana, superstitious, romantic, adept and zestful. He shoots and fishes, an alligator destroys his pet and he exacts revenge.

Into this Flaherty paradise moves an oil derrick, heralded by miraculous speed-boats and swamp caterpillars.

The entranced boy watches while the rhythmic drill is sunk and the shafts are driven down. Watches with awe as, in some of the finest sequences ever photo-graphed naturally, the well blows off its top in a fearful cascade of gas and foam. And subsequently watches as the machine triumphs and the well is joined to a pipeline.

He waves to the departing derrick and the friendly crew, another experience has come to add to his dreaming, and gone. He is back in his serene world.

Louisiana Story, full of light and beauty, is an intensification of the Flaherty manner. Slow, elegiac, inductive, it relies — too much, you may think, from the point of clarity — on visual explanation.

Flaherty spent two years in Louisiana on this film, and he has lost himself ecstatically among the stretching bayous, canopied with Spanish moss, lotus leaves, cypresses and oaks.

It is a film in which he has indulged himself to the full, in his world forgetting.

And you must surrender wholly to his luxuriation or maybe find yourself bored, not to say antagonised, by his refusal or inability to find anything new to say.

I personally relaxed and gave, and allowed the truly magnificent musical score of Virgil Thompson to tide me over the several patches that the best will in the world could not excuse.

MIRACLE OF THE BELLS: *Directed by* IRVING PICHEL: *13 September 1948*

It is providential that Hollywood's latest and crudest act of publicity on behalf of the Roman Catholic Church should appear simultaneously with a profoundly subtle French portrait of one of its saints.

Miracle of the Bells carries unseemliness into areas of sacrilege that surely Roman Catholics will not condone despite the pay-off message.

The film has been blessed by the all-powerful cabal of 13 American women's organisations. But a leading British trade reviewer cannot disguise his contempt for the film (or the public) and summarises it thus: 'Although good taste is not one of its strong suits, it should win the approval of the crowd.'

That in Trade Press terminology amounts to severe disparagement. It must be added that *Miracle of the Bells* is a slow, sleep-inviting piece of filmcraft employing a heavy-handed flashback technique.

Ben Hecht in the script vainly tries to intersperse cheap moralising with some of the satiric venom of *Nothing Sacred*. But it is coarse-grained stuff, and the story is such that nothing could lighten its repulsiveness.

It tells of the stunt funeral of the dead film star he had loved (Valli), organised by Press Agent Fred MacMurray with the connivance of Father Frank Sinatra. The method — a three-day bellringing jam session (at so much an hour) from the five churches of her humble coalmining home town. The result — nation-wide publicity, rescue of the dead star's shelved film *Joan of Arc*, and a 'miracle' caused by the crowds rocking the foundation of the Father's small church, and, like the girl in the limerick, making the saints in their niches stir.

The phoney miracle is acclaimed by the whole of the U.S.A. and welcomed by Father Sinatra on the basis that anything that brings hope to the people is an act of God. Conclusion — even God needs a good Press agent.

MONSIEUR VINCENT: *Directed by* MAURICE CLOCHE: *13 September 1948*

Monsieur Vincent depicts the extreme of human goodness in the brilliant characterisation by Pierre Fresnay of the Father Vincent de Paul who in seventeenth-century Paris gave up the rich pickings of a successful ecclesiastical career to serve 'his masters' the poor. He repudiated without criticism the vested interests of the Church he served. Incidental to the unforgettable virtuosity of Fresnay (and it is a

Painting week at the Movies — Lilli Palmer, John Garfield, Ann Todd and Ray Milland in *Body and Soul* and *So Evil My Love*

tour de force) is an evocation of squalid poverty, rapine and plague that has no equal outside the *Gorki* trilogy.

De Paul, gifted with a realistic flair for organisation, never moralises, never preaches, and in his dying invocation to a young girl follower crystallises the torturing sense of insufficiency that pervaded his life of good works.

'Remember the poor are your masters. They are terribly exacting and sensitive: you must make them forgive you your charity.' He speaks almost as if he sensed from its cradle the ominous rumble of Revolution.

Monsieur Vincent will be felt to minimise the opposition and hatred de Paul engendered in the materialistic and luxury loving Church of Rome, but it could be answered that the viewpoint is always that of de Paul, whose pity embraced all men, from the curled and scented Richelieu to the most malodorous cripple.

It is a robust, very beautifully designed, slowly moving film, informed with a haunting feel for its times, and accompanied by a faultless sound track on which music of Grunenwald is sparingly and significantly employed.

PAISA: *Directed by* ROBERTO ROSSELLINI: *13 October 1948*

It cannot be doubted that Roberto Rossellini's *Paisa* will stand as one of the few great comments on the Second World War to be made by the contemporary cinema. Outside events will impart to its London run a sombre appositeness.

Paisa, made by Rossellini in the thick of the Italian campaign, is a two-hour film about the relations of occupiers and occupied or liberators and liberated from the time of invasion to the final stand of the Germans.

Its six separate and scattered episodes, varying in quality, are unified by Rossellini's overriding insistence on the importance of the individual. His belief in men and women is evident in almost every foot of the film, through all the disillusion and irony.

The stories take place in Sicily, Naples, Rome, Florence, a Franciscan monastery and the marshes of the Po Valley. With the exception of the fifth (the monastery) each one is permeated with a sense of tragic irony and given a de Maupassant flick at the end.

They must be followed closely, for they have the inconsequential untidiness of war, the cutting is often abrupt and the detail closely packed.

Even those stories that seem to strain for fictional effect — the Sicilian girl who died avenging an American soldier and whose epitaph from his buddies is 'Dirty Little Eytie', the Roman prostitute picking up the American who treasures memories of her innocence six months before and doesn't recognise her — are saved by the sincerity of the players, Carmela Sazio, Robert Vanloon, Maria Michi and Gar Moore.

The Naples Monastery and Po Valley sequences display Rossellini's unique talents to the full. The last, brave, disillusioned and full of forlorn beauty, contains the whole core and meaning of partisan warfare and owes not a little, one would say, to Malraux's forgotten and unrecognised masterpiece *Espoir*.

Paisa, humorous and tragic, fully earns the depleted title 'great.' Its deficiencies are as obvious as its brilliance. Its title in English means *My Country*. Its American title, *Paisan*, translates as *My Pal*.

It is an all-American-Italian film, distinctly disparaging in representation of and comment on the British. And I take it that Rossellini to gain on the American market was prepared to lose in objectivity.

But the fact that the dialogue is 75 per cent in spoken American (the rest is sub-titled) should win distribution for a splendidly positive film of our tragic times.

BONNIE PRINCE CHARLIE: *Directed by* ANTHONY KIMMINS:
1 November 1948

By this time every witticism in the book will have been projected by my colleagues at Korda's £1,000,000 floperoo *Bonnie Prince Charlie*.

I have a sense of wonder about this film beside which *The Swordsman* seems like a dazzling work of veracity and art. It is that London Films, having surveyed the finished thing, should not have quietly scrapped it.

Surely those audiences who will be ballyhooed into the back-aching misery of 150 minutes in front of *Bonnie Prince Charlie*'s monumental mossy ineptitude will at last resent? Surely such a film in the circuits will be detrimental to the general habit of unselective screengazing and therefore to London Films?

Bonnie Prince Charlie with its flapping backcloths, its welter of Scottish airs and comic clansmen performs one useful service in spotlighting the talent and beauty of Miss Margaret Leighton.

TWENTY-TWO TO REMEMBER: *3 January 1949*

My list of outstanding films for 1948 is based on the simplest criterion of pleasure, received and remembered. It numbers 21 films — 22 if that artistic curio *Hamlet* is admitted on the grounds of trying.

Not one is a work of shattering filmic genius, but each possesses on its own level the common aspect of aliveness. Here they are:

American: *Crossfire, The Naked City, A Foreign Affair, Body and Soul, On Our Merry Way, Call Northside 777, T-Men, Johnny Belinda*.

British: *The Fallen Idol, The Small Voice*.

French: *Quai des Orfèvres, Le Corbeau, L'Idiot, Antoine and Antoinette, Le Diable au Corps*.

Italian: *Four Steps in the Clouds, Paisa*.

Documentaries: *The World is Rich* (British), *Waverley Steps* (British), *Farrébique* (French), *Louisiana Story* (American).

If this list has no relation to the current Trade Polls it is probably of interest to the hosts of cheated film addicts strewn all over the country to whom at least eight of the films are barred by circuits and exhibitors.

These people are intelligent Britons, won to the cinema yet maddened by its inadequacies. They are, if the trade but knew it, the real guarantee of the continued

Actor out of hand — Signe Hasso and Ronald Colman in *A Double Life*

existence of the cinema. And now, here is a letter sent to me by a reader that sums it all up, I think:

Dear Mr Winnington. — For a great many years I've been a filmgoer, about 25 years in fact, and for the greater part of that period my visits were regular twice-a-week affairs, taking the films as they came. Came a time, however, when I couldn't any longer get much enjoyment out of it, there were so many bad films, so few good ones. I stopped going finally, except for a rare Chaplin film, the Marx Brothers and Paul Muni.

There are probably thousands of people who feel as I do, but to have to put our views down on paper is usually beyond us. Two of my brothers and many of my friends are factory workers in Brum, another brother is a factory worker in Hampshire. I'm a navvy.

Then I started taking the *News Chronicle*. All the films that get your O.K. we find are right in line with our own ideas of what's a good film; the 'we' is my mother, brothers and their wives, plus a few friends we've helped to make critical.

We don't see a lot of films, but we do enjoy what we are seeing when we do.

I'm writing this at the joint request of our family to let you know you've plenty of supporters among the labouring classes like myself. We feel as you do, that the film can be a great thing with no limits to its possibilities.

The turning out of rubbishy films won't cease until the mass of filmgoers stop going indiscriminately. The only language the film producers understand is 'box office', which is where my family and I hit them.

We also get at our friends. We let them know when a good film is due at the local, they see it and nearly always enjoy it. We warn them against bad films; they see them also and usually find our advice was good. As a result they come to rely on our judgment, but the big thing is that they are now getting critical on their own account and don't just go blindly.

One told me he didn't enjoy the films half as much since listening to my advice and blames me for spoiling his nights out. I tell him he's growing up.

Anyway, thanks for your good work to improve standards of films. Keep at 'em, boy; you've lots of supporters around among us pick-and-shovel merchants.— Yours sincerely,

HENRY WILLIAMS

Rustington, Sussex.

THE WINDOW: *Directed by* TED TETZLAFF: *7 February 1949*

The opportunity has come to make the first award from my own private Film Academy. This entirely nominal prize goes to *The Window*, an American B film scheduled to support R.K.O.'s *Mr Blandings Builds his Dream House*.

The Window has no known stars unless Bobby Driscoll (*Song of the South*) ranks as such. It is the first full-length film of its director, Ted Tetzlaff, and was made with celerity at extremely low cost.

It is the story of an imaginative boy of a New York East Side tenement whose habit of telling fantastic stories encourages strong local and parental scepticism. When he actually witnesses a murder nobody will believe him except, of course, the murderers, whose one aim thence is to silence him. They nearly succeed.

This is a film with a grip on itself and the audience that never loosens. It is logical, well-shaped, cohesive, admirably acted, beautifully photographed and cut to a nicety. While asking you to make a careful note of this Cinderella of the sub-urban cinemas I will utter a blasphemy — I hold it to be, both in point of cinematic and human values, a better film than *The Fallen Idol*, with which comparison is automatic.

TREASURE OF THE SIERRA MADRE: *Directed by* JOHN HUSTON: *21 February 1949*

Film critics should of course go into literary purdah in the name of fair play and avoid reading any book that might be filmed or at least refrain from odious comparisons in their reviews.

I therefore apologise for having read the beautifully spare and matter-of-fact book by Traven on which *Treasure of the Sierra Madre* has been based.

But I think it is germane to the business of film criticism to note a major embellishment to an otherwise reasonable transcription. Huston, presumably to sweeten a harsh, masculine story, kills off a man so that the letter from his wife in Dallas can be read by a mate over his body in husky, halting tones. You can't keep a good woman out.

Now let me say that *Treasure of the Sierra Madre*, if no masterpiece is the best English-speaking film since *Crossfire*: one in which you can feel some of the old visceral strength of Hollywood.

It is a story of gold lust less relentless and memorable than Stroheim's *Greed*, because it never reaches tragedy. The corrosion of gold fever is shown eating into characters already seriously corroded by life.

Of the three down-and-outs who meet in Tampico, Mexico, raise enough cash to furnish a gold-hunting expedition, strike rich, fight bandits and, their piles of gold accumulated, run the gamut of mutual fear, distrust and hate, two (Walter Huston and Tim Holt) survive as wiser if not ostensibly better men, as poor as when they started.

The other (Humphrey Bogart), who steals all the gold and tries to kill his pal, is from the beginning so debased a human being that his decapitation by bandits is no more than an exciting melodramatic epilogue.

As open air drama depicted with wit, irony, insight and verve, *Treasure of the Sierra Madre* is a tribute to the two-fold talent of John Huston and to the clean photography of Ted McCord. Between them they bare the arid beauty of the Mexican Sierras, catch the sweltering futility of Tampico, give us a sweeping canvas of banditry and gold digging.

Bogart has his finest moments alone in a perfect little scene in a hairdresser's, but is otherwise quite outshone by the brilliant playing of Walter Huston as the garrulous old-timer steeped to his ears in the acid philosophy of a man who has won and lost several fortunes while observing with tolerance most of mankind's failings. Best of all though was the bandit chief of Alfonso Bedoya.

But I cannot forgive or comprehend John Huston's acquiescence in the musical intrusion of Max Steiner (Master of the Warner Musick) which shatters with distracting emphasis scene after scene needing only silence or the human voice.

It is becoming more and more painfully obvious that film music on English and American sound-tracks has, with the rarest of exceptions, got right out of control. Producers, apparently unable to trust actors or dialogue to convey emotion and meaning, underline every change of mood with the moaning, wilting, sobbing and crashing of full-scale orchestras.

THEY LIVE BY NIGHT: *Directed by* NICHOLAS RAY: *March 1949*

It should, I think, in all modesty be recorded that but for the observations of Gavin Lambert in *Sequence* and myself in the *News Chronicle*, *The Window* and *They Live by Night* would probably not have had a London showing, certainly not the acknowledgment of a shared programme at the Academy Cinema.

A second sight of *They Live by Night* confirms Nicholas Ray as a most sensitive and gifted director.

The unbelievable opening shot where the camera from a great height follows and descends on a fast-moving car was (as one discovered) taken from a helicopter, but it still looks like a miracle.

With remarkable pace and realism Ray then proceeds to depict guerrilla crime in America as the background to an unusually moving and tender love story. The closeness, hunger, ecstasy and agony of a first love snatched by two young victims of crime who know — while they pretend to each other — that they are doomed, is evoked with tragic poetry.

The three oldest escaped bank robbers and their hangers-on are characterised firmly and economically. Spoiled, doomed and vulnerable they move through a haze of bank robberies, cheap hide-outs, stolen cars, endless hours of boredom and short vain spells of luxury.

Throughout the film you are with hunted people, never with the hunter. It is an inside view of the hostile outside world, as seen by the criminal at its most tense and threatening, perhaps, in the brilliant bank robbery scene.

The girl and boy lovers who 'because they were not properly introduced to the life we know had to live by night' are beautifully played by Cathy O'Donnell and Farley Granger. And Howard da Silva as the gang leader, avid for the headlines that bring on the heat, is infallible.

Not a foot could go from *The Window*, as complete and compact a film as you could want, whereas *They Live by Night*, a deeper and on its top levels more brilliant film, could advantageously sacrifice ten minutes.

BLUE SCAR : *Directed by* JILL CRAIGIE: *11 April 1949*

There has been no recent full length British film with as much right to the title 'independent' as Jill Craigie's *Blue Scar*.

Jill Craigie and William MacQuitty somehow obtained financial backing and made *Blue Scar* without any distribution guarantees, gambling on the Quota Act and the urgent need of British celluloid.

Few outside the cinema world will realise the almost suicidal courage required for this act of faith.

Circuit booking as first feature, essential to the recovery of outlay, has been refused, although Sir Arthur Jarratt on behalf of British Lion is willing to distribute it.

The voice of the trade expert has pronounced that *Blue Scar* possesses no general audience appeal, though three sneak previews at large London suburban cinemas were unanimously favourable.

Blue Scar cost well under £100,000. And now its last hope lies in the decision of the Government's Film Panel.

Does *Blue Scar* entertain, inform, secure attention, touch the emotions and in fact hold the screen comparably with, say, the last dozen English or a standard dozen of American movies ? My answer is that it decidedly does.

Jill Craigie wanted to make a film about South Wales miners, so she went and lived among them, wrote her script and chose her players on the spot. Two (who play the leads) are professional players — Emrys Jones and Gwyneth Vaughan.

In Jill Craigie's honest understanding reportage lies the appeal of the film, an appeal whose freshness would penetrate, I think, into the bulk of circuit audiences.

It was the novelty of a British working-class community talking and behaving naturally on the screen that got the sneak-view audiences.

And more, perhaps: the saturnine beauty of the hills rising round the village, the sense of being in a never-ending war that knits its people together, the wry realistic Welsh talk in kitchens and clubs, at football matches and underground in the mine.

Reflecting these truths, Jill Craigie is happier than with the plot, which attempts to crystallise the instinct of the comelier village girls to emigrate to smarter places, leaving their young men behind with homelier types. They are, it appears, wrong to do this and end up in frowsty arty circles in London flats smaller than the kitchens they escape from.

Running concurrently is the theme of nationalisation about which the film does not commit itself, the idea being objective reporting of all shades of view culled from the miners themselves.

The film has plenty of naiveties. But so have many much-praised films. The music is aggressive, over-abundant and undistinguished. But that statement applies to nine films out of ten. The players all have a natural Celtic responsiveness.

Easily competing with the two eminently competent professionals are Dilys Jones, Madeline Thomas, Rachael Thomas, Prysor Williams; surpassing them is Kenneth Griffith.

Blue Scar stands in the week against an Epic, a Super-Spectacle and a Western (two in Technicolor and one in Cinecolor) and just for interest and entertainment has my money. MacQuitty and Craigie are getting a raw deal.

GERMANY, YEAR ZERO: *Directed by* ROBERTO ROSSELLINI: *18 April 1949*

Rossellini's *Germany, Year Zero* was made two years ago and first seen privately in London one year ago. In common with *Paisa*, it suffers unfairly from a wholly un-reasonable delay in presentation.

We are perhaps neither close enough nor far away enough from the circumstances that generated Rossellini's urge to testify to be moved to the full by his testimony.

Germany, Year Zero is a reflection of humanity in the deepest plight of hopeless-ness and corruption. It is heightened by macabre vistas of ruined Berlin. In a series of jabbed-in episodes Rossellini uses his camera with scorching Goya-like effect. Let us identify this horror, he says, and then start afresh.

His protagonist is a 12-year-old boy (Edmund Meschke) who, lost for ever in the hellish confusion of Berlin, is driven to delinquency, patricide and suicide. Evil submerges him while childhood still tugs heartrendingly at him. It is a tender and anguished portrait, dedicated to the memory of Rossellini's son.

Fanciers of child acting will find in Edmund Meschke no dimpled little tricks of expression evoked by patient direction. The boy is locked in himself, as casual-seeming in his terrible acts as in his attempts to play.

But inside we are always conscious of the child, panting for daylight, for a friend, for love.

Rossellini's staccato use of the camera, his crude, unfinished portraits of the boy's family and general roughness of style, will no doubt jar on those who like their films fully explained, rounded and smooth. The last two reels in which the camera accompanies the abandoned boy through the desolate streets to his death are, by any comparison, masterly.

WHISKY GALORE: *Directed by* ALEXANDER MACKENDRICK: *18 June 1949*

In the production of their first all-location comedy *Whisky Galore* (from the novel by Compton Mackenzie) Ealing Studios have nicely circumvented British Weather and British Humour.

Producer Danischewsky's Mobile Studio Unit enabled the film to be made lock, stock and barrel on the island of Barra in the Outer Hebrides during the worst summer for years, without the loss of a day's shooting.

The screenplay of Compton Mackenzie and Angus Macphail gave Sandy Mackendrick the chance to direct some of the freshest British comedy sequences of the post-war years in his first full-length feature film.

Whisky Galore makes a weak start. The sudden cessation of whisky supplies on the island of Todday in 1943 and the vain attempts of the English Home Guard captain (Basil Radford) to be taken seriously by anybody but his wife look like the prelude to all too familiar fun and games.

But with the wrecking off the island of a ship containing a large cargo of whisky,

Englishman's lament — Basil Radford, Wylie Watson, James Robertson Justice, Gordon Jackson and Joan Greenwood in *Whisky Galore*

95

the determination of the captain to safeguard any salvage and the equal determination of the islanders to rescue their chief source of health and pleasure, the story warms up.

Reversing, or rather correcting tradition, it develops into a battle between foolish Anglo-Saxon rectitude and cunning Gaelic lawlessness with the captain losing out all along the line.

Even at the height of its slapstick and Gaelic junketing *Whisky Galore* is free of the terrible affliction of self-consciousness, is gently genial with an undertinge of melancholy.

It doesn't stand aside and say 'Aren't we being funny?' as *Passport to Pimlico* and every other post-war British comedy consistently and ruinously does, and it pushes its quite tolerable love passages into the background. Consequently one leaves the film, almost surprisedly, refreshed and cheered.

For there are plenty of faults, the largest of which lies in weighing absolutely everything against the English upholder of right. He is the butt of the whole world, of his colonel, his second in command, the Excise man, and finally of his hitherto docile wife.

There is dignity in rectitude, there should be pathos as well as joy in its downfall. Radford's Captain, however funny (it is his best screen part since *The Captive Heart*), is a figure of caricature.

Filmically the best scene, aside from the naturally displayed charms of Barra, is where a Gaelic drinking song, picked up from the bedside of an old man, opens out into general celebration, though otherwise there is far too much folksy Highland musical accompaniment.

This thoroughly competent and gay film cost about £100,000 and shows no signs of makeshift. Will anyone now deny the Mobile Studio Unit as the simplest means of uncovering to a parched screen the character and beauty of the British Isles?

KIND HEARTS AND CORONETS: *Directed by* ROBERT HAMER: *25 June 1949*

The third Ealing Studios comedy, *Kind Hearts and Coronets*, is, I think, a brilliant misfire for the reason that its plentiful wit is literary and practically never pictorial. This is odd because the director, Robert Hamer, was co-writer with John Dighton, of the verbally scintillating script.

The joke is a dry sophisticated epigrammatic one on the theme of murder in Edwardian times. It opens in the condemned cell on the eve of the execution of Louis D'Ascoyne Mazzini, tenth Duke of Chalfont (Dennis Price), for a murder he did not commit.

On the other hand he had really murdered the six relatives who, with two others who died off their own bat, stood between him and the title. The cause and ingenious method of these murders is retailed in extracts from his prison diary mellifluously intoned by Dennis Price as a running commentary throughout the film. The eight obstructing D'Ascoynes are all played by Alec Guinness.

The motive was not gain or glory, but revenge for the brush-off administered by the family (they even refused her body a place in the family vault) to his D'Ascoyne mother who had married an Italian opera singer. The cause of his downfall was his attempt to follow the Edwardian custom of combining sacred ducal (Valerie Hobson) with profane suburban love (Joan Greenwood).

Of the eight Guinness portrayals four are flat caricatures perfunctorily disposed of. One — the Rev. Lord Henry D'Ascoyne — achieves a unity of brilliant acting and first-rate style. Two hover between burlesque sketch and portrait and the other — the Duke — is played straight. And his murder enacted seriously and wholly out of key is brutal and unpleasant.

The failure of *Kind Hearts and Coronets* is one of style. Neither Dennis Price, who most creditably occupies the entire film, nor Hamer the director has been able to impose the Guitry-Wilde stylism called for by Hamer the writer. This too literal film is nowhere near as clever as its words.

THE SET-UP: *Directed by* ROBERT WISE: *2 July 1949*

There are a few persons inside the British and American film industries who will acknowledge a debt owed to the forgotten war-time Films Division of the Ministry of Information.

Under that sponsorship, from whatever cause or by whatever means, the British naturalism that became the envy of American film makers forced itself out through documentary into feature films.

In that brief fermentation are the beginnings of the contemporary school of American realism. By the time Rank and the others had polished all the tentative character out of British films such men as de Rochemont, Dmytryck and Dore Schary, directly admitting their debt to the British, had caught on and amplified.

Hence *Boomerang, Crossfire, Naked City, The Window,* and this week *The Set-Up.* A dozen such movies are on the way.

Body and Soul was the first boxing film in my recollection that seriously tried to show up what is vicious in the background of the fighting ring. But for all its clamour *Body and Soul* was conventional championship stuff with pride going before a fall and love hanging on for the last punch.

Not so *The Set-up.* The central character (Robert Ryan) is a third-rate fighter of 35 headed for an ignominious punch-drunk future. He stays with the wife who loves him and hates fighting (Audrey Totter) in dingy hotels and fights in fly-blown out-of-town boxing halls. He mingles with his fellow palookas in overcrowded dirty dressing rooms sharing their infantile optimisms.

The film runs for 70 minutes and occupies precisely 70 minutes of the boxer's life before, during and after his last fight.

Indicative of the ruthless down-to-earthness of this film is the sum — fifty dollars — for which his manager and sparring partner sell this fight against a young up-and-coming boxer. They deliberately fail to warn him to lie down in the second round as arranged, being certain he will lose.

The fight, seen round by round, is the most savage ever filmed and its almost unbearable tension is heightened by shots of sadistic ringside characters — a blind man rapturously listening to the sounds of pain, an avid elderly woman lost to all pretence.

But this tension is superseded in those moments when he waits alone and deserted in the empty boxing hall for the hoodlums who have been cheated by his victory and are after revenge.

The Set-up succeeds in its honourable intentions and is an excellent example of studio-built realism in the *Crossfire* manner. And the characters of the set-up, including that first-rate actor Robert Ryan and excepting Miss Audrey Totter, ring absolutely true. Miss Totter is socially and histrionically false to the occasion.

WE WERE STRANGERS: *Directed by* JOHN HUSTON: *30 July 1949*

Nothing could have been better calculated to steady a mind rocking from a fortnight's contact with the Italian cinema (about which I am writing later) than the week's six new Hollywood films.

Superficially the violence in which five of these films specialise (and which drives an anxious colleague to threaten an Un-British Activities Committee) outdoes the violence of some of the Italian films I saw in Rome. But this extrovert boyish stuff does not begin to compare with the sense of chaos and tragedy that in those Italian films evokes both brutality and poetry.

It is apparent that anyone who desires to say anything of moment through the American screen must clothe his statement in thriller trappings, although that doesn't guarantee immunity. There is also the natural tendency in Americans to romanticise violence. The Robin Hood of modern America is the gin-swilling, quick-punching private detective.

An American director who appears to want to say something and who has the talents to do it with is John Huston.

In *We Were Strangers* he gives us an emotional, sensational, melodramatic and brutal story of the Cuban revolution of 1933 from the standpoint of a dedicated group of conspirators against a savage dictatorship.

There is so much about this film I cannot swallow — the implausibilities of detail, the convention of broken accents, the literary conversaziones, the naive doctrines of revolution.

Yet it poses a tremendous universal question — does the immense benefit to the majority that would probably result justify causing the deaths of a number of innocent persons?

In order to lure the entire Government and Police Chiefs to one spot where they can be demolished by a dynamite charge the revolutionaries select for purely topographical convenience the family tomb of a leading senator into which they construct a tunnel.

The senator is then assassinated on the assumption that the customary civic funeral will take place on the site of the tomb. The sacrifice of the hundred or so innocent spectators is accepted as the price of revolution.

But the plot is frustrated by the decision to bury the senator elsewhere and its instigator (John Garfield) is killed in a conventional machine-gun battle, thus balancing the senator and satisfying the code. The revolt, inexplicably and un-expectedly, succeeds despite this setback.

The film reaches its best levels when dealing with the relations between the tunnel-digging revolutionaries (Jennifer Jones, John Garfield, Gilbert Roland, Jose Perez, David Bond and Wally Cassell, who are all admirably played, and in the scenes between Jennifer Jones and the Chief of Police (Pedro Armendariz).

Photographed in sharp contrasts of light and shadow *We Were Strangers* contrives to haunt the mind and has therefore had its say.

Huston's direction even at its most powerful is vitiated by Antheil's clamorous music which in one passage joins in at top range with machine-guns, thunder and dialogue.

THE THIRD MAN: *Directed by* CAROL REED: *3 September 1949*

It is extremely unlikely that Carol Reed's *The Third Man* will have any challengers as the best British film of 1949. Symbolically it is joint Anglo-American already boosted as a Selznick product in the U.S.

In agreement with Reed, the writer Graham Greene went to Vienna, wrote a story, returned and expanded it into a film script. The result — a sophisticated thriller full of moods, atmospheres and ingenuities — represents the closest colla-boration between the two.

Greene's Tale of New Vienna is in light vein, an Entertainment. Naturally its form takes the hunting down of the nihilistic criminal by the seedily good character and naturally the latter encounters a succession of casually sinister figures on the way. And, naturally, under the surface lies Greene's philosophy of futility and despair.

Modern Vienna, dejected, conquered, partitioned, seething with evil under-currents and never more photogenic, is ideal ground for such activities. And for Carol Reed's observation, wit, sense of character and gift of pictorial surprise.

The plot need not be gone into but the fact that the central character (Joseph Cotten) is a hard-drinking American with no German enables language difficulties to be surmounted naturally. We are looking at everything and hearing everything through the American's eyes and ears.

With him we tour the Viennese underworld in a parade of movie tricks that are polished and splendiferous and exciting but reminiscent. Angled shots, sur-prise cutting and thrilling camera work recall Hitchcock, Lang, Orson Welles (not because he is acting in the film) and Carol Reed. The film is almost an anthology and none the less entertaining and welcome because of that.

And Reed's work with his players — Cotten, Welles, Trevor Howard, Valli (who comes to melancholy life for the first time in her film career), Bernard Lee, Paul Hoerbiger, Ernst Deutsch, Siegfried Breuer, Erich Ponto, Wilfred Hyde-White, is expectedly magnificent.

His most spectacular innovation — without which the film (for me) would have lost half its power — is the music which is played entirely on a zither. This strum-ming of a sad tense little air brilliantly opens the credits and with variations counter-

Orson Welles, Trevor
Howard, Valli and Joseph
Cotten in *The Third Man*

points the entire film. Used in different stresses against the mood and against the action it sharpens both to an extraordinary degree.

It is the fourth man of Reed's film — Anton Karas, the diminutive Viennese café player whom he persuaded to compose and play this music — who will take me back to the film.

The Third Man reveals Carol Reed as probably the most brilliant craftsman of the modern cinema, certainly as Britain's best talent, and yet as one who is devoid of the urges that make a really great director. Sensitive and humane and dedicated he would seem to be enclosed from life with no specially strong feelings about the stories that come his way to film other than that they should be something he can perfect and polish with a craftsman's love.

ANY NUMBER CAN PLAY: *Directed by* MERVYN LE ROY:
22 October 1949

Last week Mr Humphrey Bogart found his soul as a night club proprietor, which moved me to award that profession second place for general democratic glamour. A little thought, however, has caused a slight adjustment of the award.

Here is my list of those callings wherein, according to Hollywood, the American dream of male success materialises in all fullness and glory. In order of precedence they are: gambler, show producer, advertising agent, night club operator, orchestra leader.

In the crowd, well below these symbolistic figures, come reporters, private detectives, undercover men, crooners, piano concerto players, war heroes, composers, plain and fancy businessmen, plain and fancy racketeers, etc., etc., etc. Creatures of glamour certainly, but lacking the fundamental nerve, insouciance, freedom and solid glamour of the big five.

Any Number Can Play is the gambler's apotheosis. Its hero, Charley Kyng (Clark Gable), is surely the American model man, iron nerved, uxorious and white through and through. The gambling joint where his worshipping home-loving underlings wear black ties and jackets and striped trousers, is run with more decorum than a reception at the White House. And Charley can't bear to see his clients suffer and will stake them or give them their car fare home when they are cleaned out.

At his cosy home where his model wife (Alexis Smith) keeps a memory room in the cellar — containing the old iron bedstead, the phonograph, little toddler shoes and knick-knacks of their early days — things are not so good.

Charley's model son is the only person in the film who doesn't love him. He is ashamed of his father's profession. To this surly pug-nosed young man — whose hoarse voice and lack of manners mark him as the ideal collegiate type — Charley desperately explains that all American business is gambling and that it's something to be a clean gambler.

But it is not until he sees Charley stake everything on one throw of the dice and beat off a couple of gunmen that the pristine nature of Charley's patriotism becomes manifest to him. One manly loving look between them and the film has made its great testament.

THE YEAR'S BEST: *31 December 1949*

This has been an eventful year. In no other period was so much printed space given to hard news about the cinema, or to such a variety of wise and silly comment on the film situation.

Not uninteresting as it turns out is the comment made by the films themselves. Fifteen of the twenty-three films I have picked as the best of 1949 happen to have been modestly budgeted affairs, made with more than usual freedom from interference. Some of them were written off before they were started, some were shelved and rescued. Less than half had the confidence of the backers.

Both choice and order are, needless to say, personal and based on the enjoyment derived from witnessing some sort of realisation, however small, of the inimitable uses of the cinema camera.

Surveying the year one notes a desperate shortage of good French films, a total lack of good documentaries, a falling off in American musicals, an enhanced scarcity of comedies.

The year's most glorious casualty was Mr Rank's independent frame method and its most distinguished flop — Messrs David Lean and Alfred Hitchcock. The two worst films were the British *Bad Lord Byron* and *The Romantic Age*. Also to be recorded is the steady improvement of *This Modern Age*.

The awards of my one-man Tribunal go to: *Bicycle Thieves* (Italian), *Louisiana*

Story (American), *Goupi-Mains-Rouges* (French), *They Live By Night, The Window, The Set-up, The Search* (American).

Cry of the City, Moonrise (American), *The Third Man* (British), *The Blum Affair* (German), *Germany, Year Zero* (Italian), *Act of Violence, Treasure of the Sierra Madre, Easter Parade* (American), *Whisky Galore* (British), *Letter to Three Wives* (American).

Yellow Sky (American), *Kind Hearts and Coronets* (British), *Home of the Brave, Pinky, The Reckless Moment* (American), *The Small Back Room* (British).

GIVE US THIS DAY: *Directed by* EDWARD DMYTRYK: *January 1950*

From the day he arrived in England, trailing the glamour of his indictment, Edward Dmytryk has been steadily built into a small legend. British technicians dazzled by a combination of flair, instinct and easy efficiency by no means rare inside the B belt of Hollywood where Dmytryk learned his trade, critics moved by his victimisation into overestimating both *Crossfire* and his contribution to it, and others merely taken by his charm and enthusiasm, have pushed the legend along.

Two things surprised me about Dmytryk when I first met him: his insistence on making 'Christ in Concrete' if not in America, in England (despite the fact that better stories had been suggested to him) and his meagre knowledge of the noteworthy achievements of the last ten years of the cinema, for which he offered no real excuse. The compactness and vigour of *Crossfire*, for which Dmytryk is generally credited, owed as much at least to Adrian Scott, the producer, and John Paxton, the writer. With *Give Us This Day*—Messrs Geiger and Bronston can be considered as producers only in the commercial sense, and Ben Barzman's script is an obvious deficit — Dmytryk is on his own with Pietro di Donato. And in those conditions he has done no more than I, for one, anticipated with a story that is sticky with contrivance and forced symbolism. Donato's 'Christ in Concrete' is a dated and unhappy crossbreed of American shockeroo writing and Italian poetising about breasts and thighs, hunger and love and childbirth, strung to a sensational allegory of Brooklyn bricklaying in the Great Depression as a climax to which the central character, Geremio, is impaled, emasculated and suffocated in wet concrete on a Good Friday in the attitude of crucifixion. The film stretches the agony even further by giving the widow 1,000 dollars compensation — the purchase price of the house she and Geremio had been vainly trying to buy during their nine years of marriage.

Using but one Italian (Lea Padovani) in the half American, half British cast, and not more than half a dozen back projections of New York, Dmytryk has created history by acceptably creating in an alien studio the atmosphere of a particular locality of his own country, a feat that has defied some notable European directors in Hollywood. The film opens promisingly with Geremio staggering drunkenly home, too late for the birthday feast prepared by his fading wife and family, and in a fit of angry guilt striking her for the first time in their married life. Outside again, he smashes down his hand on to a spiked iron railing and repairs to his mistress for comfort and some heavy talk about the purpose of life. Flashback to the young

Hero or dypso? — Kathleen Byron, Jack Hawkins, Michael
Gough, David Farrar and Leslie Banks in *Small Back Room*

Geremio in prosperous times (1920, when bricklayers were allowed to work one
week in three) discussing the philosophy of Love and Life on top of a building with
his four Italian buddies (they were like 'five sticks in a bundle') and deciding to
import his beautiful bride from Italy. All through the film is clotted with this
verbal imagery, overlaid by the unavoidable music of Benjamin Frankel, and it is
only in the *simplest* scenes which stress in *simple* terms of the cinema the minutiæ
of poverty and love, that we are at all powerfully moved. When Geremio brings
home the bonus and Annunziata chalks another twenty dollars towards the house
on the wall of their tenement flat, or when she refuses a doctor (because he will
cost money) in the agony of her first confinement, the film is momentarily released
from its fictional prison house. These and some minor sequences make it clear that

with the right producer and with his hair up, Dmytryk might make some first class films in England or anywhere.

Dmytryk insisted on cutting *Give Us This Day* himself and he has left in at least three spare reels. But no amount of trimming could affect the film's unsatisfactory structure. What could be done, without leaving an inexplicable gap, with the dreary episodes concerning Geremio's golden hearted and faithful mistress (Kathleen Ryan) whose significance is as obscure as her occupation? Unless, I hate to suggest this possibility, it's another slice of religious allegory.

Without Lea Padovani (Annunziata) whom I saw looking quite different in Vergano's *Il Sole Sorge Ancora*, the film would have lost most of its warmth. Apart from Kathleen Ryan, Charles Goldner's organ-grinding portrayal of an elderly Italian bricklayer and a Hollywood trip among loveable wops at the wedding breakfast, the cast fits painlessly into the creditable Italian-Brooklyn background. Painlessly, but in no way memorably, unless it were for the tight characterisation of an ambitious contractor from Sidney James. Sam Wanamaker as Geremio symbolises Dmytryk's failure: virile, often touching, he never acquires the tragic status that might have saved the film, as one likes to imagine Henry Fonda would have done.

It is said that, and I don't doubt it, *Give Us This Day* if shot exclusively in a Hollywood, instead of a British, studio would have had no more, probably less, veraciousness. But it clamours for the sort of space that cannot be contrived in a studio and only a concentrated narrative development could have made us oblivious to that lack. [. . .]

BICYCLE THIEVES: *Directed by* VITTORIO DE SICA: *January 1950*

I saw *Bicycle Thieves* in Rome during a July heatwave and in between two other movies. It was mid-afternoon, the private cinema was small and badly ventilated and my interpretress was nearly fainting with the heat. In addition to these small influences against over-enthusiasm there was a disposition to caution induced by the unquestioning praise already poured out on behalf of the greatness of de Sica's film. Within five minutes my Italian friend — who had not seen the film before — was forgetting to translate and I was forgetting to remind her. We were held, silent and possessed, by a film that spoke after so long the fundamental language of the cinema.

Bicycle Thieves was conceived, written and directed in strict accordance with de Sica's principles of realism: that is, he used, with one small exception, non-professional actors and shot the whole film in the streets and buildings of Rome. His command over his material must stagger any film director, producer or executive who sees it. Those who had begun to doubt themselves and their medium will be re-invigorated by his concentration of white-hot integrity. Scores of opportunities for emotional, pictorial or dramatic luxuriation have been left begging while de Sica, concerned only with the perfection of his whole structure, ruthlessly strips down his components.

In novels, as well as in films, the power of the Italians to reflect the human tragedy of the war and its aftermath has been, among all the belligerent nations, the most poignant and immediate. This is not merely due to proximity. A sensitive, volatile and easy-living race, not really interested in war or in causes, or in the acquisition of glory, who always took the easy way and grabbed the wrong end of the stick has inevitably found a hellish nemesis. Despite all the tourist rediscoveries wretchedness abounds in Italy and obsesses the honest writer or film maker. Nobody has depicted as movingly or as realistically as have Rossellini, de Sica, Vergano and Lattuada, the agony of ordinary people caught in succeeding waves of misery, the sources of which are never clear to them. And although the almost totally uncontaminated naturalism of their method was to some extent imposed by technical and financial limitations, it was and will remain their greatest strength. In *Bicycle Thieves* de Sica has mastered and advanced the method as decisively as Chaplin advanced himself as an artist with *The Gold Rush*.

The Rome de Sica lays bare to us is as far from the Rome of the ecstatic traveller as the Blackhorse Road. Not a fountain or a statue is to be seen. But it seethes with life. It is life. The small tragedy of poverty it depicts is happening daily in every city in the world, marking and moulding the faces and figures of the poor.

The film covers one day of intense experience in the lives of an Italian workman, his wife and his small son. The man is in a stunned but not yet hopeless condition through a long spell of unemployment. He is young and still has dreams of artisan comfort and respectability. He is kind, friendly with his fellows and placatory towards the young wife of whose temper poverty has taken a quicker toll. He lives in a suburban tenement in Rome and, as the film opens, has just been given the bill-posting job that puts an entirely new aspect on his life. The job is conditional on the recovery of his bicycle from the pawnshop, which rescue he effects by pledging in exchange the last household asset — the bed linen; the pawnshop piled high to its vaulted ceiling with the bicycles and bed linen of others makes all the comment needed on the state of the local employment market.

The great day of liberation starts with the man giving his son a lift on the handle-bars to the filling station where the little boy works instead of going to school. He cannot let go of the precious bicycle for a second, even taking it through the door into the depot office where he collects peaked cap, ladder, paste and brush. De Sica makes every action of this man important, exciting and intimate. He is so human and vulnerable and real that we know his luck can't hold and that the dirtiest of life's tricks is waiting round the corner. It is even a sickly sort of relief when the bicycle is stolen by a small local gang of petty thieves as he is pasting up his first bill — a glamour picture of Rita Hayworth. A futile chase in which the thief escapes and the police prove useless is the prelude to a desperate Sunday search, with his son, for the bicycle. The hunt takes them in and out of shabby pavement marts where the rows of second-hand and dismantled bicycles are seen as in a nightmare. They are soaked to the skin in a sudden vicious rainstorm. In a gesture of angry irony the man takes the little boy into a middle-class restaurant and spends the last of his lire providing them with a meal identical to that being consumed by the superior little boy and family who have thrown contemptuous looks at their rags. This scene is beautiful pantomime, primed with Chaplinesque pathos. The boy, bright with urchin instincts and at the same time unspoiled, is tuned in with all the sensitivity of childhood to his father's misery and anger. He is played by Enzo Staiola in an adorable unforced performance free from the trick archness that brings in the cash to Masters Henrey and Davis or Miss O'Brien. The man is played by Lamberto Maggiorani, a metal worker who still carries with him the sour taste of unemployment. The truth and power of this 'amateur' acting absolutely justifies de Sica's virtual exclusion of professionals from his picture.

The thief whose vacuous face was photographed on the man's mind is eventually spotted and again escapes. The pursuit takes the man and the boy into a church hostel where meagre food is handed out to the dispossessed in return for a payment of prayer and thanksgiving. And into the antiseptic state brothel where the girls, interrupted in the sacred siesta hour, provide the righteous uproar of a group of invaded nuns. The final running down of the epileptic thief brings no lightening of the man's load of despair. The locality is hostile and the bicycle has already been disposed of. Returning home defeated he sees a bicycle leaning against a door and his bitterness forms into purpose. He sends the son off to the tram and clumsily makes off with the bicycle — uphill. He is caught but reprieved by the workman owner. In a silent desolation the man and boy (who had missed the tram and witnessed his father's shame) trudge homewards through the grey dusk.

The miracle of the movie camera has brought us close into the feelings and lives of people whose validity we never question and whom we will never forget. More truly and vividly (because of his greater discipline) than did Donskoi in his superb *Childhood of Maxim Gorky*, de Sica reveals the hopes, despairs and stifled goodness of the poor. And although his characters' faith and optimism have been shattered de Sica, like Gorky, throws over his scene the glow of compassion and hope. His understanding reaches through his bitter irony and embraces all, the thieves, the prostitutes, the fortune-telling tenement harpies, the policemen, even the ridiculous ballet of seminary students holding up their skirts in the rain.

LETTER FROM AN UNKNOWN WOMAN: *Directed by* MAX OPHÜLS:
7 January 1950

Film distributing companies now and again find themselves nursing an ugly duckling. On their hands is a slightly unorthodox film with no obvious box-office smell and no exploitation lead from Hollywood. Baffled and frightened they consign it quickly to whatever booking it can get outside London, without airing it before the Press.

Their timidity can cost the distributors hard cash, for quite often the abnormality consists only in the film being above average and therefore above their heads. The duckling may easily be a swan that will lay bigger eggs after a little special nursing. A fact which Press criticism would most surely and usefully bring to light (as indeed it has done in several instances).

Showing currently in local cinemas is a film which incomprehensibly missed having a Press show or a proper London booking.

Incomprehensibly because it tells — only with added taste and style and feeling — the sort of story Hollywood has glamorously aimed at many times. And still more incomprehensibly because it has undisputed star value in the shape of Joan Fontaine and Louis Jourdan.

The film *Letter from an Unknown Woman* is a romantic tragedy of Old Vienna from a story by Stefan Zweig. Its plot is sufficiently hallowed in fiction to be hardly worth repeating — a girl loves the great pianist, gives herself to him, is forsaken and forgotten, has his child, marries, and, writing to him from her death-bed telling of her unquenchable love, inflicts upon him a sense of unbearable failure and loss.

It is fascinating to watch the sure, deft means by which the director, Max Ophüls, sidetracks seemingly inevitable clichés and holds on to a shadowy, tender mood, half buried in the past. Here is a fragile filmic charm that is not often or easily accomplished and to which the sensitive playing of Joan Fontaine is perfectly attuned.

Ophüls, the most interesting European director in Hollywood, displayed in *The Reckless Moment* a singular adaptability to the American scene. *Letter from an Unknown Woman* however, reverts to the mood of his best-known European film *Liebelei* and is undoubtedly the more sparkling and intact work.

INTRUDER IN THE DUST: *Directed by* CLARENCE BROWN:
22 January 1950

Three recent Hollywood films have familiarised us with White mistreatment of the Negro. In each case the Negro's social value was high, his (her) disposition exemplary. As candidates for White patronage they could not have been worthier or more docile.

The fourth of the Negro cycle, M.G.M.'s *Intruder in the Dust* has a more awkward victim-hero. He simply throws the ball back to the Whites. The problem, he says in effect, belongs to those who out of guilt and fear have created it.

An old man, arrogant and difficult, an 'independent' Negro who owns land, he sits calmly in gaol while three white persons of uneasy conscience clear him of a false charge of murdering a white man and save him from a lynching. (Juano Hernandez plays the part superlatively.)

Their act brings no easy solace to the rescuers — a man, a boy and an old woman (David Brian, Claude Jarman, Jr, Elizabeth Patterson) — nor anything more than a dignified acknowledgment of a debt from the Negro. For it has made them disturbedly aware, as he always was, of the sickness behind White intolerance.

The horror is almost casual: the lynching preparations, started before the arrest is made, have the surface air of a homely town occasion. As the man says to the boy about one of the leaders:

'He's got nothing against Negroes. All he wants is for Lucas to act like he expects a Negro to. Then he'll be lynched with no hard feelings on either side. He'll even contribute to a fund for his wife and children.'

Intruder in the Dust is from William Faulkner's novel and most of it was shot under his supervision in his home town, Oxford, Miss. And in an appreciable endeavour to catch the languor and rot of small town Southern life, and perhaps with an eye on Faulkner's poetic inflexions, Clarence Brown has stylised his film almost to an extreme.

But it is effective. He has made a really good movie that is also and incidentally the first honestly worked out 'racial' film I have seen.

THE MIRACLE: *Directed by* ROBERTO ROSSELLINI: *26 January 1950*

The Italian film, *The Miracle*, which was refused a British censor's certificate and passed by the London County Council after certain sub-title cuts, is now showing at the Academy Cinema, Oxford Street.

The Middlesex, Essex, and Sussex County Councils have already banned the film as being offensive on both moral and religious grounds. Other county councils are expected to make similar objections.

The Miracle, directed and part-written by Roberto Rossellini, lasts 40 minutes and is dedicated to the art of Anna Magnani, who is the only professional actress in the cast and who is never absent from the screen.

Nannina, in the story, is an extremely simple-minded peasant girl of devout religious faith, who tends goats on the hills above her village on the steep southern coast of Italy.

A passing tramp who offers her wine appears to her as the miraculous manifestation of St Joseph, her special and particular saint.* Overcome by exultation and wine, she falls asleep.

Her ecstasy when she discovers herself to be pregnant is at first tolerated but later mocked by the villagers, who form a procession, force a basin on her head as a halo and pelt her with garbage. She escapes to the mountains.

When her time is near she struggles agonisingly up to the little church on top of the mountain. The doors are locked, but she finds shelter in the porch and her child is born. Her ecstasy is undiminished.

Anna Magnani's Nannina is a figure of immense pathos and power. With her shapeless rags, clattering tins, indescribable bundles and gauche movements she retains dignity and beauty as one can think of no other actress doing. Her performance is a tour de force.

The mock procession and its cruel warning echo of chanted Avés from below which reach the ears of Nannina just as she is about to turn to the villagers for help and the scenes inside and outside the church with the beggar Cosimino were instances of Rossellini at his top-flight of inspiration.

The straggling village looking straight down on the sea is another Italy, as remote from Rome or Naples as London.

The Miracle is simply as I have described it, a parable of faith, directed only against cruelty and intolerance, even if they should be found in the Church. It contains not one item that could be construed as offensive to taste, morals or religion.

But, as a matter of interest, the L.C.C. cuts were a quotation from the Bible addressed by Nannina to 'St Joseph', a reference by her to her 'Blessed Infant' and the Avés in the first procession which have been slurred over on the sound-track.

But the L.C.C. would not permit the Academy Cinema to follow its custom of

---

* Played by Fellini, who also collaborated on the script.

issuing a linocut poster of the film, which is something of a loss to the hoardings of London.

HOME OF THE BRAVE: *Directed by* MARK ROBSON:
PINKY: *Directed by* ELIA KAZAN:
LOST BOUNDARIES: *Directed by* ALFRED WERKER: *February 1950*

Hollywood's first three 'colour-bar' films have already grossed more than 7,000,000 dollars at the American box-office. Here is a gauge of the readiness of audiences to welcome any sign of freshness from an industry that has gone tired on them. And here too, is evidence of the quickness with which that industry can still recognise, exploit and control a trend. The trend emanates from the conscience which, to the advantage of the cinema, has always dogged Hollywood. The trail was laid with *Crossfire* and *Gentleman's Agreement*, dramatically effective films that flirted with the 'Jewish problem'. Making them called for courage and discredited their producers at the time. To their box-office rehabilitation *Home Of The Brave, Pinky, Lost Boundaries* and other 'racials' in progress can be credited. The flirtation has been transferred to the safer areas of the 'Negro problem' where a multifarious, multi-coloured selection of special cases offer themselves for dramatisation.

Of the three 'cases' under review the most heavily emotionalised and the most spuriously solved is that of the full-blooded Negro hero of *Home Of The Brave*, an adaptation of Arthur Laurent's play in which the hero was a Jew. Yet the fact

Rita Hayworth, Orson Welles, Everett Sloane and Glenn Anders in *The Lady from Shanghai*

that James Edwards *is* a Negro as much as the eloquence of his acting makes him easily the outstanding figure of all three films.

We see him first in a familiar setting — a Pacific Army base during the war — stretched out in a critical state of amnesia and paralysis while the army psychiatrist stands over with the hypodermic syringe. Drug-induced flashbacks trace the root of his sickness to that moment of extreme danger in the jungle when his childhood friend — the only White man he trusted — bites short the odiously familiar expletive 'Why you yellow bellied N . . .!' An unbearable sense of guilt for the momentarily felt joy when his friend is killed piles on to an already formidable racial neurosis and cracks him down.

The tough friendly psychiatrist and the Negro's conscience-stricken White 'buddies' effect the cure — by persuading him that his joy was an instinctive reaction of relief at his own safety, an emotion experienced in similar circumstances by the best of White soldiers. A lush Hollywood ending guarantees his future as a happy Negro bartender and nullifies the sympathy and intelligence that have made plausible an essentially theatrical conception of the problem. In fact the admirable qualities of direction, acting and writing in Mark Robson's film only emphasise its abortiveness.

The sell-out in *Pinky* is subtler. Pinky (well, but not brilliantly played by Jeanne Crain) is a Negro girl of unblemished White pigmentation whose old darkie grand-mother (beautifully played by Ethel Waters) has pinched and saved to send her to college. There she had fallen into the easy temptation of passing as white, and as such falling in love with a white doctor (William Lundigan). Returning as a graduate nurse to the cabin in the South, the sensitive and civilised Pinky is subjected to the full litany of racial prejudice, from both sides of the bar. Both Negroes and Whites hate her white skin and city manners. The film valuably succeeds in showing the roots of that prejudice to be as deep on one side as the other.

Pinky's ordeal is brought home by the director, Elia Kazan, in vivid, compelling incidents — the instantaneous change from servility to savagery by the police when Pinky, involved (and out-acted) in a brawl with Nina Mae McKinny, tells them she is coloured; the scene in the store; her pursuit at night by two drunken white men.

But Pinky's dilemma — shall she forsake her race and become 'white' or proclaim it and lose her lover? — is side-tracked into never-never-land. There is a dying, wise old *patronne* (Ethel Barrymore) to restore her to proper Negro pride, and leave her the family mansion. There is an upstanding Southern judge to uphold the will and flout a court seething with lynching fever. And a final celibate solace for Pinky — since the world's most polyglot Democracy cannot abide a hint of miscegenation — is running her mansion as a super clinic for Negro children, manned by a Negro staff.

All this apart, the cardinal crippling evasion of *Pinky* lies in the selection of an established white film actress to play the heroine. Thus is the audience insulated against the shock of seeing White and Negro embrace, against any effect of realism. I do not doubt that *Pinky* will leave Negro baiters comfortably purged and as rabid as ever, and I have even less doubts as to its effects on Negroes. As for average audiences: they will come from *Pinky*, touched, entertained and unperturbed by a well made and well acted film drama.

Lost Boundaries is a Louis de Rochemont (*Boomerang*) production, based on a Readers' Digest true account of a New Hampshire family. Though it is the soberest and least artistically titivated of the three films, its message is the same — black is black and white is white and never the twain shall meet.

A young, talented, light-skinned Negro doctor, through lack of professional openings, accepts a lucrative practice as a White doctor in Keenham, New Hampshire, 1922. He and his family are accepted unquestionably as White, and as the years pass he becomes a beloved and leading citizen. His attempted enlistment as a medical officer in the Navy discloses his race and forces him to confess the fact to his son and daughter, who have developed into healthy American campus types. The shock drives the son on a feverish Odyssey through Harlem, from which he returns resigned and ready to accept his new status. Both he and the girl break off relations with the White persons they love, and the father publicly announces himself as a Negro.

Keenham, New Hampshire, is on its mettle, but an emotional appeal by the Rector in church brings toleration, and the people make it clear that 'a man's ability, honesty and kindness have nothing to do with the colour of his skin'. (The love affairs of the son and daughter are left in the air.) All of which, high-minded and sincere though it may be, looks more like a claim for the fineness of Keenham (for doing no more than a Christian community could do and keep face) than one for the worthy doctor who had served it for years. It is indeed a special case, calculated to improve White conceit and preserve the bar. The film is directed flatly and unimaginatively by Alfred Werker; the doctor and family are played mainly by unknown and apparently white actors.

I praised these films at the time for their courage in approaching an evil any civilised man wants to see ironed out flat. But the unease that was there has crystallised with second thoughts. Films that raise such issues and baulk them are not merely negative but dangerous. And it is necessary to say so firmly, since they are trading heavily on their 'progressiveness'. When a racial film is ruthlessly honest in its issues, or when it unambiguously implies equal rights and status for the American Negro (including the assumption that intermarriage with Whites is no less unobjectionable and irrelevant than between Jew and Gentile, Catholic or Protestant), or when it just so much as documents a plain, typical story, without recourse to a fake solution; then will be the occasion, I think, to bring out the word courage.

ALL THE KING'S MEN: *Directed by* ROBERT ROSSEN: *15 April 1950*

To the glory of winning the 1949 Academy Award *All the King's Men* adds that of deriving from the Pulitzer Prize-winning novel of Robert Penn Warren.

Produced, written and directed for Columbia by Robert Rossen, it has been for various reasons one of the most promising films on the horizon. It turns up as a fascinating but curiously disappointing work.

Henry Fonda, Dolores del Rio and Pedro Armendariz in *The Fugitive*

The subject of both book and film is, for all the disclaimers, the late Huey Pierce Long, Governor of Louisiana, who achieved complete totalitarian power over that state and fancied himself, not without cause for encouragement, as dictator of the U.S.A.

Book and film fight shy of exposing to the full Huey Long's vicious methods of intimidation. Or of throwing the light on his fantastic pie-in-the-sky electioneering programme which stole so many hick hearts.

In each case the picture is one of unrelieved chicanery, corruption and decay. The power-obsessed demagogue's claim that out of evil he constructs good (witness the roads, hospitals, schools), is a familiar slogan — the end justifies the means. It is not positively repudiated.

Rossen's method of projecting Willie Stark in a rapidly moving series of near-newsreel sequences fails to probe or develop the character and therefore fails to indict.

Though Oscar-winning Broderick Crawford shows up well as Willie Stark in those moments when he has breathing space his abrupt transitions from scene to scene, from grass-seed idealist to ruthless politician, make him a stock, one-dimensional figure. The overwhelming magnetism that gave him power over voters, politicians, friends and lovers must be taken on trust.

Similarly those around him — the disillusioned reporter (John Ireland) who becomes his henchman, the patrician girl (Joanne Dru) who becomes his mistress, her ineffectual doctor brother (Shepherd Strudwick) who becomes his assassin, and the aristocratic judge (his only opponent) whom he blackmails into suicide — are characters seen in snapshot form.

In contrast the stage actress Mercedes McCambridge (also an Oscar winner on this occasion) as Stark's hardbitten political aide-de-camp and mistress impresses on the scene a vital, fully articulated character.

On the positive side — though it has dislocated the film's purpose — Rossen's staccato factual approach (recalling aspects of *Citizen Kane* and *Boomerang*) gives a vital atmospheric view into the political-social atmosphere of the South.

He shot the film in all weathers and it gains enormously. His crowds and locations are real (extras and studio work were cut to a minimum), his angles dramatic and his sound track discriminating and inventive. *All the King's Men* is dramatically inferior to *Body and Soul*, but it consolidates Rossen, the ex-writer, as a director and naturalism as an accepted style in Hollywood.

THE DIVIDING LINE: *Directed by* JOSEPH LOSEY: *May 1950*

William Thomas and William Pine, producers of *The Dividing Line*, are long successful B film factors who have turned serious. The director, Joseph Losey, once made a name with experimental films (he was associated with the distinguished 'Living Newspaper'). Now after many fruitless years in Hollywood he seems to have got what he was looking for.

The story, anything but new in American movies, is of mob violence, persecution of the innocent and the shocking extremes of savage unreason into which Mothers' Day-observing U.S. taxpayers can be so suddenly whipped. The film is from a straight screenplay by Geoffrey Homes.

The fury is aimlessly unloosed on the Mexican fruit-pickers across the tracks by some upper-class young toughs in a dance-hall brawl. A respectable young worker, defending his girl, confusedly strikes a policeman. Fleeing in panic he collects unjust accusations of rape and murder. The front pages and television whoop it up and try him before he is caught.

Three defendants are mustered on his side — the young newspaper owner (MacDonald Carey), the Mexican journalist (Gail Russell) and the rich father of one of the toughs (Paul Hoyt): a lynching is only just avoided and 'The Union's' offices are well and truly wrecked by the mob.

Notable are Losey's reticences, his juicy play with sundry small characters (so much more succinct than Rossen's comparable attempts in *All The King's Men*), his low-keyed evocation of a small Californian town, the photography, editing and playing. (Lalo Rios as the young Mexican is an outstanding newcomer.)

The Dividing Line has a glow reminiscent of the work of those pioneers of American photography, Brady and Walker Evans.

SEVEN DAYS TO NOON: *Directed by* JOHN BOULTING: *13 September 1950*

A burningly topical theme is the basis of a new British thriller, *Seven Days to Noon*.

The theme is the doubt and disillusion that is prone to assail the atomic scientist when he contemplates the destructive possibilities of his life's work.

In this case the scientist (played by Barry Jones) suffers a complete mental break-down and becomes obsessed by fanatical and misguided purpose. He abstracts a destructive weapon from the secret Government laboratory he controls and issues an ultimatum to the Prime Minister — unless the Government announces the total abandonment of atomic warfare and the destruction of its stocks of atomic weapons he will detonate his bomb in London at 12 noon on Sunday next. The destructive range of the bomb is ten square miles.

It is Monday and Scotland Yard, alive to the seriousness of the threat, institutes a widespread search for the missing scientist by every method at its command. At the same time the War Office organises the immediate evacuation of London.

The action swings from the scientist to his pursuers and the tension mounts. A broadcast from the Prime Minister warns the public who exhibit all the well-known attributes of the British when faced by crucial danger. Posters of the missing man emblazon the walls and buses. Yet he is both cunning and lucky in his encounters and evades capture right up to the sensational climax at five minutes before zero-hour.

The film is extremely well made by the Boulting Bros. (produced and edited by Roy Boulting, directed by John Boulting) from an original story by Paul Dehn and James Bernard.

The evacuation is staged with remarkable skill and the London scenes are probably the best ever photographed in a British feature film. In the last two reels when the military are converging on Westminster through a deserted city in the hunt for the fugitive the beauty of London is seen at its most poignant.

In every respect — cutting, editing and playing — *Seven Days to Noon* is the Boulting Bros.' best film. The performances of Barry Jones as the scientist and Olive Jones as the faded brassy actress who gives him unwilling shelter, are only excelled by that of Joan Hickson as a chain-smoking cat-loving landlady.

Elsewhere perhaps there are some concessions to the cheap laugh that is considered invaluable in British movies.

Seven Days to Noon is a first rate thriller that does not pretend to a serious message, but yet will leave a query in the mind. Was the scientist as mad as all that?

ASPHALT JUNGLE: *Directed by* JOHN HUSTON: *7 October 1950*

Director/writer John Huston has one of the most vividly individual talents practising in Hollywood. So far he has exploited it best in the development of melodramas that, while liberally furnished with plot and action, essentially turn on character (*Maltese Falcon, Sierra Madre*).

It is clear that Huston has now acquired an itch to say something serious though it is anything but clear that he knows what he wants to say. His social conscience, given an emotional outing among Cuban revolutionaries in *We Were Strangers*, reappears in *The Asphalt Jungle* (part-written and directed by Huston from a novel by W. R. Burnett). This can fairly be described as a gangster movie turned inside out.

A group of criminals plan and effect a big jewel robbery and it is their hopes and

Un-American activity — Anne Revere, Gregory Peck, Dorothy McGuire and John Garfield in *Gentleman's Agreement*

fears, weaknesses and strengths, loyalties and treacheries that supply the film's tension.

The 'hero' (Sterling Hayden) is a small-time crook with a weakness for gambling on horses and a dream of buying back the old farm in Texas: his devoted moll (Jean Hagen) gives everything and asks for nothing. The leader (Sam Jaffe) is clever and courageous, but he cannot resist young women. And the safe-cracker is a loving father and husband.

Even the bad crook among the good troupers, the double-crossing big business backer (Louis Calhern), is allowed his domestic humanities and a dignified death. A plea is also made for the corrupt police-lieutenant.

The purpose of all this is obscure. Obviously Huston is giving us a view of the criminal as a human being lost in the concrete jungle, but he vitiates his detachment by a sentimentality that becomes positively mawkish in the long-drawn-out finale of the dying hero's return to the old farm. Huston has preached a sermon without a text.

But on the way he has given us some crisp characterisation delineated in exciting movie technique (seriously disrupted, incidentally, by pointless censor's cuts) and perhaps the best robbery ever staged in Hollywood. Only by Huston standards does this generally impressive film fall short.

CITY LIGHTS: *Directed by* CHARLES CHAPLIN: *28 October 1950*

The revival of Chaplin's *City Lights* is in some ways a greater event than its first appearance in 1931. For this superb film has matured with the passing of time (and the increase of our own disillusionment) and it sheds a new glow of revelation.

Clearly one of the world's ten great movies* *City Lights* is the consummation of Chaplin's genius. The comic inventions are richer and apter, the irony bites deeper, the melancholy is profounder than in any other of his films or in any other film comedy made. It is the summing up of Chaplin's tragi-comic view of humanity and it is the legitimate parent of *Monsieur Verdoux* (where the bedraggled victim is allowed to hit back with a full armoury of bitter paradox).

City Lights is everybody's film, irresistibly funny and deeply sad, with the most poignant ending of any movie ever made. It is a silent film to which Chaplin has added his own relevant sound track and musical score and a minimum of sub-titles.

But by a perfection of timing and miming he gains through 85 minutes your total surrender. For he has made the closest approach to sheer mastery over an intractable medium in the history of the cinema, so that his jokes, his shafts of satire, his sentimentalities, universal and timeless, have the durability of great art. They cannot be repeated too often. They stay for ever in the mind.

City Lights for the record is the one in which Chaplin champions the blind flower girl (Virginia Cherrill), saves the life of the drunken millionaire (Harry Myers) who fetes him when drunk and rejects him when sober, is involved in a brilliantly composed boxing sequence and touches at the end the summit of human pathos.

THE MEN: *Directed by* FRED ZINNEMANN: *December 1950*

First casualties of the cold war are those small outposts of reason which, up to 1949, managed to hold a front in newspapers, radio and films. Films now must not only fight their way through the industry and through the intransigence of distributors: they must also face vague but powerful political pressures. These pressures will of course increase. As a small sign, two not overtly political films — both in differing degrees impressive — have had difficulties in surmounting a distributor resistance which went beyond the normal timidity of the species.

The subject of both films — one an American feature, the other a British Government sponsored short, *The Undefeated* — is the plight of severely maimed ex-soldiers. A valid enough theme of our times and useful, one would think, even in an atmosphere echoing with war drums, for the films are honest and sanguine. But it seems to have been felt that a film which shows a man so incapacitated by war that his readjustment demands the highest exercise of self-discipline and faith, might be damaging to the recruiting drive. The fact that in each case the man *does* regain self-belief and a sense of social responsibility is not so important as the fact that his ordeal mirrors the eternal nightmare of the serving soldier.

For the hero of Fred Zinnemann's *The Men* is a paraplegic whose injury has made him, almost certainly, impotent. One approaches a film of this sort almost

* My list of the world's greatest films, fought out with colleagues Gavin Lambert and Lindsay Anderson, amounts to nine (we cannot decide on the tenth). They are *The Childhood of Maxim Gorki* (Russian), *The Grapes of Wrath* (American), *Earth, Road to Life* (Russian), *Zéro de Conduite, Le Jour se Lève* (French), *Bicycle Thieves* (Italian), *Italian Straw Hat* (French), *City Lights* (American).

with eyes averted, aware that to make it endurable a purpose well above the reach of a sensation-mongering Litvak or a sentimentalising Wyler, is called for. Stanley Kramer, Zinnemann and the scriptwriter Carl Foreman have realised this purpose. *The Men* is the most distinguished film to which any of them has put his name.

Apart from all other considerations, a film which tackles the normally 'unmentionable' and sells out, is a bore. We all used the word 'courageous' to cover the apathy occasioned by the beggings and dodgings of the Negro cycle (*Intruder in the Dust* excepted). *The Men* does not sell out and is marked by the sort of courage we had ceased to expect from English-speaking movies. Not surprisingly, the force of its integrity has informed almost every aspect of the production (I make an exception of Dimitri Tiomkin's background music).

The Men plunges without preliminaries into the heart of its subject and disdains the use of a single flashback. Advancing soldiers are cross-cut into the credit titles while a drum beats on the sound-track. An officer signals them on, a gun rattles: the wounded officer, groaning on the earth, dissolves into the same man lying on a hospital bed in America, hopeless, bitter, crushed — a paraplegic. Zinnemann then cuts to another room in the hospital (which specialises exclusively in the treatment of paraplegics) where the wives and girls of the patients (among them the officer's girl, Teresa Wright) are being informed by the principal doctor (Everett Sloane) that their men, paralysed from the waist down, are as helpless as babies and will have to be trained anew in the primary physical functions. They will also, he informs them, with the rarest of exceptions, be impotent.

The officer, Ken Wilozek (Marlon Brando) insulated in despair, is at first unapproachable even to his fellow patients, whose armour against the vacuum of the future is a front of ironic self-mockery. Gradually Ken submits to training, is admitted to the bitter camaraderie of the ward, consents at last to see Ellen. By sheer persistence she imparts to him some of her own unfounded optimism and at last persuades him to agree to an engagement. But by that time she has herself become obsessed by doubts of her fitness for so awesome a responsibility. The doctor will not reassure her, her family oppose the marriage, she is as much in need of help and understanding as the crippled Ken.

On the wedding night the fears of Ken and Ellen build up into an emotional climax, the causes of which neither can understand. This scene in which two persons who love each other deeply pour out the fruit of all their torment in irrational words of hate is a hallmark of the truth of the film. It is one of the few love passages of the cinema to encompass the pitiful ache of human love.

Ken, returning in a fury of misery to the security of the hospital, is moving unconsciously to his own moment of realisation. Following a drunken spree he is expelled by the self-governing committee of the hospital, as a means of bringing home to him his responsibility to his wife. He returns to her and they face life together, the implication being that their biggest battle now lies before them, that they are reasonably equipped to fight it, and that if they win they will have touched the summit of love because they will have transcended self in a way that is permitted to few.

Such is the bald story of a remarkable film which explores the relationships of a number of human beings living in circumstances of unusual tension and stress, while affording a dramatically realistic view of the mechanics of their existence. Most of the men are played by actual paraplegics and the film is dedicated to them. The key parts are played by professionals who, with Marlon Brando, gave a good deal of study to the behaviour of paraplegics in the leading U.S. hospital for that affliction. Zinnemann's authority with the non-professional players is expectedly flawless and it is only with his main characters that a literary note is occasionally detected, sometimes in crosstalk between the men, and in an odd scene or so. Zinnemann's refusal to make concessions is exemplified in the scene between Ellen and her well-meaning, un-understanding commonsense parents, as in the wedding night quarrel: situations that would have fatally trapped most Hollywood directors.

This is not to depreciate the powers of the hospital sequences where the slow process of readjustment is harassed by treacherous hopes, sudden inexplicable physical collapses and occasional tragic ventures into the world of women, moments when the bravado to which the men cling deserts them.

The film depends a good deal, of course, on Marlon Brando, whose combination of style, depth and range comes like a blood transfusion into cinema acting. But there is also Everett Sloane's dedicated physician, afflicted with bouts of impatience and disillusionment, to help us drown the memories of Dr Genn and so many other film medicos. And the only star of the piece, Teresa Wright, begged for the part and did herself a favour since she has never before looked so much like an actress.

Round *The Big Clock* — Charles Laughton, Elsa Lanchester, Maureen O'Sullivan and Ray Milland

The Men was produced under Stanley Kramer's method of exhaustive preliminary rehearsal before shooting, the reward of which is to be seen in a pre-cutting tautness that pays compliments to Carl Foreman's writing (aside from his virile dialogue) as well as to Zinnemann's direction. We must make the most of *The Men* for, as with any other honest statement about war and its effects, the net outcome is pacifist. And that is a courageous thing today.

ALL ABOUT EVE: *Directed by* JOSEPH MANKIEWICZ: *8 December 1950*

A Letter to Three Wives discovered Joseph L. Mankiewicz as a writer/director with a fresh and welcome line on smart screen comedy. His new film, *All About Eve*, is longer, smarter, more sensational, but in comparison, as movie and as comedy, disappointing.

Eve (Anne Baxter) is a young stage actress who worms her way from obscurity to fame almost overnight by a process of biting every hand (and there are a number of willing ones) which feeds her.

In her career of blackmailing, chiselling and lying she is ably assisted by a villainous and improbable dramatic critic in an astrakhan collar (George Sanders) who has a degenerate admiration for her ruthless will to succeed.

The fact that Eve exposes herself so early in the film as a slut and so obviously (except to her victims) is detrimental to a sustained interest in her goings on. It is indeed on her principal benefactress and victim, leading New York actress Margo, that the interest of this $2\frac{1}{4}$-hour film centres.

This vain, gaudy, hysterical, neurotic, self-pitying, prodigally emotional but always warmly sympathetic creature of the theatre — obviously modelled on Tallulah Bankhead — is brilliantly, and I mean brilliantly, played by a Bette Davis unflattered by make-up or lighting. It is the best thing she has done for years, if not in her whole career.

Elsewhere the film depends on a quick-fire stream of juicy epigrammatic wise-cracks relating to the theatre — which had all the actors at the preview audience in fits. These are evenly distributed among the cast (Celeste Holm, Gary Merrill, Hugh Marlow, Thelma Ritter, Gregory Ratoff) after Miss Davis has had the pick through an undisciplined sprawl of theatrically conceived scenes.

All About Eve has plenty of surface cynicism, but no detachment, no edge and no satire. Boiled down it is a plush backstage drama that allows Miss Davis to get her man, Miss Holm to keep hers and Miss Baxter, in an artistically unjustifiable would-be clever climax, to get her deserts.

SUNDAY IN AUGUST: *Directed by* LUCIANO EMMER: *19 January 1951*

All film-makers have to strike a compromise between pleasing themselves and pleasing the box-office. It can be done and the discipline thus imposed on him can be beneficial to the film creator. But when the economics of the thing are considered it is almost a miracle that a good film comes our way at all. And that when it does more often than not it should come from Hollywood.

The plight of the Italian film-maker is a special one. He established a great reputation after the war by reflecting with the utmost sincerity and the utmost realism the emotions felt by Italians and the conditions of their life. But this reputation was made outside not inside Italy.

His films were adored abroad and cold-shouldered in his own country where the taste was and still is for the most blatant types of Hollywood films and Italian imitations of them. If he makes a film that pleases him in any way, he must place all his hopes on the foreign market. Admire then the tenacity of the Italian director or producer who keeps the realist tradition alive.

Sunday in August comes as the first Italian film of note since *Bicycle Thieves*, and as the first feature film of Luciano Emmer, a young man who has made a distinguished name with a technique of filming the works of great painters. Its producer, Sergei Amidei, is the scenarist associated with some of the best known Italian post-war films (*Open City, Paisa*). The method is naturalistic, the cast is largely non-professional and the locations authentic.

It is the story or rather the stories of five separate groups of people who go on an August Sunday outing from the blistering streets of Rome to the beach of Ostia. Like all films employing this compendium formula (not one of my favourite forms of narrative) the tendency is to diffuseness. But it has the sparkle of all such days won from the routine of life, as well as all the confusion, heat and discomfort.

Most successful of the episodes concern the large family who sweat and toil and quarrel on their way to, on and back from the beach and swear, as before, they'll never do it again and the inarticulate romance started between the young daughter and the boy she meets on the beach. Least successful is the spiv episode.

All the stories are fairly obvious, indeed, the film cannot but remind you of Carol Reed's *Bank Holiday* and its several descendants, but the great difference lies in the way they are filled in with flesh and blood. It is the truest film of its sort we have seen and its freshness, humour and optimism should guarantee it a good reception at British box-offices.

PANDORA AND THE FLYING DUTCHMAN: *Directed by* ALBERT LEWIN: *2 February 1951*

The scene of *Pandora and the Flying Dutchman* is a small village on the coast of Spain where beautiful, wilful, tempestuous Pandora (Ava Gardner) is the toast and tease of the wealthy Anglo-American colony.

At the inception of the story (told as a flash-back through the beard of English archaeologist Harold Warrender) one of Pandora's admirers slips himself a lethal dose and dies on the floor out of unrequited love.

To recover from this slight annoyance Pandora goes for a blow in the racing car with which racing motorist Nigel Patrick is about to tackle the world's record. 'Do you love me enough to throw this car over the cliff?' she asks. With a look of doglike rapture he pushes it into the sea.

It isn't that she's a destructive girl, explains the Warrender beard on the sound

Pageant week in Hollywood — Ingrid Bergman and Tyrone Power in
Joan of Arc and *Captain from Castile*

track. She's just waiting for Something that Fate has in Store for her, and she has to fill in the time.

Fate starts clicking the moment Pandora, impelled by some strange force, swims naked to the yacht which has mysteriously sailed into the bay and which is manned exclusively by the stern and well-fed person of James Mason.

Mr Mason as it turns out is none other than the legendary Flying Dutchman condemned to sail the oceans for centuries in a handsomely-appointed, self-running modern yacht (and, incidentally, mix with the best society at his ports of call) until he meets the Woman whose Love will Rescue his Soul.

When he does meet her she isn't notable for her tact: 'Are you fond of the sea?' she asks.

The film might have been enjoyably silly but for Albert Lewin's strivings to be classy and an air of third-rate decadence that hangs about it. On their own account can be enjoyed the Spanish scenery, the photography of Jack Cardiff, the personality of the actor-bullfighter Mario Cabre and (if your tastes lie that way) the looks of Ava Gardner.

This is a joint Anglo-American production and one of the occasions, I think, when we might be generous and let Hollywood have all the credit.

A WALK IN THE SUN: *Directed by* LEWIS MILESTONE: *23 February 1951*

The London success of Lewis Milestone's 22-year-old *All Quiet on the Western Front* has been repeated in local cinemas.

It is a film with the minutest allowance of sex-appeal, its acting style dates absurdly, but the hatred of war survives. And this is the secret behind its box-office triumphs.

Nearly five years ago 20th Century-Fox commissioned and subsequently disowned Milestone's World War II epic *A Walk in the Sun*. Since when no British booker would touch it. Now Eros Films have rescued and Paramount are showing this considerably distinguished war film.

A Walk in the Sun doesn't declaim against war and is free of the self-pity that suffused his earlier and famous film; though there is a proneness to certain emotional stresses and extravagances. The prevailing mood is one of desperate acceptance, masked by flippancy and warmed by the interflow of true comradeship — the fighting soldier's only dividend.

Taken almost verbatim from the novel by Harry Brown, the film gives an account of one platoon of the Texas Division on its first day in Italy after the Salerno beach landings in 1943.

With the lieutenant and sergeant killed before they start, the platoon moves slowly and fearfully towards its objective — an inland farm — isolated and exposed to everything the unseen, unknown enemy can throw at it.

Various things happen — veteran sergeant cracks up under the strain of a year's fighting, low-flying planes attack armoured cars and tanks approach and are overcome until eventually, without knowing why or how, what's left of the platoon forcibly occupies the farmhouse.

The sense of purposelessness, of blindly serving a plan whose shape and outcome you will never know dominates the action and is summed up by one of the men: 'We've got a grandstand seat only we can't see nothing. That's the trouble with war you can't see nothing. You have to find them by ear.'

The men — Dana Andrews, Richard Conte, John Ireland, Herbert Ridley and eight other leading characters — are defined and differentiated without recourse to low comedy or high sentiment. The dialogue they speak becomes an individual refrain, used repetitively and prodigally in a deliberate attempt to gain something like the effect of blank verse.

The attempt is successful and the poetic feel is heightened by the bold use of Earl Robinson's ballads as a sort of intermittent chorus.

Milestone's direction is outstanding; as in *All Quiet*, he can bring both tension and clarity into scenes of confusion. The film as it stands (115 minutes) would profit by a total cut of the initial scenes in the landing craft and by a slight paring down elsewhere. But either way *A Walk in the Sun* remains a notable war film, if not the most notable war film to come from America.

STORM WARNING: *Directed by* STUART HEISLER: *2 March 1951*

Some of the most exciting American films of this decade have been based on the never-failing situation of One-Man-versus-the-Mob.

And in order to show how the courage and integrity of an individual can move mountains of injustice, Hollywood sometimes doesn't hesitate to lift the lid off hair-raising scenes of cowardice and corruption in everyday American life.

Boomerang, the prototype, told of the near escape of an innocent man from a politically framed-up murder charge and was based on fact. Warner Brothers' *Storm Warning*, which is a story of what could happen to an innocent passer-by in a small Southern town, might easily have been, if you ignore the final collapse into unnecessary melodrama.

The stranger (Ginger Rogers), a travelling model, drops off one evening at Rockport from an overland coach to visit the sister (Doris Day) she has not seen since her (the sister's) marriage. The atmosphere in contrast to the cheerfulness of the bus is strange and hostile; the cabman refuses to drive her, the lights go out in the shop windows, the streets empty. The rain is coming down.

And then, alone and on foot in the deserted town, she is the terrified and unseen witness of the prearranged Ku Klux Klan murder of a Yankee journalist who was engaged on writing an exposure of KKK activities. She can, moreover, identify the three leading killers.

The second shock comes when, sick and revolted, she meets her brother-in-law (Steve Cochran) and recognises him as one of the killers.

The entire town is in thrall to the Klan and her testimony is the only means by which its solitary opponent, the district attorney (Ronald Reagan), can break its power. If she testifies she wrecks her sister's happiness.

Finally she is absolved from this responsibility by the moral collapse of the vicious brother-in-law, but there the producers falter and arrange a chase and

All keyed up — Humphrey Bogart, Lauren Bacall, Lionel Barrymore, Claire Trevor and Edward G. Robinson in *Key Largo*

pursuit finale in which all the undesirables, and the sister, are conveniently shot to death as the fiery cross of the Klan symbolically breaks and falls to the ground.

With the aid of an exceptionally good script, admirably handled by the director, Stuart Heisler, all the players excel themselves in this (for these song and dance exponents) strange territory. Ginger Rogers most effectively mingles an air of distaste, fear and indignation with a model's worldly-wise slant on things — but where was that expert witness on un-American activities, Mrs Rogers, looking when her daughter made this film? Steve Cochran intelligently epitomises the cloaked or shirted underling, given a licence to bully.

Storm Warning treats of the Ku Klux Klan as a racket purely and does not even hint at its political viciousness. It was photographed, incidentally, at Corona, California, by Carl Guthrie and is a good example of a melodrama fitting into its background and theme. If it isn't one of the ten best films of 1951 I shall be surprised.

LA RONDE: *Directed by* MAX OPHÜLS: *June 1951*

The release of *La Ronde* in London is exceptionally good timing. For Max Ophüls' film, gay, stylish and civilised, has already in a way become a part of the Festival which its Curzon run is likely to outlast. The immediate success of *La Ronde* is due neither to the X certificate nor to sensational reports of its wicked daring (useful as these factors will no doubt be in recovering the large price paid). There was an audience waiting for the film before the critics had time to write about it, an audience who had sensed the very special expression of a very personal talent.

I am unacquainted with Schnitzler, but he has clearly been as delicately and firmly bent to the design of Ophüls as was Stefan Zweig in *Letter from an Unknown Woman*. *La Ronde* is a comment, romantically phrased, on the deceptions of love. It is framed in the stylised elegance of Hapsburg Vienna at that period when, the days of power over and the decline well advanced, it earned the title of 'gay' and launched a thousand musical comedies. But, in all of the nine episodes which are linked together in a roundabout of love, the situations and the dialogue take us wittily, painfully and poignantly close to the life we know today. The thesis: that in the pursuit of love we deceive first ourselves and then our partner, who repeats the process, and so on and so on.

Thus the prostitute gives herself free to the soldier who can't be rid of her too quickly or too rudely in order to seduce the maidservant who, when he has become vulnerable to her through love, betrays him with the young master. And he in his next step to manhood forsakes the maidservant to seduce the young wife, who returns guiltily to the sanctimonious husband who is deceiving her with the shop-girl he has set up in an apartment. She in turn becomes a ready victim of the egocentric poet who, tired as soon as he has started the affair, resumes his amorous duel with the actress whose ruthless self-love is even greater than his own. She in turn avidly pursues the Count whose coldblooded ceremonial dissipations lead him out of her arms into those of the prostitute of the original episode. And what more ironic and fitting than that on his way out the Count should run into the original soldier on his way in — seeking the only comfort procurable?

It will suffice to list the players in the order of their appearance and to state that, with the exception of the last two, they give the faultless, apprehensive performances without which the whole delicate structure would have crashed. They are Simone Signoret, Serge Reggiani, Simone Simon, Daniel Gélin, Danielle Darrieux, Fernand Gravey, Odette Joyeux, Jean-Louis Barrault, Isa Miranda, Gérard Philipe.

The story is set in motion by Anton Walbrook, unrecognisably polished and sympathetic after his years on the English screen. As master of ceremonies, commentator, and minor participant in the piece, he steps from the present day into the romantically misted Vienna of the past, and in the deserted square starts the merry-go-round (literally) and the first adventure to the tune of a waltz by Oscar Strauss. This haunting waltz tune recurs throughout the film and becomes an ironic signal of the act of consummation; of love's triumph or defeat, whichever you will.

Though Ophüls can leave you in little doubt — for the episodes build up to an increasingly bitter comment, and the two final scenes cruelly mock the plight of their trapped victims. Yet he is less successful with these culminating scenes than with the open and gaily cynical earlier passages which prepare the way. To be fair, there are signs of some clumsy and harmful cutting in these two stories, but to be equally honest there are greater signs of serious miscasting in the selection of Gérard Philipe for the Count and Isa Miranda for the actress.

In the exchanges between the young wife (Danielle Darrieux) and the husband

(Fernand Gravey), *La Ronde* touches the apex of brilliance. The cutting, the magical movement of the camera round the beds, the dialogue, the acting, contribute to a wickedly amusing double exposure of the delusions of marriage and of adultery. Ophüls was never happier, nor for that matter was Danielle Darrieux.

It is not really surprising that Ophüls can still invest the cliché of Old Vienna with all the elegant raptures that Lubitsch, among so many, could never encompass. But to do it with so little ostensible elaboration denotes the true romantic artist. And this is not to demean the invaluable contributions of d'Eaubonne (décor) and Matras (camera).

To me *La Ronde* suggests a Mozart *Theme and Variations*, at once formal and gay, cynical and tender, romantic and ruthless.

NO RESTING PLACE: *Directed by* PAUL ROTHA: *13 July 1951*

With the decline of Hollywood as a film exporting centre — TV having engulfed it, or vice-versa, within the next few years — it will probably be left to Europe to keep the cinema alive. It is even possible that sheer necessity will set the British industry on the path it should have taken long ago.

The call then, if there is to be a future at all, will be for improved quality and quantity on very much decreased budgets, and this means a new sort of film. The precision ground works of Carol Reed, the Ealing comedies, the box-office roughage of Val Guest and Herbert Wilcox are all in their ways valuable to the future industry. But far more interesting and important than anything else at the moment is the small-scale pioneering movement as represented by Paul Dickson's *David*, Pat Jackson's *White Corridors*, and this week by Paul Rotha's *No Resting Place*.

Rotha's *The Film Till Now* is the standard work on the art of the cinema. And in his first feature film he has applied with great sincerity theories he has enunciated in that book. The critic has become creator and is doubly vulnerable.

With *No Resting Place* Rotha has proved that it is possible to make a film drama, employing professional and non-professional actors and using real locations (interior and exterior) throughout while grappling with the worst weather conditions in Irish memory — at under £60,000 and well within schedule. The film shows no signs of stringency or makeshift.

Shot in Ireland and based on Ian Niall's highly readable novel, it is a realistic story of Nemesis. The illiterate, itinerant tinker (Michael Gough) who accidentally kills the gamekeeper is defeated in the end as much by his own divided nature as by the relentless shadowing of the obsessed police guard (Noel Purcell). His plight is that of all outcasts who defy Society and are broken by it.

The lush Irish backgrounds are an unfailingly lovely setting for this slow, somewhat aloofly presented tragedy. It is good to look at and listen to — the natural Irish voices free of whimsey and blarney, the natural sounds punctuated with identifiable bird song, the sparse pastoral music of William Alwyn. And there are fascinating glimpses of the tinker's strange wayward life and flashes of real insight in the direction.

If Rotha, through his own austerity, has failed to generate the passion that would have made *No Resting Place* a landmark, it is none the less a milestone (it has incidentally given Michael Gough the best acting part of his film career and discovered to the British a fine actress in Eithne Dunne).

Producer Colin Lesslie's act of courage in backing this fresh and unusual film with every penny he possessed has been fully justified. He has made his point and put us all in his debt.

STRANGERS ON A TRAIN: *Directed by* ALFRED HITCHCOCK: *September 1951*

When, nearly ten years ago, Alfred Hitchcock broke away from his Daphne du Maurier phase with *Shadow of a Doubt,* there were premature congratulations. He was first in with the real location melodrama, and it looked as if he might have returned to his older and more entertaining style. The succeeding Hitchcock films, popular, adept and replete with useless trick effects, have been, however, peculiarly depressing in that their hollowness has derived from Hitchcock himself, and not — as in the cases of some other expatriate directors — from Hollywood. Hitchcock, one has felt, no longer believes there's much point in making films, and satisfies a jaded urge mainly in the setting up and surmounting of pointless technical obstacles. To a whole generation, unacquainted with most of his work in the *Blackmail — The Lady Vanishes* period, Hitchcock's reputation must have seemed inflated.

His new film, *Strangers on a Train,* to some extent restores the situation and recalls the old virtuoso of the art of suspense. Here again fear and paranoia are let loose in the open against normal backgrounds, and the tension mounts and writhes through ordinary humdrum human activity to its bizarre, sensational climax. The story, adapted from Patricia Highsmith's novel by Raymond Chandler and Czenzi Ormonde, is an intriguing one.

It opens juicily with the apparently chance encounter between two young men, strangers, in the saloon of a Washington-New York express. One of them, Bruno Anthony, a playboy type (who has, it turns out, contrived the meeting), lays a harebrained proposition before the other, Guy Haines (Farley Granger), a popular tennis star. Banteringly, but with an underlying air of deadly seriousness, he suggests a murder pact. The inconvenient and unpleasant wife of Haines, who refuses to release him to marry a Senator's daughter, is to be murdered by Anthony. In return, Haines is to dispose of the equally inconvenient father who stands between Anthony and the full expression of his personality. The absence of motive — there being no link between the executor and the victim — will guarantee two perfect and useful murders.

Sensing madness, the half-amused, half-horrified Haines escapes from his embarrassing companion, leaving his cigarette lighter behind in the confusion, and proceeds to an abortive meeting with his wife, a small-time slut admirably portrayed by Laura Elliot. A violent quarrel, during which he threatens her, is overheard by witnesses. The scene is now laid for a murder in the grand Hitchcock manner. The paranoiac Anthony, following Mrs Haines that night on a jaunt through the fairground Tunnel of Love, catches up with her on an ornamental island and neatly throttles her. Ingenuity is stretched to the limit when the murder is seen as a reflection in a lens of the victim's fallen spectacles. With these in his hand, Anthony then confronts the horrified Haines, demanding fulfilment of the rest of the bargain.

The film begins to sag when Haines fails to develop as a plausible character. Vacillating and cowardly before the blackmailing threats of Anthony (which an ounce of normal courage or acumen could have demolished), he makes unsuccessful play for sympathy as a hero. The bad casting of Farley Granger is not the only lapse; the tempo has diminished and the flaws of logic obtrude. And the sequences through which Anthony stalks and badgers Haines (Robert Walker gives a polished and chilling performance throughout the film), are further slowed down by dull interplay between Haines and the suspicious Senator's daughter. One scene produces some of Hollywood's greenest psychiatrical corn. Anthony, an uninvited guest at the Senator's socialite reception, is thrown into a psychotic trauma by the chance resemblance of the Senator's younger daughter (Patricia Hitchcock) to the late Mrs Haines, and half-strangles a playful dowager. This strange behaviour is looked on by the company as no more than harmless eccentricity, and he is politely asked to leave.

In contrast, Anthony's home background is evoked with a malignant skill that bears out the hand of Raymond Chandler in the script. The atmosphere of over-heated, opulent decay is typical. There is real horror in the scene where the Senator's daughter (colourlessly played by Ruth Roman) confronts Anthony's doting mother (a brilliant performance by Marion Lorne) at her easel with proof of his criminal lunacy, and encounters a bemused, apathetic and immune old woman, as crazy as her son.

The action finally resolves into a race against time. Now thoroughly out of control, Anthony is rushing to plant the lighter at the scene of the murder; Haines must win a tough championship game before catching the only train that will enable him to intercept Anthony. This is pure Hitchcock sleight-of-hand, but pretty to watch. Anthony's feverish attempts to recover the lighter he has dropped down a drain are brilliantly cross-cut into the magnificently photographed tennis match.

The climactic life-and-death struggle on the madly accelerated roundabout comes, however, like an expected blow on the side of the head from a blunt instrument. A lot of murderers have had their final run across a lot of parapets, along a lot of sewers, up a lot of ladders, down a lot of tunnels and in and out of a lot of funfairs since Hitchcock started it all up.

Strangers on a Train confirms Hitchcock's utter dependence on his script — in this case the best he has had for years — and a basic superficiality which prevents him from developing the psychological conflicts his characters do no more than suggest. His power of observation and his flair for surprise, counterpoising of the realistic against the bizarre, are still in evidence, but beyond a wider (and effective) use of close-ups he makes no innovations or advances. But in spite of its many and obvious lapses the film will certainly be classed as one of the successes of the year.

FILM CARTOONS GROW UP: *5 October 1951*

It has been evident for some time — even to the film critic, who sees only first feature films — that Walt Disney has been superseded in the field of the short cartoon film.

On his own territory of furiously invented physical mishap and mayhem he has been ousted by the commando-trained creatures of the M.G.M. and Warner cartoons. *Tom and Jerry*, *Tweetie* and *Bugs Bunny* are rougher and noisier than Donald Duck at his roughest and noisiest. They are equally deficient in grace.

The magic went out of Disney with Mickey Mouse to be recaptured now and again in portions of his full length films. But neither Disney nor his imitators have ever really used the full licence of the animated cartoon. (With the exception of Disney's *Baby Weems*, when he used drawings rather than pictures.)

By filling in the whole frame three-dimensionally they lose the inimitable freedom of the flat drawing and become illustrators instead of cartoonists. Thanks to Columbia the distinction can be appreciated at your nearest local cinema.

For over a year there have been appearing at the rate of one a month some remarkable Columbia cartoon films that leave the Disney school cold. They are

Slave girls not good for Tarzan — Lex Barker, Cheeta, etc, etc in *Tarzan*

made by the United Productions of America, whose president and source of inspiration, Stephen Bosustow, was 'laid-off' from the Disney Studios in the 1941 economy drive.

The first U.P.A. film I saw, *Ragtime Bear*, conformed to Disney literalness but with some positive differentiation — an absence of vulgarity, an increase in wit. Since then it has been fascinating to watch the development of U.P.A. away from the literal Disney conception into uninhibited cartooning without any sacrifice of box-office.

The recent *Gerald McBoing-Boing* (Technicolor) won an Academy Award and has had a great box-office success. Yet it is cartooning in a most fastidious and sophisticated style, reminiscent in a way of the Steinberg-Bemelmans school of drawing. Here is a perfect sound track, a sense of composition that can effectively leave blank whole sections of the frame and a captivating story (about a small boy who speaks in sound effects instead of words).

The latest U.P.A., *Trouble Indemnity*, continues the adventures of the charmingly myopic retired banker Mr Magoo with a similar wit in both drawing and story. With these two films Bosustow and his group of artists have found their form. The future is theirs.

THE BRAVE BULLS: *Directed by* ROBERT ROSSEN:
THE BULLFIGHTER AND THE LADY: *Directed by* BUD BOETTICHER:
October 1951

How many films have been able to assimilate the 'colour' of Mexico? Perhaps two. The chiaroscuro is too rich, the pictorial character of the place is a snare. To romanticise with a guitar, to paint with the lens, to go primitive; Mexicans themselves cannot resist it. Nevertheless the signs are pointing to Mexico as a new area of creativeness in the cinema. The present Mexican Government is an enlightened one, and is likely to be re-elected. It can see the value of bringing in the disinherited Hollywood writers and directors. It can subsidise films as uncompromising as Buñuel's harsh and beautiful *Los Olvidados*. In the meantime Mexico's proximity, comparative cheapness and eyefuls of photogenic legend and landscape have emboldened both Columbia and Republic simultaneously to satisfy the current location-fever and tackle the forbidden subject of bullfighting. Any film made for Anglo-American audiences on this theme is crippled by the ban imposed on actual scenes of bullfighting. Both films suffer in this respect though both, in their ways, testify to commendable intentions. They make at least pretensions of disclosing the mystique of bullfighting.

Robert Rossen's production for Columbia of Tom Lea's *The Brave Bulls* is the more ambitious and the less successful film. Repeating and exaggerating all the faults of *All the King's Men* it is completely overcome by local colour. A primary weakness of script (by John Bright) which (I take it) tries to reproduce the book chunk by chunk, is turned into nothing less than chaos by Rossen's surrender to tempting local detail.

The central figure, Mexico's most adored torero, Luis Bello (Mel Ferrer) is timid, disillusioned, fearful that his fighting courage has given out, when he falls under the spell of a fickle socialite (Miroslava). The liaison does not increase his confidence and when she betrays him with his friend and manager (Anthony Quinn) the matador hits bottom. A hint, however, that the manager's betrayal springs from the highest motives is not pursued, and he and his paramour are perfunctorily killed off. At the same time Bello's young brother is waiting for his first chance in the bullring and Bello is being importuned by the shabby little owner of the arena where he killed his first bull, to pay a gala visit there as leading matador.

The link between these separate themes is Bello and it is never joined because Bello is not allowed to develop as a character. His conflict is within himself and the narrative should move implacably to the real tragedy and real climax of man-versus-bull. This theme also is lost on the way in a series of snapshots, vivid at times, and informative, but entirely on the surface. The camera work of Floyd Crosby and James Wong Howe is excellent and the soundtrack, over which the traditional overture of the bullring is used as a leit-motif, is tremendously effective.

The Bullfighter and the Lady, produced by John Wayne and directed by Budd Boetticher, puts more effective emphasis on the dedicated isolation of the matador through a simpler and firmer narrative. A young American variety star (Robert Stack) sees the great torero Estrada (Gilbert Roland) in the ring and is seized with a fever to fight bulls. He becomes a pupil and friend of the matador and through this device a certain amount of simplified information about bullfighting is imparted — though not nearly as much as can be gained by looking at Goya's etchings. Through Roland's magnificent playing something can be sensed of the intense and purified approach of the matador to the bull, his equal partner in the art that reaches per-fection in death.

Robert Stack is an agreeable ash blond actor who, with Joy Page, balances the film for the box-office with a love interest and somewhat blurs the point of the film by becoming a leading matador in six short lessons.

The censor, who will allow far crueller treatment of animals than bullfighting to be glorified on the screen, has, one suspects, stepped hard on this film. The mutilated newsreel shots of the ring — though edited by John Ford — are quite useless since they all avoid the 'moment of truth'. Nor in either of these films is there any explanation of why, when or how the bull is killed.

RED BADGE OF COURAGE: *Directed by* JOHN HUSTON:
16 November 1951

As replacement for the stage show at the Empire on Sundays, M.G.M. have seen fit to show one of the most remarkable war films ever made. This film, *The Red Badge of Courage*, adapted from Stephen Crane's unforgettable novel about the American Civil War, was written and directed by John Huston as the fulfilment of a great ambition.

It was cut in Hollywood from 80 to 69 minutes and is obviously a problem child. Though its immediate fate is uncertain it will, I believe, be showing in 10 and 20 years' time with other film classics.

Anton Walbrook, Ronald Howard, Yvonne Mitchell and Edith Evans in *Queen of Spades*

It sees war through the eyes of a young Unionist recruit (played by America's most decorated soldier, Audie Murphy) who is dreading action yet aching for it, and who covers up his fright with braggadocio.

The enemy attacks and terror forces him to run, but his absence isn't noticed. Against a second attack he reacts in a fury of hysterical courage. He is a hero until he overhears a general referring to the regiment as mule drivers.

His pride after he has led an action in which the enemy is routed is again depleted when he hears that the real battle took place somewhere else. And finally on the march he has made his adjustment to war, in the confusion and hysteria of which cowardice and heroism can go equally disregarded.

Directly inspired by the wonderful Civil War photographs of William Brady, *The Red Badge of Courage* excels in pictorial representation of, let it be admitted, a highly picturesque war. But it also inducts you into the heat and chaos of battle in a way that hasn't been equalled since *All Quiet on the Western Front*.

The film does not attack war so much as show its illogicality and its unchanging aspect. For the general who visits the lines cracks the self-same jokes as generals cracked at Waterloo and on the Western front. And fears and heroisms and acceptance are met in the same terms.

MISS JULIE: *Directed by* ALF SJÖBERG: *30 November 1951*

One is reminded this week, almost with a shock, of those times when Swedish silent films had so much prestige that France and Germany were imitating them and Hollywood was coveting (later to acquire) the directors and players who made them.

The reminder is a Swedish film, *Miss Julie*, which impressively succeeds in bringing up to date those early individual traits. High among them was the sort of pictorial lyricism which, in its enslavement to dialogue, the talking film has now almost completely surrendered.

The striking achievement of Alf Sjöberg, the writer and director of *Miss Julie*, is not merely to have redeemed and daringly employed this visual language but to have done so whilst adapting a play consisting almost entirely of dialogue between two persons.

It would be a mistake, however, to class *Miss Julie* as a brilliant extension of Strindberg's play. It is a fresh work that uses Strindberg as raw material for its own design and purpose.

The scene is a spacious Scandinavian country estate at the end of the nineteenth century where on Midsummer Eve is witnessed a tragic fulfilment of sex and class hatred and long buried sins. Left alone in the house the Count's daughter is seduced by her father's valet after she had provoked him with mixed motives of vengeance (against men), lust and disdain. But his adoration and subservience turn into contempt as his mistress abjectly begs for kindness in her shame.

He relents, but even as they plan to elope their hatred flares out, there can be no respect or love between them. As her father returns Miss Julie kills herself.

The tragedy, enacted in the heavy somnolent atmosphere of the Midsummer

Eve Feast, is set in motion by the junketing of the peasants whose repressed animism breaks loose and suffuses the whole scene. From the opening shot Sjöberg casts a strange spell which diminishes only in the final confused passages between Miss Julie and the valet.

Sjöberg's luminously lyrical style, contributed to by brilliant cutting and camera movement, reaches a peak in the childhood flashback sequences which touchingly explain the misery and discord of the lovers. His handling of this tedious but necessary device is daring, poetic and authoritative.

Miss Julie is warmly and movingly played by Anita Björk, an actress with an original style of looks that fit the period, and the valet by Ulf Palme. I suspect that both of them have been made more sympathetic than Strindberg intended.

But then, again, I suspect the film, which is a consistent pleasure to the eye, regardless of subject or sub-titles, to be a finer work than the play could ever be.

CLOSE-UP ON 1951: *28 December 1951*

In the hush that encompasses the virgin week of Christmas — the only week without a new film — the film critic looks back over the year and gains strength.

He can, on this occasion, seeing how much better he fared than in 1950, allow himself a little extra optimism respecting the films of 1952 and gaily wish all his readers and all the Film Industry (including Sir Michael Balcon) the happiest of New Years.

It was a hard job last year to find five top flight films. Today my choice of the eight best feature films of 1951 comes as readily as the Academy of Motion Picture Arts' annual discovery of the greatest film ever made. In the absence of Carol Reed no British film qualifies.

The Winnington Academy Award (1951) goes then to Max Ophüls' *La Ronde* (France) for style, civilised wit and three perfect reels. To Becker's *Edward and Caroline* (France) for uncommon virtuosity of writing, acting and direction, upheld within a structure so fragile that the drop of a pin could have been disastrous; also for its equally uncommon, unsentimental love of human beings.

To Luciano Emmers' *Sunday in August* (Italy) for a robuster vote of confidence, registered with no less skill, in the human race. And to Sjöberg's *Miss Julie* (Sweden) which takes the reverse (and low) view of men and women with the freshest and most dashing of cinematic effects.

To John Huston's *The Red Badge of Courage* (America) for the brilliant pictorial innovations and to Lewis Milestone's *A Walk in the Sun* (America) for the humane perceptiveness with which they depict the plight of the civilian-soldier amid the confusion and illogicality of war.

And finally to Billy Wilder's *Ace in the Hole* and Henry Hathaway's *Fourteen Hours* as representative (with typical virtues and shortcomings) of the bright, caustic, ruthless, inimitable journalistic school of American film-making.

It has been an odd year containing some odd unclassifiable films. One of the most important was Paul Rotha's *No Resting Place* which tore down the myths of British film-making costs and laid a trail for future British films.

Two others whose intrepid international purpose was blurred only by political expediency were the Swiss *Four in a Jeep* and the Franco-Italian *Unwanted Women*.

After these about fifteen good to medium-good feature films represented solid entertainment of one sort or another. In this group four British films unambitiously figure, though only one of them — Pat Jackson's *White Corridors* — offered serious professional challenge. The others are *Encore, The Lavender Hill Mob* and *Lady Godiva Rides Again*.

On the Hollywood films, it seems, one can already feel the grip of the Un-American Activities Committee. *Storm Warning, The Sound of Fury* and *The Breaking Point* essayed tough themes but failed to follow through. *A Place in the Sun* vitiated its American tragedy in Boy and Girl romance.

On the medium-good list must also go Hitchcock's *Strangers on a Train*, though it loses speed on the gradients, and the two musicals *An American in Paris* and *Fine and Dandy*, both irresistible though one is too fancy and the other too mechanical.

Top place in the Winnington Museum of Artistic Curiosities goes to *Tales of Hoffmann*, and second place to *Pandora and the Flying Dutchman*. The worst bad films were *Rommel* and *Steel Helmet*, the funniest bad film *Another Man's Poison*, the most charming bad film *Paris Waltz*.

Historically if not aesthetically interesting were the return of Russian films with *Ballerina* and the arrival of the first post Civil War Spanish film *Don Quixote*.

But two short films did make history: *A Visit to Picasso* and *Gerald McBoing Boing*. The former as well as being the finest and gayest film on painting ever made is the apotheosis of the artist. The latter is a brilliant rediscovery of the cartoon form so long misused by Disney and his imitators.

AFRICAN QUEEN: *Directed by* JOHN HUSTON: *4 January 1952*

The strongest and most natural talent operating in Hollywood today is that of John Huston, who both writes and directs his films (three of the most recent have been *Treasure of the Sierra Madre, The Asphalt Jungle* and *The Red Badge of Courage*). He is prolific, experimental and courageous: he understands men, women and actors: he loves to reproduce the face of nature.

The New Year opens auspiciously therefore with John Huston's first British film — *African Queen*, a deceptively straightforward adaptation of C. S. Forester's novel. Nothing is harder to film successfully — or more welcome when it is — than this sort of open-air romantic adventure.

The masterly simplicity of C. S. Forester's tale faced Huston (also part-writing the script with James Agee) with a task worthy of his powers. It is confined almost entirely to the deck of a decrepit flat-bottomed river boat cruising through labyrinthine river and swamp and to the relations of the two people manning it — a prim English spinster missionary and the gin-swilling Canadian captain of the African Queen.

Driven into unwilling intimacy by the 1914 war (it is German East Africa) they escape the Germans by a series of miracles after astonishing feats of endurance and, of course, fall in love and live happily ever after once they have sunk the German launch with home-made torpedoes.

Huston shooting in African locations, keeps the story afloat through thick and thin, taking everything, like his two lovers, the hard and satisfying way. He does not abate one detail of dirt, heat and discomfort. He is rewarded by performances from Humphrey Bogart and Katharine Hepburn that are outstanding and represent, in both cases, a complete break from tradition.

The missionary's awakening warmth and tenderness, timed to a hair-breadth by Miss Hepburn, will be irresistible to audiences of every shape and size in Britain and the U.S.A.

African Queen makes history as the first jungle film above schoolboy level, though a satisfying quota of wild life and a wealth of exotic African scenery are given the benefit of some of Jack Cardiff's finest Technicolor photography.

The faults are obvious — the film is 15 minutes too long, the ending is forced and facetious and one cannot swallow the first abrupt transition of the two antipathetic characters into their new and shining selves. They are shortcomings I can forgive a genial, captivating and exciting movie.

Nearly three years ago in this paper I wrote an appreciation of *Sequence* as the brightest and shrewdest film periodical to be read. This week brings us the last issue of *Sequence*, and I can face its passing with gratitude but few tears.

Its irreverence and youthful dash had degenerated into coterie-writing reflecting the unhappy dilemma of the intellectual who tries to invest the cinema with a complexity it cannot as yet support and thereby damages it no less than he who will not admit it as an art.

As a sign directors like John Ford, Thorold Dickinson and Jean Cocteau are canonised and aestheticised out of all sense. *Sequence* has gone, but this critical party line dangerously survives.

OUTCAST OF THE ISLANDS: *Directed by* CAROL REED: *19 January 1952*

Once every three years or so film critics relax with a sigh of gratitude and the ranks of Wardour Street are reverently hushed — a new Carol Reed film has been given to the world.

And the Golden Boy of British films has not failed, until this week, to repay that veneration, sometimes with a major work, but always at least with one dazzling new trick and a film that is polished until it shines.

The trick of *The Third Man* was the zither accompaniment which imparted a raffish melancholy to a nondescript, if stylised, melodrama.

The trick of Reed's new film, *Outcast of the Islands*, is Kerima, the Egyptian girl, who as a native enchantress does not speak or act and is its one triumph.

The film is taken from the early novel of the same name by Joseph Conrad, which describes the degradation of a white man in Borneo in the old days of sail.

Willems, vain, unscrupulous, self-deceiving and ripe for disaster, meets it in the

Donald Houston, Jean Simmons and baby in
Blue Lagoon

arms of a native girl of sulky beauty and strong character (the prototype of all the Tondelayos of ensuing South Seas fiction).

Under this baleful spell he wickedly betrays his friend and benefactor, Captain Lingard, and, cast out forever from white society, is left to rot with the alien creature he now hates and fears.

Without expanding these characters (being far more concerned with rich, full prose) Conrad yet managed to give them and their story a feel of inevitability and fitness. As literary figures they move naturally in their literary orbit.

The figures which Reed has created from a script ingeniously packed by W. E. C. Fairchild with most of the book's detail, are theatrical, incongruous and one-dimensional. They are outcasts from reality, condemned by the exacting camera.

Sir Ralph Richardson's Lingard with marcelled beard and wig and wooden as the figurehead on a ship's prow, Robert Morley's petulant Almayer, prodigiously overplayed, Trevor Howard's slouching, expressionless Willems, and George Colouris' comic opera native are all reproved by Kerima, mute and wet from continuous baths in the river — but dynamic.

They look strange against the exotic natural backgrounds of Ceylon and Borneo, where a lot of the film was shot, and since the dialogue was lifted straight from Conrad, who wrote in his own stilted, declamatory style, they sound even stranger.

The truth is that the dilettante Reed is beaten by his realistic and often beautiful

Eastern backgrounds as much as by Conrad. The sort of artifice by means of which he has been able, so far, to disguise an increasing distaste for the rude turmoil of life tends to look garish in the open air. Typical instances are the revolving umbrella of Wilfred Hyde-White and the hammock torture of Robert Morley.

And he is quite unable to extract from Trevor Howard an illusion of the all-consuming passion on which, after all, the whole story hangs.

In the final assemblage of indoor and outdoor material Reed has used all his great skill to gain atmosphere and tension. But it is sleight-of-hand.

SECRET PEOPLE: *Directed by* THOROLD DICKINSON: *9 February 1952*

The opening of Ealing's *Secret People* coincides exactly with the appearance of a book which meticulously details the hows, whys and whens of this particular film's genesis.

The idea of such a book came from the director of the film, Thorold Dickinson, and it is in a sense a manifesto.

Making a Film (Allen and Unwin) was written by Lindsay Anderson (critic and editor of *Sequence*), who sat in as one of the film unit and recorded day by day, minute by minute, the complex process of creation. The complete shooting script is also included.

One admires Mr Anderson's energy, loving care and patience. Like the man who writes the Lord's Prayer on a pinhead, he has performed a feat that need never be repeated.

But the academic value of the book would have been considerably greater if the author's wide-eyed wonder at being part of a real film unit and his hero-worship of Thorold Dickinson did not permeate every page.

'Thorold, do you ever find it difficult to direct a film?' Mr A. enquires of Mr D. And the reply: 'Yes, very . . . it's terribly difficult to direct a film you don't want to make. That's why I've made so few . . . This comes from here — from the guts.' Or this on the film's progress from one of the unit: 'Madly, madly smooth. Thorold's a dream.'

Splendid, if the finished film carries but a little of the glory so portentously invested in it by Mr Anderson and fellow Dickinsonians in other periodicals. For this is the film Thorold Dickinson has been longing to make for ten years and can thus be regarded as embodying his dearest principles.

That *Secret People*, after all the creative agonies recorded by Mr Anderson, should turn out to be a confused, uncoordinated spy-thriller concealing a tentative message deep down below some strained effects of style is another tragedy of British film hopes.

Secret People is intended to show the corruption of the individual by violence, even when it is employed in the highest of causes. And the 'secret person' is the unknown self concealed in the outer person who emerges to resist the act of violence to which the outer person is committed. The message, much quoted, is Auden's 'We must love one another or die.'

To illustrate these by no means startling truths Valentina Cortese figures as a refugee from a dictatorship resembling that of Mussolini. She has fled to London in 1930 after her father has been murdered by the dictator.

Seven years later, a British citizen, she encounters her one-time lover (Serge Reggiani), who is also her late father's successor as leader of the opposition underground, now a terrorist party.

Love (not politics) persuades her at his behest to plant a bomb under the visiting dictator at a London party. And when the bomb misfires and kills a waitress her horrified reaction — to inform the police — is the normal one for a non-party girl.

In fact it looks just like the old story of the nice girl and the gangster, especially when she dies with a knife in her back, saving her little sister from a similar fate. Since the lover is never shown as other than a heartless thug or the girl as in any sense politically active, where is the corruption and where is the regeneration? And where is the point?

Mr Anderson's book discloses that Sir Michael Balcon was much perturbed over this vital flaw.

Dickinson's isolated studio scenes — the Paris café, the London café, the garden party, the conspirators' meeting — testify to a finicky stylist but they don't hang together. And the practical plot details involving such mundane things as the planting of the bomb, the behaviour of the police and the conspirators, the coercion of the theatrical agents, cannot stand scrutiny.

Valentina Cortese's performance is occasionally moving, Reggiani's negligible, Audrey Hepburn's negative and Charles Goldner's (as a lovable wop) straight out of *Give Us This Day*.

Good advice to Thorold Dickinson, in view of *Secret People* and *Man Of Two Worlds*, might be to try directing a film he doesn't want to make.

A STREETCAR NAMED DESIRE: *Directed by* ELIA KAZAN:
27 February 1952

As a play, newspaper serial or film Tennessee Williams' morbid tribute to sex, decay, violence, poverty and sex seems to throw out an irresistible enchantment.

It is a story of people living in the deepest caves of the human jungle. Unredeemed ugliness and brutality are relieved only by the primitive gratification of the senses.

The scene is New Orleans, and Elia Kazan (producer and director) gives us some theatrically composed settings lit by the fitful glow of neon lights outside and underscored by the despairing beat of the Blues that were born in New Orleans.

Like boys diving in the mud, Kazan and Williams slap on the dirt. The disintegration of the prostitute ex-schoolmistress Blanche Dubois, pitifully trying to keep up pretences in the Kowalski apartment, should be a harrowing experience. It isn't.

And for that we can't altogether blame Miss Vivien Leigh, who works tremendously with ravished make-up and fluttery hands to little effect.

Where Dostoievsky or Strindberg or even Zola could shatter us, Tennessee Williams leads us to a dead end. He throws no fresh light on human suffering, invokes no pity, filches no hint of beauty from the degradation.

His 'significance' is no more than an obsession with sex frustration and defeat for their own sake.

Elia Kazan's transcription of play to film is painlessly professional and loyal to the text. One is not surprised to hear that the film is an improvement on any stage version.

He has not, however, fully succeeded in accommodating the cinema medium to the torrent of undisciplined words on which Blanche Dubois is borne to her destruction.

Out of this shockeroo piece the performance of Marlon Brando is terrific. As the primitive, defiant, repellent Kowalski, 'the Polack' who resents and rapes his sister-in-law, Brando burns with a sullen glow that one will not easily forget.

And as Mrs Kowalski, enslaved by his virility, Kim Hunter brings us the one small spark of human warmth.

A Streetcar Named Desire has an X certificate.

RASHOMON : *Directed by* AKIRA KUROSAWA : *15 March 1952*

When it comes to banditry in the woods the Japanese are several moves ahead of Walt Disney. The story of *Rashomon*, the first Japanese film ever publicly shown (I believe) in Britain, is set in motion by the actions of a ferociously realistic bandit (Toshiro Mifune).

It was awarded the Grand Prix in last year's Venice Festival and it provides a strange, savage and enchanting experience.

It is impossible to determine to what extent *Rashomon* typifies Japanese film making. Very likely, as in the case of the Italian classics, native audiences look at it coldly.

However that may be, the director, Akira Kurosawa, has brilliantly assimilated Western techniques into the formal style of the East. The fusion is a happy one — a felicitous oriental wedding between the silent and the sound film — that adds something to both.

Rashomon is based on a modernised fable by the liberal writer, Akutagawa, who committed suicide in his thirties.

By a ruined temple gate in eighth-century Japan a priest, a woodcutter and a servant discuss a mysterious local crime, while sheltering from a torrential rainstorm. The priest is horrified, the woodcutter confused, the servant cynical.

The facts are simple: a bandit who is under arrest had intercepted a nobleman and his beautiful young wife while they rode through the forest. Desiring the wife he had tied up the husband, raped her before his eyes and then killed him.

But the truth is complex. The wife and the bandit while admitting these facts tell different stories in order to reflect the greatest possible credit on themselves. The spirit of the husband conjured up by a medium adds yet another version.

Finally, the woodcutter confesses to being an eye-witness and his story, animated by guilt and envy, also differs.

The acting, owing much to mime, has an intensive force, an abandonment and passion, that will shake dialogue-fed Western audiences. The sub-titles are barely necessary. Yet the film is full of subtleties, of poetic changes of mood as the eye of each successive character transforms not merely actions but scenes into conflicting, contradictory patterns.

Kurosawa bitterly rips the veils from human frailty, sparing only the woodcutter in a sentimental epilogue. But with the eye of an artist he records a beauty that mitigates the abjectness of his victims.

I am not sure about that ending, though perhaps it does unconsciously reveal the dichotomy of the Japanese; the swift, inscrutable change from barbarous cruelty to unabashed mawkishness.

Nor am I sure about the Japanese variation on Ravel's 'Bolero' which accompanies the bandit's story. In any case I shall go back and find out.

VIVA ZAPATA!: *Directed by* ELIA KAZAN: *29 March 1952*

Mexico is a dangerous country for film-makers. The clouds and the cactus so easy to become arty about, the primitive squalor so easy to be poetic about. A country for disillusioned Hollywood producers to spread themselves in.

Eisenstein, John Ford, John Huston, John Steinbeck have all fallen for the siren song, Mexicana. Now Elia Kazan (directing) and John Steinbeck (writing) bring us a two-hour saga of peons v. rurales, of revolution, counter-revolution, train-wrecking, shooting up and the machete in the back — *Viva Zapata!*

General Emiliano Zapata, a Mexican Indian and to this day an enigmatic figure, united with General Pancho Villa in 1909 to overturn by force the despotic Diaz Government. For eight years the two of them maintained uneasy control until Zapata was betrayed and murdered. Zapata is still a legend among the people for whose rights he fought and who are still dispossessed.

Steinbeck's version of Zapata (Marlon Brando) is idealised. The brigand-liberator — whose inventive methods of torture are recorded, whose personal assassinations make a long list and whose bigamously wedded brides littered the countryside — approximates to a cross between a highly monogamous American liberal and the new sheriff who has come to clean up the town.

But that isn't of outstanding importance in view of the fact that the film faces some hard political truths. Zapata witnesses to the corrupting effects of power, the intransigence and apathy of liberated masses, the dreadful disillusionment of the post-liberation processes and the (nearly always) unbridgeable gap between the idealist man of action and the cold professional revolutionary.

Steinbeck may over-simplify and soften and blur these points, but they linger. He is a sentimental victim of the spell of Mexico which he can't resist expressing in chunks of poetic dialogue — as witness the terrible wooing scene between Brando and Jean Peters — when the treatment should be hard and direct.

The strength of *Viva Zapata!* is in Kazan's direction backed by Joe McDonald's magnificent unromantic photography which yield some superlative sequences. And Marlon Brando.

Arguments as to whether or not Brando can act in the theatrical sense are irrelevant. Brando conveys power, which, in the cinema, can transcend acting — as in *Streetcar* he transcended Vivien Leigh. Here it is the power of an illiterate Indian given to few words, whose rare, swift eloquence can startle, whose rage can scorch — the power to rouse, lead and safeguard a whole countryside.

Anthony Quinn as Zapata's lecherous, tyrannical brother might be said to form with Brando a composite portrait of the real life Zapata. Jean Peters as his inamorata forms a well-bred vacuum for the box office.

SINGIN' IN THE RAIN: *Directed by* GENE KELLY *and* STANLEY DONEN: *12 April 1952*

Gene Kelly is one of Hollywood's half dozen originals. Beyond the exuberant dancing style and a personality that comes over from the screen in waves is the talent that made *On the Town* the first homogeneous film musical.

Kelly's knack of conveying that one day he is liable to create the first great musical and push the cinema a long way forward persists in *Singin' in the Rain*. Though the film is structurally inferior to *On the Town* its best sequences are more pointed and its numbers — borrowed from a past heyday of musicals — are gayer.

A mildly satiric story concerning the beautiful blonde film star (Jean Hagen) whose mute beauty has launched a thousand fan clubs and whose incurable Brooklyn accent nearly ruins the film company on the advent of the Talkies; some affectionate ribbing of the tricks, clothes and mannerisms of the old-style musical; all rather broad and obvious but pleasant and at moments electrifying.

Tab Hunter and Linda Darnell in *Island of Desire*

As, for instance, in the brilliant main solo dance in the streets through a flood of rain, a sequence which compares with Kelly's dance with his reflection in *Cover Girl* and revivifies one of the best remembered of early vintage numbers — 'Singin' in the Rain' from *Hollywood Review 1929*.

It is far better than those items we remember so tenderly from past films. The main strength of those old Hollywood musicals was the fact that they were able to hire music from composers like Berlin, Cole Porter, Kern and Gershwin, with whom there is no modern to compete.

Kelly's most dangerous weakness is a taste for artistic ballet, a taste which ran riot in *An American in Paris* and here expresses itself in two unworthy slow-motion dances — one in some forbidding Dali type decor — with Cyd Charisse, whose own not inconsiderable skill has no chance to display itself.

After Gene Kelly the film belongs almost entirely to Jean Hagens's cunningly balanced disparity between pneumatic-drill voice and glamorous face.

CRY, THE BELOVED COUNTRY : *Directed by* ZOLTAN KORDA :
26 April 1952

Take any obstinate scorner-of-the-cinema to this week's new films and if he remains unconverted his is an aberration that will never be adjusted. And he will be the poorer man.

Two of the films adventure as only the cinema can into the troubled and complex field of European and native relationships in the lands of South Africa and India. In their utterly different ways, though neither has the full proportions of great screen art, they leave you richer, wiser and for ever affected.

The third film puts within the reach of millions — or of that proportion of them sanctioned by an X certificate — one of the most scorching American plays of its age.

A month ago in this newspaper (27 March) I extolled the courage and integrity of *Cry, the Beloved Country*, a joint adaptation by Zoltan Korda and Alan Paton of the latter's best-selling novel. It is the story of the tragic pilgrimage of an old Negro preacher in search of his son and his sister in the squalor of Johannesburg's shanty-town.

Its effect is to bring home with almost unbearable closeness the plight and nature of a warm, kindly native people that has lost its traditional way of life and is being poisoned by inhuman penalisation. It shows, too, the loveliness of the country which no longer holds for them a living.

Much of its strength derives from the fact that *Cry, the Beloved Country* disdains sensational 'exposure' of White brutality and intolerance. (The Rev. Michael Scott's factual film was far more shocking in this respect.) It does not preach or propagand. It tears you to shreds.

The Whites in the film are good people, visited no less than the Negroes by guilt and fear and confusion. But it is the latter who suffer and are disinherited and driven into crime and misery. Only the enlightened Europeans, says this film which makes a plea for Christian understanding, know that degradation is indivisible.

Alternately amateurish and inspired, the film makes its own pace, its own laws, sustained by players who invest its characters, White and Negro, with subtlety and nobility. They are, among others, Canada Lee, Charles Carson, Sidney Poitier, Joyce Carey, Edric Connor, Vivien Clinton and Michael Goodliffe. Sidney Poitier as the young priest and Charles Carson as the white father are outstanding.

THE RIVER: *Directed by* JEAN RENOIR: *26 April 1952*

I went to the Press show of Jean Renoir's *The River* and failed to respond. I suspected my own mood, saw it again and surrendered completely. As soon as possible I shall see it again as an act of pleasure.

Made in India and based on an autobiographical novel by Rumer Godden (who worked on the script), *The River* unfolds like a dream — a dream of adolescent love by the banks of the Hooghly River in West Bengal.

Two white girls (Patricia Walters and Adrienne Corri) and their half-caste friend (Radha) experience in their various ways the ache and joy of first love when Captain John (Thomas E. Breen), a young American who has lost a leg in the war, arrives on a visit.

The stranger wallows in self-pity and departs, the girls have made the dizzy flight from childhood to womanhood, a small brother dies, the mother of one of the girls has a baby, the river flows on. Life opens out.

Adolescent girlish love — a favourite theme of women novelists and *New Yorker* writers — has a limited appeal. And none of the players here — young or old — comes particularly to life (the American is a plain boor).

Yet a belief in life and a way of life, strange, spiced and full of bright childhood dreams in the markets, temples and walled gardens of India, break out of a fragile Anglo-Indian *après-midi*.

The River is unfailingly pleasing to the eye and the ear. It is one feels, however flavoured the mood, a true India, seen lyrically but with love and understanding by a Frenchman (an Indian critic praises it as compensating for Kathleen Mayo and Beverley Nichols), who revels in its people, vistas, trees and rivers, its music, feasts and ceremonial.

LOS OLVIDADOS: *Directed by* LUIS BUÑUEL: *3 May 1952*

The theme of juvenile delinquency has inspired some unforgettable films. *The Road to Life, Shoeshine, My Universities, Children on Trial* have probably had a longer lease of life than many of the better-known film classics. One does not need to be a sociologist to see why this should be.

The most savage and in some respects the most artistically impressive of them all *Los Olvidados* (*The Young and Damned*) opens today at the Academy. It is the work of a Spaniard, Luis Buñuel, who shook the *avant garde* of the 'twenties with his surrealist films, and who has been missing from the screen for eighteen years.

Buñuel shot the film in four weeks in the slums of Mexico City and used only two professional players. One of these, Estella Inda, as the young mother, raped at the age of 14 and unable to give to the son who resulted the love that might have saved him from crime and tragedy, touches the main spring of the problem and emerges as a universal figure of despair.

For the rest, *Los Olvidados* is a catalogue of juvenile crime and horror never far from nightmare, retailed with a fluid power of composition and a microscopic care for detail. One is reminded throughout that Buñuel is a compatriot of Goya.

Buñuel is explicit: delinquency is caused by lack of love which is caused by poverty. In stating this he makes absolutely no concessions other than to his right to shock us out of our seats — as big a compromise as any, perhaps.

And this is just what he fails to do, although every harrowing incident is taken from the Mexican police files and every character has the rare ring of authenticity. For his protest has no anger, warmth or pity, and I found myself coolly admiring the art and style of a film that left me more or less emotionally unaffected.

The censor deserves a special credit for passing, with an X certificate, a work of art so violently unorthodox.

HIGH NOON : *Directed by* FRED ZINNEMANN : *3 May 1952*

The traditional Western ends with the marshal cleaning up the town. *High Noon* takes it on from there.

The marshal (Gary Cooper), now a solid and newly married citizen, is warned at 10.30 of the impending arrival by the noon train of the vicious killer who had terrorised the town. With three bad men he intends to liquidate the marshal, who had sent him up for murder.

Deserted by everyone (including his Quaker wife), Cooper sweats it out alone minute by minute, the story's action being synchronised with the running of the film. It ends as we suspected it would.

But it is futile to mourn the tragi-ironic ending that would have made this an outstanding film. Allowing for the tritenesses and the monotonous ageing Cooper front there is some fine tension and consistently high craftsmanship. And, surprisingly, an excellent folk-tune motif from that old studio musick-master Dmitri Tiomkin.

AAN : *Directed by* MEHBOOB KHAN : *19 July 1952*

I have known that in India nearly three hundred films are produced each year and that it is nothing for an Indian fan to see one film fifteen times or more. I have gathered by reading exotically outspoken Indian film reviews that Indian taste favours the gaudy and romantic, is set against realism, and guided by star appeal.

That was the extent of my knowledge of the world's second largest film industry until this week. *Aan* is the first Indian colour film made, the first Indian sound film to be publicly shown in Britain, and as good an example as can be seen (I am assured) of slap-up Indian film production.

Aan is an epic, cut down from its original $3\frac{1}{4}$ hours by one-third and suffering a little perhaps in clarity since director Mehboob Khan is giving us comedy, tragedy, romance, costume, spectacle, slapstick drama, dancing, sex, music, rodeo and horse-opera; sometimes all together in one scene.

Peasant girls are faced with the choice between poison or being eaten by lions to save their honour and high-born and heroines have their dashing peasant lovers flogged. Drunken princes gloat over dancing girls, camels stampede, forts are fired, sword fights abound and Democracy triumphs over Tyranny.

And then, just as you are thinking that even Mr Mehboob must have gone through the pack, he flourishes his ace — a dream sequence.

Twenty years of Hollywood cliché are freely and ingenuously packed into a film that remains intractably Indian and innocent. Its most Eastern touch, curiously enough, is the presence of a Cadillac in the courtyard and the wearing of riding breeches and boots to denote noble breeding.

Acting that relies on the crudest silent film technique, a sound track that cheerfully embraces Indian music, Western serenades, sambas and foxtrots, a parade of dazzling Indian beauties queened by the young star Nimmi, give to *Aan* a piquancy which is quite separate from art. It should do well in the territory of Cecil B. de Mille.

But it does not of course begin to explore or exploit the life and culture of India. Nor is there any evidence of this having been done by any one of India's five hundred-odd producers.

MANDY: *Directed by* ALEXANDER MACKENDRICK: *2 August 1952*

Alexander Mackendrick is a director who stepped straight in from documentaries to make the best of the Ealing comedies — *Whisky Galore*. His subsequent and more ambitious comedy, *The Man in the White Suit*, while to some extent missing fire, gave distinctive proof that talent not luck was behind this remarkable feat.

Mackendrick's third film *Mandy* is a drama of affliction and triumph. It shows him as a director of warmth and sensibility who can win vivid performances from intelligent actors, or from a seven-year-old child. He is a stylist, too, and, with crossed fingers, I prophesy a very bright future for him.

Mandy, played by Mandy the daughter of broadcaster David Miller, has grown to the age of six in a forbidding world of silence. Born deaf she is unable to discover the use of her perfectly normal vocal chords. She has no means of communication with the outside world.

Her middle-class parents (Phyllis Calvert and Terence Morgan) are helpless until the mother takes Mandy to the Royal Residential School for the Deaf in Manchester, which specialises in teaching deaf children how to lip-read and speak, and is the foremost school of its kind in the world. The father and his family oppose the move on snob grounds — the school is free and unlovely — but the mother persists at the cost of separation from her husband. Gossip is aroused by the close interest taken in Mandy's case by the Headmaster (Jack Hawkins) and the machinations of an anti-progressive councillor (Edward Chapman). Domestic crisis of a familiar brand ensues.

The film is both inspired and trite. With Mandy herself, who gives a phenomenal performance (no less heartrending in the triumph of her first spoken syllable than in her locked-in loneliness), with Jack Hawkins (whose harassed untidy headmaster and maker of unsung miracles has depth, strength and purpose) and with Dorothy Alison's jewel-like playing of a dedicated nurse Mackendrick can and does go to town.

In the key passages with these players, in the school itself amongst the real deaf children, his film is, I venture to state, unsurpassable.

Mackendrick, however, is bound by the script (of Nigel Balchin and Jack Whittingham) to retail a domestic story which impinges on Mrs Dale's territory. Miss Calvert is adequate to the task and Mr Morgan a dead loss. But Mackendrick has triumphed over this weakly motivated story by the strength and integrity of his tribute to the ideal of selfless devotion which mankind can set against its suicidal destructiveness. And by the poignancy of the central drama of Mandy.

Peggy Evans, Dirk Bogarde, Jimmy Hanley and Jack Warner in *The Blue Lamp*

Serge Reggiani and Simone Signoret in *Casque d'Or*

GOLDEN MARIE (CASQUE D'OR): *Directed by* JACQUES BECKER: 6 September 1952

The convention of French screen-love in general reverses those of Britain and Hollywood. English-speaking love finds its fulfilment off-screen, in the future, the lovers being brought into each other's arms by the last reel to start a new life together. They uphold success, breeding, middle-class morality.

French lovers, beaten by life before the film has started, taste their brief hour to the full before death brings them the only true and lasting consummation. And because the incurably romantic French taste insists that love is sweeter when it is doomed and more brilliant when it shines out of squalor, French heroes and heroines are displaced proletarians, outside the law but full of wistful dreams.

By a coincidence two French films appearing together this week with the same heroine, Simone Signoret, illustrate perfectly the use and abuse of this convention.

Jacques Becker is a writer-director whose high standard of accomplishment has been unfailing in widely dissimilar films (*Goupi-Mains-Rouges, Edward and Caroline*). In *Golden Marie* he is the alchemist who turns lead if not into gold at least into silver-gilt.

Golden Marie is a legendary courtesan who flamed in the Apache underworld of Paris in the 1900's. Most of the men who loved her met violent deaths. As the climax to this film, she sees from an attic she had hired the one love of her life (Reggiani) executed at the guillotine.

As a prelude to this powerfully realised scene there are knife fights and lyrical interludes of love-making in the country, betrayals, murders, escapes and celebrations in the cafés.

There would be nothing to distinguish all this from the picturesque routine of cabaret Apache life, but for the grip of a director with style at his finger-tips and a gift of giving his narrative a smooth and beautiful flow. Becker has made the period come to life in scenes that catch the glow of the painters Renoir and Monet.

But the film also depends on Marie. Simone Signoret's mocking animated beauty fulfils all the demands and gives aptness to the title, as well as lifting the lugubrious, walrus-moustached Reggiani well above his class.

I have indicated that *Golden Marie*, which I have seen twice, is a film not to be missed on any account. Yet the sum total of all its considerable artistry gives a strange effect of emptiness. What was the purpose? What was the content after all? It's a compliment to Becker that one asks these questions only as an afterthought.

LIMELIGHT: *Directed by* CHARLES CHAPLIN: *18 October 1952*

As one who has the unusual distinction of not having written a word about Charles Chaplin (other than as a reviewer of his films) I feel that I need make no apology for returning in this column to his film *Limelight*.

Limelight passes the one great test of a work of art — it stays with you and flourishes. It is a film of essence. As you dwell on it the weaknesses dwindle and you know you cannot rest until you have savoured once more the sweetness and melancholy of its intuitive genius.

You are beset, too, by an urge to return to it and discover if you can how far Chaplin himself is implicated in his portrayal of the eternal trouper, with his trite Thoughts about Life and Love, his flamboyance, his self-pity, his generosity.

I am profoundly conscious of two things in *Limelight* — its pessimism and its tribute to love. The tragedy of Calvero is the tragedy of man, while the sentiment, strong, sweet and selfless, that links Calvero and Terry as they wander before the clumsy back-projections of London, is man's unfulfilled dream. Not often is the cinema empowered to uplift sentiment so surely and so shamelessly.

As a last word I must warn you of the comedy act gloriously shared by Buster Keaton. This is so overwhelmingly, devastatingly funny as to be physically painful.

The unique fecundity of Chaplin which had already spilled over into ballet (superbly danced by André Eglovsky) and music-hall song and dance, here crowns the day with surely the one new comic gag in the world.

MIRACLE OF MILAN: *Directed by* VITTORIO DE SICA: *22 November 1952*

An unusually full week is crowned by a distinguished Italian film. *Miracle of Milan* (*Miracolo a Milano*) is a fable, fantasy or fairy tale created by Vittorio de Sica and his inseparable writing collaborator Zavattini (they made *Shoeshine, Bicycle Thieves*) around the theme of poverty and goodness.

The superb opening reels — employing as is seldom done the great pictorial-poetic resources of the cinema — show the orphan Toto discovered in a cabbage patch and adopted by a wonderfully kind sprightly old woman; learning from her to believe in the essential goodness of people; disconsolately following her funeral hearse through wet dismal streets; and being conducted wonderingly into the State orphanage.

Toto grown-up (Francesco Golisano) meets a harsh world which growls at his 'Good morning', but finds friendship and charity among Milan's down and outs in their unspeakably decrepit shanty town.

And Toto's indestructible faith in life invigorating this hopeless community transforms it into an estate wherein happiness and humility, humour and tolerance flourish together.

The gushing of an oil well on this forgotten piece of ground brings in Big Business, savagely satirised by de Sica, as it employs first trickery and then tanks and tear-gas to oust Toto and his friends.

They are saved by his suddenly acquired power to work miracles (vested in him by his old foster-mother flying down from above), but ultimately this is of no avail.

There is no place in this world for the poor, says de Sica, and no place for goodness since it resides only in the poor and dispossessed. So it ends with them all flying off on broomsticks, to a 'land where "Good morning" really means "Good morning".'

It cannot be pretended that de Sica's miracle-working sequences equal the gloriously logical fantasy of the preceding reels. But despite the later confusions this remarkable film, which should captivate a large general public, is sustained to the end by rare emotional purity and an organic sense of comedy.

The music, a song and theme by Cicognini will have a strong popular appeal. It's the sort that stays in the head.

THE CRIMSON PIRATE: *Directed by* ROBERT SIODMAK: *27 December 1952*

A minor but regular form of Hollywood myth is the pirate film or sea-opera. It is an innocent convention requiring only a change of torsos and a large expenditure of dollars with each fresh version.

All film pirates are either Crimson or Black, with occasional deviations into Purple or Red, and this must be conveyed in the title which, together with the cast list, is ample information for the critic to pass on to his readers, whether they be addicts or otherwise.

This hitherto happy situation has been upset this week, first, by the seasonal shortage of subject matter in celluloid, and secondly, by the method Warner Bros. have adopted in handling the most expensive pirate film on record.

The story runs that having half made *The Crimson Pirate* on conventional lines they decided to guy it and a tongue-in-cheek introduction by Burt Lancaster — the most agile buccaneer since Douglas Fairbanks — bears this out.

The result of this dichotomy is a not altogether consistent blend of piratics and knockabout burlesque. The fact that the latter is frequently conducted with some spirit and expertise may not exactly console the fans who like their pirates straight.

The film is packed with extra gimmicks. These include an eighteenth-century scientist (James Hayter), whose prophetic inventions enable Buccaneer Burt to take the island by amphibian assault, aerial bombardment, machine-guns and flame throwers, a specially built ship which really sails, Eva Bartok, and a democratic message.

THE MAN WHO WATCHED THE TRAINS GO BY:
Directed by HAROLD FRENCH: *27 December 1952*

There are certain books which read so much like film scripts that one wonders why film producers don't leap at them and put them absolutely untrammelled into celluloid. One of these is, or was, Simenon's *The Man Who Watched the Trains Go By*.

Those responsible for this transcription are Raymond Stross, an exhibitor turned producer and a British director, Harold French, who also wrote the script. The world which separates them from Georges Simenon is vast and apparently unbridgeable.

The Last of Mrs M, *or* the Shadow of the Genn — Cathy O'Donnell, Leo Genn, Greer Garson and Walter Pigeon in *The Miniver Story*

Simenon wrote a well-knit and tense story of the breakout into crime of a respectable Dutch costing clerk. His style was detached and sardonic, his characters pitiful, seedy and human.

The clerk's sordid little fling in the underworld of Paris, his cunning game with the police and his encroaching madness were made real by closely observed detail.

The film gives us Claude Rains in his *Phantom of the Opera* mood engaged in a duel of wits with an improbable and humane police inspector (Marius Goring) and wooing a glamorous demi-mondaine (Marta Toren) in the heavily Continental atmosphere of a British studio. It is wordy, over-acted, evasive and boring.

LES JEUX INTERDITS : *Directed by* RENÉ CLÉMENT : *3 January 1953*

At the Academy Cinema the year ends not with a whimper but a bang. René Clément's *Les Jeux Interdits* (the English translation, *The Secret Game*, is, incidentally, apter than the French title) has been misleadingly described by colleagues as an anti-war film.

It is this only by deep implication, with the far-reaching clarity of an art which disdains the sermon or the message. The film testifies rather to the strength of innocence which can discover a shrine in the midst of ugliness and death. It is the apotheosis of first love.

On the stampede by road out of Paris in 1940 a five-year-old girl sees her parents and her dog shot to death by German machine guns. Her uncomprehending grief centres on the dog.

Clutching its dead body, she wanders through the fields and is met by the 11-year-old son of a small farmer, who takes her into his home. There they witness the death of the elder brother who has been kicked by a stampeding horse.

Believing that dead people are buried in cemeteries for company and to keep them out of the rain, the unreligious city girl and the superstitious peasant boy begin their secret game and build a cemetery for the dog, adding a mole, a beetle, a lizard, a hen and whatever dead small creature they can find.

They rifle the village cemetery and church for crosses which they plant on the graves of their animals, gabbling the prayers they do not understand. Discovery brings terrible punishment. The girl is torn away to an orphanage, her stored up grief breaking out in a heartrending cry for the boy as she hears someone call his name, Michel, on the railway station.

The boy is bereft. He has had his vision of beauty, his great love, and, that over, he will become hard and rough and stupid as life envelops him.

The idyll of this boy and girl is developed with unfailing delicacy and a brilliant perception of the ruthlessness and vulnerability of children. The entrancing little girl (Brigitte Fossey) is wonderfully responsive to the light and strong direction of Clément. She projects an irresistible and uncloyed child-appeal.

But the boy (Georges Poujauly) is something more — an actor in his own right — and it is through his performance that one is privileged to rediscover the sweet dreams and bitter anguish of childhood.

The tragedy is sustained by pity, irony and humour and its dreamlike quality is

Carmen Miranda in *Something
for the Boys*

heightened by a spare guitar accompaniment, based on folk music and played by
Narciso Ypes, which steals in faintly and forlornly.

The scene is sunlit and lethargic, but war is in the distance and the earth is all the
more precious because of the nearness of the shadow.

A few small touches that are over plausible, the somewhat stagey stampede
scenes in the beginning and the overdone bucolic comedy, are comparatively minor
faults in a film through whose tragic comprehension clamours an unquenchable
faith in life.

LE PLAISIR: *Directed by* MAX OPHÜLS: *7 February 1953*

The outstanding commercial success of *La Ronde* has produced a not altogether
unexpected reaction from Hollywood. Backed by Columbia Pictures its Austrian
director, Max Ophüls, has been persuaded into an endeavour to repeat the pattern
with *Le Plaisir*. It is a disappointing film with some consolations.

Using three Maupassant stories to point the paradoxical deceptions of pleasure,
Ophüls tends to stress the obvious with a Teutonic broadness that has the effect of a
constant nudge in the ribs. Cynicism and sentimentality substitute for irony and
melancholy, particularly in the centrepiece, 'La Maison Tellier'.

This, it may be recalled, is the famous story wherein the popular local *maison*
is unexpectedly closed while Madame and her five young women repair to a First
Communion in the country.

The subtleties and humour of the situation as well as its pathos are borne under

153

by the over-ornate style and the note of forced gaiety by which Ophüls, away from his Viennese background, seeks to disguise a fundamental uncertainty.

Indeed, the outstanding sequences — the sunlit drive through the country, in the Renoir manner — are those in which Ophüls breaks away from the story.

The first episode, 'Le Masque', opens brilliantly. A series of long skilful tracking shots sweeps us into a quadrille at the gala ball and the frenzied masquerade of an old man who will not relinquish his youth. But the story ends inconclusively.

It is in the final episode, 'La Modèle', concerning the love of an artist and his model that Maupassant is best served and the artificiality of the style least over-powering.

A commentary by Peter Ustinov, as the ghost of Maupassant, explains to us with a neatly simulated French accent what we know is happening on the screen and emphasises, lest anyone should be in doubt, that it is all very French and very naughty.

A formidable cast includes Claude Dauphin, Gaby Morlay, Danielle Darrieux, Pierre Brasseur, Jean Gabin, Daniel Gelin and Simone Simon.

DIARY OF A COUNTRY PRIEST: *Directed by* ROBERT BRESSON: *18 April 1953*

It is a considerable time since I have been held so emotionally spellbound as by *The Diary of a Country Priest*. The director, Robert Bresson, who makes a film every several years only under the deepest inner persuasion, has imparted to this French version of Georges Bernanos's celebrated novel all the stored-up force of his unclassifiable art.

Judy Holliday in *Born Yesterday*

The young country priest, a boy, racked by an incurable stomach complaint comes to his first parish. It is a poor, rain-soaked village on the Pas de Calais and its inhabitants resent, trick and mock their new priest: because of his youth, because of his unworldliness, because of his simplicity.

As the elderly neighbouring priest explains to him: "They don't hate your simplicity. They defend themselves against it. It burns them.'

Existing on a diet of stale bread soaked in the cheapest wine the priest records his agonies, his depths of loneliness when the ability to pray forsakes him, the senseless scandals and jealousies which pursue him to his death.

Narrated in uncompromising diary form the film envelops you in its intimacy, its intensity, its complexity, its slow, relentless rhythm.

To play the priest Claude Laydu, a young Belgian actor (now Swiss), lived for weeks with priests, underwent a severe diet to develop the look of a mortally sick ascetic and became so fully identified with the part that it will be impossible ever to forget his almost medieval anguish; or to doubt that *The Diary of a Country Priest*, is the profoundest, and the noblest, of all religious films.

PICKUP ON SOUTH STREET: *Directed by* SAMUEL FULLER:
31 July 1953

While the output from most Hollywood companies has been almost halved, 20th Century Fox alone keeps up the old regular flow of flat films. They are clearing the decks for the miracle of CinemaScope.

The three 20th Century films which this week share the distinction of cornering the August holiday market offer serious indications, however, that the barrel-scraping process has begun. This, of course, won't worry 20th Century. The effect of such films will be to make the most unexacting audiences restive, dissatisfied, ripe for change, ready for the mammoth art of the horizontal screen.

Pickup on South Street is concerned to demonstrate to the American filmgoer the unspeakable nature of the 'Commie'. [*Communist, fellow-traveller, radical.*]

It does this by causing a cheap pickpocket (Richard Widmark) to steal the purse of a street-walker (Jean Peters) who is the 'innocent' dupe of a Red spy ring. The purse contains Government secrets on microfilm and the F.B.I., who are trailing the girl, stand by as helpless witnesses. A sluttish stool-pigeon (Thelma Ritter) is invoked separately by the girl and the police to trace Widmark, who is aware of the value of his haul and ripe for some blackmail.

The police are violent and cynical; the pickpocket will not hesitate to knock a girl unconscious; the stool-pigeon would sell her own grandmother, the girl is a drab. They would betray each other at the drop of a hat; love of country, religion, loyalty, are alike empty of significance, in their hard and vicious world.

Yet they cannot stomach 'Commies' at any cost and such uncomprehending hatred brings its rewards. It unites and legalises their natural brutality and brings a clean record for the pickpocket, wedding bells for the girl, a heroic death for the stool-pigeon.

There is nowhere to be found any criticism, even by implication, of the moral code of these jungle patriots. It is enough that they are Red-haters. But some of the dialogue in which these topsy-turvy ethics are expressed was too much for the London audience with which I saw the film. Lines like 'I took you for a regular crook, I never figured you for a Red' drew some very loud laughs.

CinemaScope embraces Victor Mature

WORLD WITHOUT END: *Directed by* BASIL WRIGHT *and* PAUL ROTHA: *28 August 1953*

On next Monday evening British television screens will show a new and important 60-minute documentary film, jointly directed for Unesco by Paul Rotha and Basil Wright.

Viewers will see history in the making in more senses than one, for this will be the first full-length film to have cut deliberately loose from cinema exhibitors and gone straight on to the air. (I am not counting the première at the Edinburgh Festival.)

It is a sign, too, of a new period of richness in televised cinema, since Paul Rotha has by now established himself as TV documentary chief.

The film *World Without End* simultaneously penetrates Mexico (Paul Rotha) and Thailand (Basil Wright) to point the parallels which mark the semi-primitive lives of their peasant inhabitants.

The problems are different, yet they are the same: problems of disease, education, child-welfare, diminishing natural resources. To meet them a new co-operative force has arisen under the general title of the United Nations Educational Scientific and Cultural Organisation. *World Without End* shows us the work being done — democracy in action.

The Mexican and Siamese sequences are smoothly dovetailed together by linking shots, by music or any means at hand — a remarkable feat as both directors were working thousands of miles away from each other.

The Wright/Rotha work is cohesive, at the same time the style of each director is absolutely typical and identifiable.

The story has to fight, to some extent, against Rotha's indulgence in pictorial anthologising and Wright's almost mystical passion for the Orient.

Both are engrossed in academic pattern-making though the most telling sequences — such as the Yaw-scuring episode in Siam — are those in which artistry is abnegated in favour of plain narrative.

But all quibbling aside, *World Without End* is an engrossing and humane film furnished with some lovely folk-music and an admirable score by Elizabeth Lutyens.

SHANE: *Directed by* GEORGE STEVENS: *4 September 1953*

It is a film critic's venerated axiom that there is no such thing as a bad Western. If challenged on this he will elaborate on the themes of movement, pattern, simple heroics and authentic American folklore. Yet the number of Western films that he will admit into the acknowledged front rank of screen art remains countable on the fingers of one hand.

These are invariably the films (e.g. *The Virginian, My Darling Clementine*) in which a feeling for history and character operates below the action and the gun play; whereas the regular dude Western gaily scoffs at historic fact, motive and probability.

Shane is an exceptional Western film. Its plot — that of the notorious gunman (Alan Ladd) trying hard to live down his past, but forced to fight again because his friends are menaced by bad men — is probably the oldest on Hollywood's files.

But into this framework George Stevens has fixed, as near as anyone could, the Wyoming of 70 years ago; a place of conflict and growth; primitive, brutal, opulent and breathtakingly beautiful.

The bad men are all the more terrifying because they are sometimes shown in the guise of human beings and because they have some sort of a case. The realism of the fights matches that of the Settlement — bare and crude — utterly void of gilded saloons, can-can girls, debonair gamblers or singing cowboys.

He has even softened the Ladd cockiness into a passable semblance of taciturnity.

The Ladd brashness is further softened by a small boy (Brandon de Wilde) who hero-worships him while Mr Ladd makes sheep's eyes at the boy's mother (Jean Arthur). Stevens takes his time over the domestic interludes, but he packs in some reasonably intelligent characterisation. His settlers who sing 'Abide with Me' indiscriminately at a celebration or a funeral are beautifully caught.

Stevens's currency is goodness, badness, cowardice, courage, adventure and other sorts of love than the sexual variety. It adds up to quite a film.

Joseph Cotten, Françoise Rosay and Joan Fontaine in *Long Encounter*

Articles 1946–52

Florentine frolics — Phyllis Calvert, Stewart Granger and Patricia Roc in *Madonna of the Seven Moons*

Previous page: Marlon Brando in *Viva Zapata!*

Grierson, Pioneer

NEWS CHRONICLE: *19 September 1946*

John Grierson is the man who coined the word documentary to describe the non-studio film that chooses 'the living scene and tells the living story'. He was for years the prophet and master of British Documentary and his influence permeates that great tradition.

Now the small stock of the cinema's literature is enlarged and enriched, the believer's faith reinvigorated, by a collection of John Grierson's past writings inadequately titled *Grierson on Documentary*, edited by Forsyth Hardy.

He is, as you will find by reading this ardent affirmation, a brilliant and original mind, gifted with a pen that all of us will envy. His belief in the cinema glows from every page, edged with wit, deep in knowledge and experience earned in sustained and ceaseless battles against the powerful tyrants who see and would use the film only as a shoddy trade.

This book displays Grierson as a major critic in all phases and at all levels of the film. What he foresaw in 1926 has come true in 1946, and he is every moment alive to the dangers and the opportunities and the weaknesses of the enchanting thing we call cinema.

'There is one thing the cinema precisely possesses. It began in the gutter and still trails the clouds of glory with which its vulgar origin was invested. But as we ask it to go deep, be sure we are not just asking it to go middle-class. . . .'

This lucid work comes at the right moment, at the turning point of British films.

Critic's Prologue

PENGUIN FILM REVIEW, NO. I: *1946*

The half-centenary of the cinema came in a flood of bad films. Films that frequently provoked in me a positive rage simmered down into a three-line crack in my reviews: films with meaningless titles, meaningless dialogue, meaningless plots set in quivering jellies of music. A situation that drove a colleague to suggest that the normally intelligent cinema-goer really needed a Film Digest — a recent one might contain the sequence of the Duke's tottering triumphant passage through corridors and up the stairs to welcome his son and heir in *Kitty*, the dance of Gene Kelly and the light Indian girl in *Anchors Aweigh*, the alcoholic ward scene in *The Lost Weekend* — a little hoard from a hundred thousand feet of film that might run for forty minutes, a year's cinema-going without tears condensed into three hours.

The critics are in bad odour with the industry because they will complain about the low quality of the films they have to review, although there is a parallel tendency to overpraise the faintest appearance of merit. There certainly is no denying that film criticism in Britain has taken on a new sharpness in the last several years, owing, I think, to three causes:

First: we in Britain have been involved in six years of total war and we are now as remote in outlook from the citizenry of the Middle West of America as we are from that of the Fiji Islanders (and American films to succeed must primarily satisfy the former community).

Second: the British cinema has been born, and for all its immaturities and hesitancies encourages us to resist the wholesale possession of our screenspace by celluloid that is 75 per cent geared to the lowest tastes of a less matured and less experienced people. Though there is nothing to support the accusation made constantly in the American Press that British film critics are engaged in a vendetta against Hollywood; it is absurd to imagine that we should want to do without the gusto and aliveness of the best and even the good average of Hollywood films.

Third: there is judged by Hollywood's own standards a failing of those qualities I mention above, a bankruptcy of inspiration and the development of a blatant and monotonous insincerity, bitterly commented on by the few serious critics of the films who write in the American Press.

The cinema then as represented by Hollywood faces the turn of its first half-century in the lowest possible condition of creative energy. Let us be comforted that it can descend no farther. The artist has been so humiliated, hectored and bedevilled by Big Business that the poor degraded hack must be revitalised, nourished, cherished, respected and allowed to create again, for however much they may pretend to the contrary, the film cannot live without ideas from men with creative imagination.

That piece of wild optimism (not as insane as you may think) opens what I well believe to be a great opportunity for me to practise in this publication an extended, more detailed and more analytical form of film criticism than the writing of a weekly review in the Press allows; a four years' run of bad films cannot impair my passionate belief in the film, in cinema, in movie or in whatever abstract you use to define the moving picture. As an art it is so fantastically new that many otherwise intelligent persons deny its right to the title. They haven't the wit to envision the future creative giants of the film, compared with whom Griffith and Chaplin will be as the first scrawlers of animal drawings on cave walls are to Rembrandt, nor have they the apprehension of what a deeply universal need the cinema fulfils.

Right, it's cheap and shoddy, and made by ten-year-olds for teen-year-olds. Good, then it must be freed from sordid enslavement by entrepreneurs who use it for the sole purpose of making big, wonderful, easy, painless money or dream of selling their country's goods to the world by the cinema. Only a demand from the people themselves can free the film aesthetically.

Meanwhile it might be appropriate to make a quick survey of the cinema as it stands now in the darkest phase of its short history. In a whole year there have come from America only three films of pronounced individuality and charm. Two new feature films and several documentaries from France (all I have seen) reveal insufficient evidence to judge if her power to present a theme and tell a story specifically in terms of the cinema and in the incomparable French idiom is undiminished by the years of occupation. A solitary film *Lermontov* shines through the over-simplified textbook propaganda which Soviet Russia seems to regard as the first necessity of her studios.

It is a long way back and it will be a long way forward to films of the greatness of *The Childhood of Maxim Gorki*, to me the world's most beautiful film, because of its sublime understanding and compassion. Switzerland surprised us with her first two films, *Marie-Louise* and *The Last Chance*, and startled the industry with their popularity, for they are both intelligent and humane.

British films have come to possess a craftsmanship and freshness above that of the regular flow from Hollywood. By contrast they seem miracles of taste and intelligence, tending to produce overlavish praise from starved critics and a complacency within the studios: in the long fight ahead the biggest threat they face might seem to be from within. But of that more later.

The first of the three American films I refer to above is of course *The Southerner*, which may be regarded as a freak picture, viewed without much enthusiasm by its sponsors and unlikely to have any widespread effect on subsequent picture making. It is a grand picture, finely shaped and finely acted, remarkable in that it registers the first complete success of a French director (Jean Renoir) on alien soil. The theme is that of humble people waging a dual struggle against man and nature for their small piece of earth. Its note is compassionate and sanguine, there is in it none of the bitterness of *The Grapes of Wrath*. Renoir's pacifist acceptance and humanitarianism pervade the picture. Nor is there any of the falseness which abounds in *Our Vines Have Tender Grapes*, a film which took in a number of persons. Here is the American pseudo-pastoral, relying for most of its appeal on the winsomeness of Margaret O'Brien and Jackie Jenkins and doing a fine job of sales promotion for America. Lovely photography added to its spurious appeal. Experts on the film are suckers for photography, and when they rave about a film like this, it's almost like claiming that a shoddy book is worthwhile because of its beautiful type-setting. Good photography, important as it may be, is in this year of grace a rudimentary right, though I remember that the photography of some of the great films was for this reason or that less than good, without in any serious way imparing the total work.

But apart from fine photography which both these films have, apart from the contrast of true and false values, in one there is a classic shape in the seasonal flow of life through a year — spring, summer, autumn, winter with water as the dominating element — water scarce, water torrential, water the desired, water the fierce and murderous. The other is a honey-coloured cliché dressed in mock simplicity with smooth editing to clothe its lack of shape and rhythm. But it is a sure bet that *Our Vines Have Tender Grapes*, getting the box-office by its unscrupulous appeal to the adolescent adult through the wide artfully artless eyes of these two young experts in the art of giving grown-ups what they want, will define the structure of many future essays in phoney Down to Earth.

Before I pass to the murkier aspects of recent Hollywood film production, I will pay yet another tribute to a film of small pretensions and large heart, *Sunday Dinner for a Soldier*, one of the truest pictures to come out of America — true in its unsentimental delineation of near poverty with all its simple hopes and joys and refreshing in its handling of child actors.

After that, with a forward and backward glance at the immediately past and future delicacies from the conveyor belt, the first word to occur to me is 'music'. Music in films has crept from background to foreground. There is nearly as much music in the straight drama as in the overt musical. In the series of Love and Ever films — *Forever in Love, This Love of Ours, Forever is To-morrow, To-morrow is Forever*, as in *Our Vines Have Tender Grapes* — the music takes on a peculiarly lush and odious potency, formlessly weeps at us with strings from the opening credit title and pursues us after the finale. It accompanies inexhaustibly the inexhaustible dialogue, basic English of Romance, stunning us with its sweetness as the words of high passion stun us with their starkness. 'Gee, you're a swell kid!' 'You're not so bad yourself.' Howya, beautiful?' 'Howya, handsome?'

And the taming and subjugation of musicians goes on — first Stokowski and then Iturbi, recruited into musicals as embarrassed uncles to young love — they are more photogenic and distinguished and funnier than Benny Goodman and Tommy Dorsey as they render the dearest numbers of Wurlitzer virtuosi on thirty grand pianos with mirrors and smug nods and winks at Miss Durbin or Miss O'Brien.

The concerto film, at its best in *The Seventh Veil* (because it conceded that a brilliant pianist might put music before love) and at its worst in *Love Story* (because the music was as much of a bore as the story) is less ominous than the musical biography, of which large numbers are on their way.

With *A Song to Remember* there was a revolting and stupid distortion of fact and some beautifully recorded music of Chopin. Will the other great composers on the list receive any better treatment? There is absolutely no reason to suppose they will, because their love life was never rounded or orthodox and too interesting to fit into the sort of pattern that would make tolerable the intrusion of 'highbrow' music on to the sound track.

Even the civilised French cinema, in *Symphonie Fantastique*, turned the life of Hector Berlioz into a sort of Hollywood romp with all the old cherished clichés, and of Gainsborough's projected *Paganini*, with Stewart Granger in the lead, my forebodings have a nightmare quality.

The lighter sort of musical biography is eminently more suitable for concoction into box-office. There the nearness of the composer's death can be made into a valid excuse for romanticising the details, there the nature of the music itself renders it reasonably palatable in the backstage setting that gives us just another

The show must go on — Merle
Oberon and Cornel Wilde in
A Song to Remember

musical good or bad, unvaried in outline and utter respectability as it ranges from
Yankee Doodle Dandy to *The Dolly Sisters*.

A word here for the noticeably superior understanding by British producers of
the function of music in films. At least half a dozen of our composers have specialised
in the writing of music for the cinema. They have evolved scores that are full of
character and meaning and are yet unobtrusive; you rarely find the music in British
films blurring or disturbing the dialogue. But few film makers here or in Hollywood
seem able or inclined to employ the golden instrument of silence, few indeed
anywhere have more than the glimmering of a notion of the possibilities of the
sound track with its endless vocabulary of all the noises of life.

What I principally note in Hollywood films is the loss of a vital sense of adventure.
Many things can account for this, but mainly we must blame the total industrialisation of film manufacture from script to finished movie. Rarely does the writer see
more than a vague ghost of his original conception after it has been picked at and
mauled at every turn.

Paramount, in giving Billy Wilder his head with *Double Indemnity* and *The Lost
Weekend*, gave a new stimulus to American films. These two films were sordid,
harsh, salty and alive; they specialised in detail of environment, the characters

165

moved and talked in a meticulously observed background, and the films themselves moved according to some sort of a design. They have started the new trend of 'psychological thrillers', films which in the nature of things must import the documentary feel we crave for and miss in other films with ostensibly worthier objects. This quality contains the true essence of the cinema, the high-lighting and wedding of detail to action, action where the camera not necessarily the character is allowed to range free. Incidentally, the music in both of these films was so good as to be almost unnoticeable. Recent examples in this genre, such as *The Blue Dahlia* and *Scarlet Street*, have failed to approach the shady, shoddy poetry of *Laura* or *Double Indemnity*.

The situation though is not as bad as it would seem; there are Wilder, Wellman, Ford, Sturges, Zinnemann, Capra, Lang, Kanin, Wyler, Siodmak, Renoir(?), Minnelli and other directors with first-rate movies, by any standards, to their credit. At least half of them have been out of commission during the war, and they come back to an industry acutely conscious of the threat of British films which get the praise of 'highbrow' American critics. That is the sort of stimulation that good British movies can effect.

I have held consistently to the belief that British films should aim at the British market and that now is the exact time to plan for doing this. Mr J. A. Rank's method of open attack on the American market by making the epic film to dazzle Americans will, I am certain, lead in the end to pleasing nobody and losing grasp of

Corn in Egypt — Stewart Granger, Vivien Leigh and Claude Rains in *Caesar and Cleopatra*

Britain's great moment. While *Caesar and Cleopatra* doesn't frighten Hollywood (if it does me), the success in Britain of *The Seventh Veil* and *The Captive Heart*, and of even those Gainsborough horrors, *The Wicked Lady, Madonna of the Seven Moons,* and *Caravan,* most emphatically does.

The recent triumphs of British films in Britain should not be allowed to intoxicate us. They are good, very good, but they lack sweep and they lack writers and they lack actors. By that I mean that very few of the characters in British films really come alive. They are of the stage rather than of the world where the movie camera should focus, and they often give our films the ethereal glow of anaemia. We are likewise in our class-consciousness unsuccessful at depicting the ordinary men and women of Britain in character or voice, accent or behaviour. Our comedy is non-existent and we don't know how to make musicals. (Look how that great comic Bud Flanagan has not merely been neglected but positively insulted by the films they have put him in.) But perhaps the worst crime of the British film industry is its cheap and inane approach to Britain's great traditions.

It is appalling that an ugly hodge-podge of servant girls' lore like *The Wicked Lady* should mock at our own past, while a contemporary American film *Kitty* handles it with reverence and loving care, intelligence and charm.

It is in *Brief Encounter, Journey Together, I Know Where I'm Going, The Way to the Stars, Dead of Night* that you sense the magic possibilities of the British cinema, fragile, encompassed, hardly daring to breathe. And when I meet a director or writer who says to me with passion and certainty, 'I'm going to make a film that will shake the daylights out of you even if it isn't box-office', I shall feel we might have started.

To finish there is the heartening success of Leopold Lindtberg's *The Last Chance,* that Swiss-made parable of internationalism. It is a brave and good film, and it asserts for the first time in any film made about this war that compassion is all-important. Moving and tragic, it pleads for international unity through its story of the succouring of a band of refugees by three Allied officers at the risk of their own lives. It is not a great film because it never fuses into passion, does not leave you held and haunted afterwards. That is how those few films I deem great affected and still affect me at each showing.

The Cinema

MACDONALD MEDLEY: *1947*

The critic of films is in a difficult position. He has little in the way of tradition to refer to: good films are rarely looked at by the circuits and reach only special cinemas in London or small film societies in the country. So, when he permits himself to talk of the movie as an art he is apt to be ridiculed. Indeed, the search and waiting for a sequence, even a single shot, to sustain him in his faith are long and exhausting. I am going to try and define the good movie as I see it. The one film in the hundred (literally).

The movie critic has to grow and grope while the cinema grows and gropes. But the world lies before him because, obviously, the film cannot remain in its present condition of suspended animation. It must go forward, it cannot go back any further.

When people who love the medium talk about it, it is tacitly accepted by them that ninety-nine out of a hundred current films are worthless, though perhaps in their various ways sometimes entertaining. This is not high-brow precocity any more than their use of the word cinema as an abstract. But it's a word to bring shrieks from the paid hack writers of the trade and their counterparts in the Press who carry without a blush the title critic. What is cinema? Pudovkin and Eisenstein have written obscurely and endlessly about it; others have written obscurely and endlessly about them; the days of 'Close-up' lie behind us like a thick, dark forest through which we have fought our way and survived.

A man who has written more lucidly than most about films and one who has contrived to make several good ones himself, said to me he knew he was looking at cinema when he felt a prickling up and down the spine. He's right. There's no mistaking that moment of sudden apprehension when the camera lens, like the poet's eye, invests an ordinary scene with sudden terror or beauty. Just such moments are jewels to enrich the general pattern of the film.

The job of the fiction film, like that of the novel — and it is closer to the novel than to the play — is to tell a story entertainingly. But imagine a world in which all novels were confined to the æsthetic level of Ethel M. Dell and Charles Garvice, with occasional upward and ambitious flights into the higher worlds of Hall Caine and Marie Corelli. For that's roughly the situation which one hundred per cent commercialisation of the cinema has led to. Worse, for the average present-day film very rarely succeeds in being a film at all; even if it's had a smart script written for it, it looks and sounds like a tricked-up play. Cinema is not there; cinema, which lies in the mind of the writer and the lens of the camera. The movie camera can move through time and space; it can make stones act as it can make men and women who never had a second's training: it can bring Samarkand to the people of Saskatchewan in rich and intimate detail; it can make the same building look large or small, friendly or menacing: it can go where the human eye longs to travel and never could reach: it can give us the whole world, and it gives us the beggarly literalness of the illiterate.

How weary we are of their verbal conventions, the worn words never charged anew, the close-up, passionless kisses, the sickly orchestras that help along the emotional onanism. In all the war films made in America and Britain I remember only three love scenes without embarrassment. They were the proposal in the pub in *Millions Like Us*, the return of Raymond Massey to his wife from a convoy in *Battle of the North Atlantic* and the wedding breakfast in *Under the Clock*. These scenes had a clipped, documentary reality which related the broken accents of true love to the background of the film and gave them poignancy. But of the lighter moments of love on the screen one can hardly bear to tell, for gaiety is as rare as wit or lust or tenderness. In all movie sequences where one or other of these qualities could be detected, there also was cinema. I will mention the delicious personality evoked by Carol Lombard in *Nothing Sacred*, where love had wit and lightness, the sordid yet refreshing lechery of *Double Indemnity*, the jive session of *Phantom Lady* which became a danse macabre of the sidewalks. These films were circuit bookings. They were not popular because they flaunted the deadly conventions and formulæ of box office.

The gradual conditioning of world cinema audiences to a middle-class attitude of mind has gone hand-in-hand with the industrialisation and monopolisation of the cinema. Let's say the three movies above might be considered sordid and cynical and therefore against public morality. But what about *Sunday Dinner for a Soldier*? This was a film which avoided obnoxious sentimentality only because it really tried to be a film. It had a story where by all the laws of Hollywood we should have wallowed, instead we were moved and charmed. *Sunday Dinner for a Soldier* showed us more of America in its ninety minutes than any of the domestic comedies and tragedies which Hollywood companies so proudly ballyhoo. It was booked for one week at the Tivoli, was given an enthusiastic press (somewhat to the embarrassment of the film company) and taken off just as the public were beginning to warm up to it.

Here again was that wedding of documentary and fiction which makes the true movie. Let us say that in the novel plot characterisation and style are the three chief ingredients. Who can deny that style is what gives the book its flavour? So in the movie visual description, the poetry of the camera, makes the rest banal or beautiful.

Style, the method of telling, is what separates a good from a bad script. Style, though, is the element most rejected by the movie kings and their hosts of satellites in favour of star glamour, vulgar elaboration and spectacle. Script is the heart and soul of a film, no good script is entirely ruined by bad direction or indifferent photography or acting. Good script, plus good direction give you the rare film on which we advocates of a new art pin all our faith.

The importance of style, of the approach of one man, is amply demonstrated by that long suffering director, Jean Renoir. His film *The Southerner*, which appeared in London at the tail-end of August, made history. It was the first time a French director had managed to breathe in Hollywood. This sincere and tireless practitioner in celluloid proved that the artist cannot be killed by the machine; he made a film about American life so obviously authentic, so compelling in its statement that it gave the London critics a fresh lease of life. They were able to praise with honesty and enthusiasm. A Frenchman looked at American life and made it live: he presented an American scene not often penetrated by the glamour seekers and bulldozers of the studios: he delineated something utterly American with utterly Gallic emphasis. Therein he testified to the art of the cinema, taking a theme that a hundred hacks had made unbearably familiar to us: making it alive with tenderness and within the emotional and mental scope of any audience anywhere in the world.*

* How happy Winnington would have been at the great acclaim of Renoir in Britain in recent years; special seasons of his films at London's National Film Theatre and elsewhere, and tributes to his artistry on the recent publication of his autobiography. And he is alive to receive them. — P.R.

It was no *Grapes of Wrath,* no passionate indictment like that great film, of the *nouveau riche* capitalism of America, but in its quiet implications it was in some ways better. Here the basic coinage of work and pleasure, struggle and aspiration was given a new edge by style and approach. Grief, for instance, in all its loneliness — we see a man walking over a field away from his wife, who is sobbing helplessly on the ground. This is cinema, an oblique statement cut into two dimensional montage. Emily Dickinson wrote:

> Tell all the truth, but tell it slant,
> Success in circuit lies,
> Too bright for our infirm delight
> The Truth's superb surprise.

Circuit indeed. The word has now become abominable to us sad and hopeful movie-goers: for circuit bookings are the first big obstacle to the showing of good films. Who is going to make satisfactory and intelligent films without the necessary commercial reward or exhibition, and so concentrated vertically is the film industry in Britain and America that distributors are mere paid servants of the film makers, who own the cinema throughout from the celluloid to the plush cinema seats. From the making to the showing the same barbarous mentality is in control. If a good film here and there escapes into the cinemas it is by accident, or else a luxury allowed to a film-maker whose name is wasted. Artists in films as in other creative fields are simple if savage people. They can be bought like the Ashanti with a bead necklace or a top hat or fine promises.

There are many people of great professional skill in the creative side of the cinema; honest craftsmen who have a pride and belief in their jobs. They are men of the people and they reach out to the people. But in between is a vast industrialised enterprise which tells its artists and craftsmen what to do and its customers what to like. It must do this because its aims are purely and simply money making on the lowest level plus an unco-ordinated and in its way logical notion that good films are dangerous. They are dangerous because of their instantaneous impact on the minds and emotions of the world's citizenry. Educationalists have proved that the visual image makes a deeper impression than the verbal or aural image. In this small country 30,000,000 people see films every week. They see eighty American films to twenty British or other films. They absorb a large amount of the message or propaganda behind them. For don't make any mistake, negative propaganda is as powerful as positive propaganda.

Which brings us to that crucial and burning question of British films. Cynics and hard-boiled critics have long given up worrying. They see Mr Rank happily consolidating deals with America and engulfing every vestige, mechanical and creative, of our considerable cinematic resources. It is significant that at a time when the envelopment of the British cinema by Mr Rank was in its early and less obvious stages that the Americans were frightened of our films. The fear has diminished. We seem to be making just the sort of films which please Hollywood while displaying all our past weaknesses and dispensing with the new-found strength and purpose that came to us during the war.

Critical Survey

PENGUIN FILM REVIEW, NO. 2: *1947*

For some time now I've been troubled by an uncomfortable urge to overpraise British films, to wish them, almost, into realms of thought and feeling they inherit but never fully enter. It is not enough that they overtop the normal Hollywood production — and they have done that since 1942 — in discretion and discrimination and taste. It is, I think, their heritage to invigorate the whole business of film making. Britain has the biggest start of all countries on the new paths of the cinema: with lots of stories to tell on celluloid, and the ability to tell them and the places to tell them in.

As proof of this, I ask you to note a definite break from discreet miniature and delicate water-colour into full canvas. I ask you to pay attention to the first *big* British film to have been made, a film that confidently sweeps our cloistered virtues into the open.

The film is *Great Expectations*, and its première should roughly coincide with this issue of *Penguin Film Review*. It is a landmark in the history of British films: not only because it is taken from the most shapely, mature and filmable of all Dickens' novels, not because it has the best photography I've seen for years or because the casting is nearly perfect or because of its knife-edge cutting or its furious pace, but because it casts a complete spell derived from some inner power.

Cineguild, the Rank unit which made *Great Expectations*, has asserted itself as the most finished of all British film studios from *In Which We Serve* to *Brief Encounter*. It is a closely co-ordinated unit that has grown up together in experience and resists separation. Anthony Havelock-Allan, Ronald Neame and David Lean represent the source of its strength, though, I should say, it is the latter who supplies the nervous force of its pictures. Some time ago I wrote to the effect that when this outfit should break away from Noël Coward, we should recognise in David Lean Britain's leading film director. I was right.

It is fifteen years since I read *Great Expectations*, but after the film had been running for a few seconds, the old magic flowed right out at me from the screen. I was with the frightened little boy Pip, running with him across the marshes by the gibbets and into the churchyard. I caught his fears and tremblings and, though I was naturally prepared for the advent of the convict, the shock, when he irrupted, was utter. The camera turns round with Pip from the gravestone, and suddenly a close-up of the convict full on is cut in with masterly timing and effect. In the marsh scenes, here and throughout, the English weather has at long last come into its own on the screen, the celluloid itself seems saturated with wet winds, the sound track echoes the creak of bent trees and the cries of forlorn birds.

So far so good, I thought, but now we come to the narrative, the move from atmosphere into the commitment of action, the real test. And then in the cottage with Mrs Joe Gargery (Freda Jackson) savagely at work with her tongue and fists on Joe (Bernard Miles) and Pip (Anthony Wager), I realised that David Lean was in absolute control of his story.

How alive is the dialogue of the original, which throughout the film has been little tampered with, how alive are the characters, balancing on a delicate tightrope between the highly coloured Dickensian characterisation and the realism of the camera and the sound track. This is the first Dickens film that is not a Christmas Annual Coloured Supplement, full of chuckles. It is not only a matter of casting to have found a set of actors who live their parts full-bloodedly but never floridly: it is sheer direction. From the children (Anthony Wager and Jean Simmons) to such experienced interpreters as Francis L. Sullivan, Finlay Currie, Martita Hunt, the cast (with the possible exception of Bernard Miles) produces a smooth precision and zest that matches the pace and flavour of the film. In *Great Expectations*, as in most of Dickens's novels, the narrator is a mere instrument played on by events and people's emotions. He never comes alive. Young Anthony Wager, refreshingly free of precocity and 'child genius', gives the boy Pip a wide-eyed, curious, observant young-Gorki, young-Dickens quality (again sheer direction). In maturity, played by John Mills, Pip takes on dimensions and joins the scene, in the best acting performance ever given by one of the soundest actors on the British screen.

You may or may not agree with the necessary sacrifices of rich minor characters that Lean and Neame have made in their adaptation. You will, one and all, if you know the book, deeply regret that major absence of Trabb's boy. But you will have to admit that, having decided on what was necessary to his narrative, David Lean has made a nearly flawless job of telling it. I did not have the opportunity, so vital to a long review of such a packed film, to see it for a second time. But I was able to observe the ingenious tricks of cutting. Several sequences belong to the handbook of cinema: the feverish journey of Pip in a state of near delirium through the streets to his bed, the dreadful end of Miss Havisham (Martita Hunt), the death sentence in the jail. It is to be hoped the censor will have left them in.

The imaginative strength of Lean displays itself here and there throughout the film. You have the young Pip lying in the grass and playing with it while longing to be a gentleman, you have the older Pip, a gentleman, lying in the grass and playing with it wishing he had never become one, in all his misery.

The costumes and the sets show what can be done with the English scene. No pains and expense have been spared. But the point is that all this pain and cost is in the celluloid itself, clothes are lived in by the persons who wear them. The houses and streets have an air of being warmed by inhabitation.

Great Expectations, though obviously the product of devoted team work, owes its primary inspiration and influence to one man — David Lean. He had, of course, a great start with a story that for all its difficulties of adaptation is indestructible. He has made a film that will please everybody in Britain and shock not a few in Hollywood, and will be adored in Europe. *Great Expectations* deserves all the screaming publicity that *London Town* and *Caesar and Cleopatra* embarrassed us with. It is an occasion on which we can join with Mr Rank in complacency. Cineguild have shown that they deserve the best writing available in Britain and complete freedom of choice in their subjects. They have made the first great challenge to the world on behalf of Britain. They have made the first big attack.

White Cliffs of Maugham —
Veronica Lake and Franchot
Tone in *The Hour Before
the Dawn*

Rome: Open City

NEWS CHRONICLE: *23 August 1949*

Since Rossellini shook the screens of America, France and Britain over three years
ago the prestige of the Italian cinema has come to be the highest in the world,
equivalent to that of France in the period before 1939.

Yet most of us who laud them have seen only five important Italian films —
*Open City, Shoeshine, Vivere in Pace (To Live in Peace), Four Steps in the Clouds,
Paisa* — all made years ago.

These shoestring masterpieces were created in a freedom which must be
credited to the then almost complete disorganisation of the Italian film industry.
Lack of technical and financial resource was a godsend to writers and directors, who
boiled with the suppressions of years.

Would this power of taking life 'as it were by surprise' persist as the industry
developed and the anger died? As the financiers step in with who knows whose
money, must the Italian cinema follow exclusively the traditional and deadening
paths of commerce?

To find the answers to these questions I have just spent eleven very hot days in
Rome, centre of the industry. There I saw sixteen films and as many officials,
executives, writers and directors as could be found.

In that unforgettable city of slickers, beautiful women and sleek men, a noisy
concourse of Americans adds to the impression that everybody is in the film

173

business. Touts and grafters buzz round the new de-luxe industry of a defeated agrarian nation, and the price of film-making soars. It is being said, only half jokingly, that the Italians contemplate Egypt as a site for cheap film locations. British units flock to Italy, and Americans to Britain, for the same reasons of economy.

In this scene are born wild financial fantasies. Yet realistic and apparently uninhibited Italian films are still being made, though with increasing opposition from sponsors and distributors and official and religious censorship.

The directors whose names outside Italy embody all the réclame of the Italian cinema are already being disparaged as 'leftists' and 'poets'. If not yet as un-Italians. And their films hold little or no appeal for escape-seeking Italian city audiences.

Italian audiences number six hundred million a year (two-thirds of 1940 figures) and they see 400 films yearly, of which 60 are Italian and six to eight British. The all-American remainder covers a ten-year gap in Hollywood 'culture'. Faced with a situation similar to that which the British industry so tragically bungled, Italian executives show no signs of having better plans to balance imports with exports, or of having any better weapons with which to resist the might of the dollar.

There are, however, saving elements such as the absence (so far) of vertical monopolies (i.e. monopolies from production down to distribution and exhibition); and, paradoxically, the pervasive native inefficiency. In such conditions films which preserve the integrity of Italian 'neo-realism' can still conceivably squeeze through.

If this assumption seems cynical let it be remembered that it has been in the poverty belt or in states of emergency that the art of the cinema has best flourished. No streamlined film industry will tolerate such nonsense as poetry or art. The pre-war Russian cinema was a transient exception that has succumbed to other compulsions.

Films Without Heroes

NEWS CHRONICLE: *25 August 1949*

I went to Rome hoping for, and needing, some sort of restorative experience, and I was not disappointed.

There are perhaps ten Italian directors of importance, all of them young men by the standards of their profession. A high proportion, but not surprisingly so when it is recognised that the screen provides a form of expression natural to the Italian temperament. What is remarkable is that some of them have been able to maintain an almost savagely honest stand.

The smart life — and there is enough of it in Italy — makes only oblique appearances in films that are preoccupied with the brutal realities confronting the majority of Italians. The hero is, as often as not, the anti-hero — a stunned, buffeted but sympathetic and resistant victim of his times.

Such a figure is presented with staggering force by Vittorio de Sica (the director of *Shoeshine*), in *Ladri di Bicicletti* (*Bicycle Thieves*), a superlatively visual film depicting one grey, fateful day in the life of an unemployed working man and his entrancing small son.

De Sica uses for his studio the vivid, vital streets and places of outer Rome, and for his players ordinary men and women without previous acting experience. The leading player is a workman who has known the miseries of unemployment.

The tragedy of this every-day story of a stolen bicycle that means food and future to its despairing owner is left unsolved, but the conclusion is not altogether hopeless.

It is de Sica's command over his material and plot, his paring down of incident and detail to the essential minimum, that make *Ladri di Bicicletti* the greatest film since *Le Jour se Lève* (1938). It is a reaffirmation of the mislaid values of the cinema.

De Sica is clearly outstanding in the world sense. But there are other directors whose work, while in every way as individual as Rossellini's, is under better control.

One of them, Alberto Lattuada, made two violently bitter films about post-war Leghorn and Turin, *Senza Pietà* (*Without Pity*) and *Il Bandito* (*The Bandit*). In these the satire is ferocious and the disillusion complete. Yet they show exceptional technical and visual command backed by a well-developed imagination.

And Lattuada has imported these attributes (with his sense of tragedy) into a beautifully-made period film (late nineteenth-century) of social and personal conflict in the highly photogenic Valley of the Po. *Il Mulino del Po* (*The Mill on the Po*) uses only one or two professional actors and was shot entirely on location. It has an authority equal to that of the great Russian costume films.

Lattuada's next film was to have been *Miss Italy*, a social satire on Beauty Queens, but Lux Films have turned it down. His happy ending (the girl finds her soul and returns to her humble beginnings) did not appeal to them.

Qualities akin to those of Lattuada are strengthened by belief and hope in the one film of Aldo Vergano, *Il Sole Sorge Ancora* (*The Sun will Rise Again*). Surely no film anywhere has given such subtly graded portraits of Occupiers, Collaborators and Resisters as does this story of the last days of Occupation in the region of Milan? And its restrained characterisation only reinforces the power of its culminating scenes of terror and bloodshed.

Vergano, a director of fascinating potentials, is now making a film 'for greater freedom' in Poland.

To this group of directors belong the less articulated talents of Giuseppe de Santis, whose *Riso Amaro* (*Bitter Rice*) carries out his precept that only in 'the frankest and crudest approach to the problems of day to day life is the true realism discovered'.

His scene is in the rice fields below Milan, to which every year flock thousands of temporary women workers. His diffuse and sensational story is framed in a magnificently pictorial background, strewn with promiscuous and unrelated visual effects. The film has an uncontrollable sincerity.

Lurking sombrely in the shadows is the 'enfant terrible' of the Italian screen,

Badinage in Bangkok — Irene Dunne and Rex Harrison in *Anna
and the King of Siam*

Luciano Visconti, whose controversial reputation can hardly be assessed on *La
Terra Trema* (*The Earth Trembles*) — a slow, powerful, murky, chaotic and
sometimes lovely film about the oppressed anchovy fishermen of Sicily.

Nor can Renato Castellani be omitted from this elite group. His picaresque story
of derelict youth, *Sotto il Sole di Roma* (*Under the Sun of Rome*), is lightweight but
salty with character.

Among this array of bright gifts those of Rossellini might well have seemed to
pale, but his short film, *The Miracle* (a tribute to the art of Anna Magnani), easily
preserves his front place pending *Stromboli* and a comedy in process of being edited.

But without a doubt the popular hero is Pietro Germi, whose *In Nome della
Legge* (*In the Name of the Law*) strikes a beautiful compromise between realism
(Italian) and fable (American) with a dash of beloved Italian tragi-drama. This
slick job is in effect a Western put into Sicilian trappings with the Mafia supplying
the posses. It puts the ball in every slot.

Second only to Germi as a bright boy is Luigi Zampa (*To Live in Peace* —
Angelina). His *Anni Difficile* (*The Difficult Years*) is a cunning compound of pathos,
slap-stick, humour and drama that pleads sympathy for the weak, lovable little
Italian who unwillingly allowed himself to be led into the higher ranks of the local

(Sicilian) Fascisti, only to be betrayed by everybody. I found *Angelina* dubious, *Anni Difficile* is dubious, dangerous and doubly glib.

And if you should want to know what holds up the showing of these films in England the answer is simple:

(a) Italian distributing companies have inflated notions of the extent of British box-office for the films they themselves have no real belief in and

(b) Nobody in Britain has the courage or ability to exploit a large potential market for them.

Years are squandered in the sort of bargaining at which Italians excel and the heat of topicality dies from the films.

Can British Films Pay Their Way?

NEWS CHRONICLE: *22 May 1952*

Without the financial help it has been receiving from the Government since 1949 the British Film Industry would almost certainly have collapsed. It is on its feet today only by reason of that assistance which is due to end in 1954.

In an endeavour to face the question of what happens then, P.E.P. (Political and Economic Planning) have just issued an exhaustive report on the structure of the Industry.*

All previous reports have been thoroughly digested, the facts presented and the evidence sifted so that the non-expert reader, after a summing-up by P.E.P., may reach his verdict.

To the main question 'Can British film production be made to pay its way?' P.E.P. have no clear cut answer. But in two conclusions they are explicit: that no film industry outside Hollywood can exist without Quota protection, and that the nature of the home market makes impossible the continued existence of British film production without some form of Government intervention or participation.

The latter is an inevitable conclusion and it is anybody's choice as to what form it should take.

P.E.P. have done a service in presenting clearly and readably so much invaluable data, financial and economic, in one volume. In doing so they have lost sight of only one thing — the film. No one after reading this report will be in any doubt as to how and why vertical monopoly became the ruling force in British film making.

But P.E.P. are entranced by figures and percentages — never more malleable and misleading than in the balance-sheets of monopoly film finance — and pay far more attention to the number of films made than to their quality. In accepting those figures at their face value P.E.P. miss some important truths and betray the lack of a broad grasp on the subject.

On circuit monopoly for instance the report does not mention that all pictures

* *The British Film Industry*, P.E.P.

booked by the three big circuits are the personal choice of two or three men. Nor in stressing the numerical strength of the circuits does it disclose that the monopoly holds iron sway over the public as well as the producer.

Another factor ignored in this somewhat blue-eyed report is the industry's failure to seek for and back the sort of showman-producer who has always been the real strength of Hollywood.

An English Kramer (*Champion*, *The Men*, *Cyrano de Bergerac*), de Rochemont or Pine Thomas who can cut his films to austerity pattern and use his available talent to the full is surely a necessity to any solution. But there is nobody to back him.

The reader of P.E.P.'s report cannot fail to observe through its pages the emergence into supreme control over British film production of the chartered accountant.

With the exception of Sir Alexander Korda, and, in a lesser way, Sir Michael Balcon, the power is vested in James Lawrie (National Film Finance Corporation), John Davis (General Film Distributors — Pinewood), Reg Baker (President of the British Film Producers Association and Ealing) and Robert Clark (A.B.P.C.-A.B.C.) — all accountants.

Among other things it is plain to me from the pages of the report, if not to P.E.P., that the film industry has no effective means of market research and lags behind the needs of its audience. As a consequence its methods of salesmanship have failed to move with the times.

Film production is more than a matter of accountancy and no 'solution' that does not as a first duty safeguard the film itself and its audience is of any use at all.

Oh, Mr Cole Porter! — Alexis Smith, Cary Grant and Monty Woolley in *Night and Day*

The Missing Element in the Cinema

HARPER'S BAZAAR: *May 1948*

I propose here to make my reply to a question that is thrown at me at least twice a week: 'How on earth do you go on doing it?' I have been seeing something like three hundred films a year for six years, and I intend to continue this strange life as long as my enthusiasm for it persists and my eyesight holds out.

The secret is that I am a film addict in the way that I am a print addict. As I would endlessly re-read one of Miss Dierdre O'Brien's books in lack of any other print, I would join the queue for a Mark Ostret film or an American musical rather than see no films at all. It might be thought that as an addict with a platform I would be a useful gauge to the film trade. But the fact that I will hold the cinema to be an art as well as an entertainment, puts me in automatic opposition to every principle of the industry.

In these eventful years as a critic, I have noted the subjugation of Hollywood's creative minority by a terrorism that lacks only jack-boots and coloured shirts, the betrayal from without and within of the pubescent British cinema, the reduction of Soviet film art to monotonous text-book propaganda, the surrender of the French to allegory and pessimism, the sudden, though not illogical, flowering of the Italians. Through all this confusion of apparent defeat and degeneration of the film, it is possible not only to identify and rationalise the destructive forces but to increase the strength of one's belief in a mass art that has barely scratched the surface of its stupendous powers.

I have lately observed a tendency amongst some of its earliest and most enthusiastic advocates to write off the film as an art, to classify it as an artistic industry of entertainment that occasionally touches fairly high levels of emotional effectiveness, and nothing more. It is claimed that a medium to which so many unassailable specialists contribute (the art director, the writer, the producer, the cameraman, the director, the sound technician and so on) cannot achieve the essential unity or cohesiveness of a work of art.

It is irrefutably contended that the film serves a political and social need as a narcotic, rivalling or even superseding the church in the valuable respect of providing the masses with an escape dream. Nor would I attempt to deny that much of its irresistible magic lies in a primitive surrender to darkness, warmth, consanguinity and the hypnotic flicker of the screen. Social scientists may have exaggerated the ill effects of the screen on the adolescent mind and senses, but there is an inescapable hypnosis attached to the movie screen that can catch up from his plush seat a sane, balanced, even well-read, adult person, and emotionally implicate him in a novelette-in-motion that, transposed into its literary equivalent, would be scorned by a twelve-year-old schoolgirl. His mind may reject the film utterly, but he will be powerless to move while banality grips him.

This power of the screen to unify, coerce, stupefy, enthral and mesmerise audiences in every country in the world is either sinister or miraculous according to how it is used, or even, if you like, according to the progress or otherwise of humanity. Certainly a world that does not pretend seriously to seek peace, that is incapable of feeding itself, that lives fearfully from day to day, cannot be expected to exploit the dynamic art of the screen. For the screen realised and released is both pacifist and universal. It identifies man with man and place with place, it is a medium of poetry, compassion and illumination. It is an art that nobody will let grow up.

Its creators in the screen's short history have done no more than further it into luxurious adolescence, in which condition it will remain just as long as politics, finance and, more importantly, technique rule the artist.

I think we can say that film technique has nearly advanced to the point at which the artist could control his medium wholly and thus bring it into the category of an art. The missing element is the artist himself, and we will find him not as a director or producer but as a writer who inscribes on paper, with a completely visual power of writing, the thing that will be put down into celluloid by craftsmen. He will at all points control these craftsmen to the extent that in their individual spheres they are subservient to the film as a whole. Griffith, Chaplin, Eisenstein, Dreyer, Vigo, Renoir, Clair obeyed as far as they could this essential principle. But they were pioneering in an undeveloped medium, and much of their creative purpose was vitiated in technical improvisation and makeshift. The creator of the grown-up film must see in the cinema his only means of expression, and he must see his material as something far richer than the actual, as something far removed from the literal: the paradox of the cinema is that it is anything but photographic.

His medium has no bounds as to movement, time or place; he commands texture and detail, his camera lens is microscopic or telescopic, moving or static, he can quicken or slow the growth of living cells and human movement, he has a selective view over the whole of nature and a compulsion over his audiences that is god-like. And he has sound: all the words that can be spoken, all the music that can be composed, all the noises of the world. The soliloquy, the interior monologue, the imagery of the thought stream that underruns the obstructive dialogue; every device by which the novelist or dramatist attempts to chart the Individual are within the range of the movie screen. A *Ulysses*, a *Hamlet*, a *Moby Dick* of cinematography are not beyond the bounds of our vision.

The cinema is man dreaming as well as man in conflict and action with man and nature. By which I mean, the cinema is the first method of art to catch up with the speed and range of man's instantaneous comprehensive vision in that condition between sleeping and waking — the cinematograph daydream. Indeed my first surrender to the movie was at the realisation that all my day dreams were film sequences. And I was excitingly confirmed by one man above all, Jean Vigo, who, in *Zéro de Conduite*, transcended the matter-of-factness of life completely and convincingly. In this film the rituals and nightmares of schoolboy existence were seen by Vigo as in a dream-state, hectic, haunting and true beyond any realistic exploration I have seen of that terrible world. But that film had to be met more

Peter Lorre to the *Mth Degree*

than half-way and seen more than once to be fully grasped and was, in fact, dismissed tersely by a distinguished colleague who gave it 'zero for achievement and one for trying'.*

The present-day movie is forced to be painfully obvious in subject matter and technique because of the non-discriminatory methods of distribution and exhibition, but more because of the wholesale appeasement by the leading productive functionaries of box-office and business.

At no period of the cinema's history were films so flat and efficiently uncinematic. In their off-guard moments members of the hierarchy of ace directors who are powerful enough to choose their own films indiscriminately curse the cameraman, the art-director, the script-writer, the executive. Conscious of inhabiting an

* C. A. Lejeune, in the *Observer*, who had taken it from a Paris newspaper without credit. — P.R.

artistic cul-de-sac, they forbear to look within themselves, to acknowledge that they are like conductors of wonderfully well-drilled orchestras who cannot find any new or worthwhile music to play. They will argue that nobody would listen to it if they found it, that nobody would back it. But the incontrovertible fact is they do not look for it or have become too atrophied by success to recognise or fight for it.

No art is served without endless battle, and indeed the opposition to the smallest advance of the film has all the appearances of invulnerability. Yet it can and will be fought and circumvented. A man such as Roberto Rossellini, who prefers to make his films from hand to mouth in the way that he wants them made, can refuse to be bought at a fabulous price by Hollywood. The Un-American Activities Committee may appear to have crushed all creative vitality in Hollywood, yet at the same time must it not have hardened and clarified the thing it seeks to eradicate? It is reasonable to anticipate that some of the indicted Ten and others, to whom the idiotic injustice of the arraignment must appear as a savage declaration of war, will look for freedom in other places.

In Britain, by the clumsiest of machinery, some of the right things have been done at the wrong times. The 45 per cent quota could eventually be the means of rescuing the British film from its self-dedicated mediocrity after apparent disaster had hit the economics of the industry. The film thrives on disaster and stringency, especially in Britain, where by a slow process unperceived in Wardour Street audiences are sorting themselves into several levels of film-consciousness: and when audiences begin to stir, our writer-director begins to inherit.

But wherever and in however small a way the film flourishes and moves forward my first pleasure will be to clamour on its behalf in as many places as possible.

Strike-breaker Greer Garson in
The Valley of Decision

Indexes

1 FILMS REVIEWED

2 DIRECTORS OF FILMS REVIEWED

3 FILMS IN CARICATURE

Signoret, Simone, 148
Simmons, Jean, 137
Sloane, Everett, 109
Smith, Alexis, 78, 178
Sologne, Madeleine, 49
Stanwyck, Barbara, 40, 43
Sullivan, Francis L., 82

Todd, Ann, 87
Tone, Franchot, 173

Trevor, Claire, 124

Valli, 100

Walbrook, Anton, 132
Warner, Jack, 147
Watson, Wylie, 95
Welles, Orson, 100, 109
Wilde, Cornell, 34, 62, 165
Woolley, Monty, 178

5   GENERAL

Bondi, Beulah, 46
Boomerang, 69, 71, 97, 113, 123
Borchet, Ernst, 79
Borthwick, A. T., 13
Bosustow, Stephen, 130
Boudreaux, Joseph, 86
Bouverie Street, London, 11, 14
Box, Sydney, 19
Boyd, Gladys, 7
Boyd-Orr, Sir John, 36
Brackett, Charles, 85
Brady, William, 113, 133
Brando, Marlon, 117, 140, 141
Brangwyn, Patrick, 7
Brasseur, Pierre, 154
Breaking Point, The, 135
Breen, Thomas E., 144
Bresson, Robert, 24
Breuer, Siegfried, 99
Brian, David, 107
Brief Encounter, 19, 22, 61, 68, 69, 70, 167, 171
Bright, John, 130
British Film Academy, 18, 24
British Film Institute, 8
British Film Producers Association, 178
British Lion, 93
British Museum Newspaper Library, 7, 13
British National Orchestra, 47
Bronston, S., 102
Brown, Harry, 122
Brown, Vernon, 13
Buckhurst Hill, Essex, 11
Buckinghamshire, 11
Bugs Bunny, 129
Buñuel, Luis, 130
Burnett, W. R., 114
Byron, 46

Cabre, Mario, 122
Cadbury, the Family, 13
Caesar and Cleopatra, 42, 70, 167, 172
Cagney, James, 22
Cain, James M., 42
Caine, Hall, 168
Calhern, Louis, 115
Call Northside 777, 89
Calvert, Phyllis, 53, 146
Canada, 83
Canterbury Tale, A, 70
Capra, Frank, 166
Captive Heart, The, 96, 167
Caravan, 167
Cardiff, Jack, 122, 136
Carey, MacDonald, 113
Carmichael, Hoagy, 41
Carson, Charles, 144
Cary, Joyce, 52, 144
Casque d'Or, 19
Cassell, Wally, 99

Castellani, Renato, 176
Central Office of Information, British, 74
Cervi, Gino, 76
Ceylon, 137
Chamberlain, Neville, 13
Champion, The, 178
Chandler, Raymond, 19, 58, 127, 128
Chaplin, Charles, 105, 162, 180
Chapman, Edward, 147
Charisse, Cyd, 143
Chatterton, 46
Cherkassov, N. K., 35
Cherrill, Virginia, 116
Childhood of Maxim Gorki, The, 24, 106, 116n, 163
Children of the Arctic North, 53
Children on Trial, 144
Chopin, 164
Cicognini, 150
Cineguild, 171, 172
CinemaScope, 155
Citizen Kane, 65, 113
City Lights, 116n
Clachan, The, London, 11, 18, 20
Clair, René, 180
Clarence, O. B., 61
Clark, Robert, 178
Clayton, Jack, 24
Cliffords Inn, London, 10, 21
Clinton, Vivien, 144
Close-Up, 168
Cluzot, Henri-Georges, 24
Coates, Albert (Sir), 40
Cochran, Steve, 123
Cocteau, Jean, 49, 136
Cohen, Harriet, 47
Colonel Blimp, 70
Colouris, George, 137
Columbia Pictures, 111, 129, 153
Communist Party, 17
Condamné à Mort S'est Echappé, Un, 24
Confessions of a Nazi Spy, 83
Connor, Edric, 144
Conrad, Joseph, 136
Conte, Richard, 123
Convoy, Magazine, 8
Cook, Thomas Ltd., 12
Cooke, Alistair, 7, 9
Cooper, Gary, 145
Corbeau, Le, 89
Corelli, Marie, 168
Corri, Adrienne, 144
Cortese, Valentina, 138
Cotten, Joseph, 99
Covent Garden, London, 84
Cover Girl, 143
Coward, Noel, 48, 61, 171
Crain, Jeanne, 110
Crane, Stephen, 131
Crawford, Broderick, 112